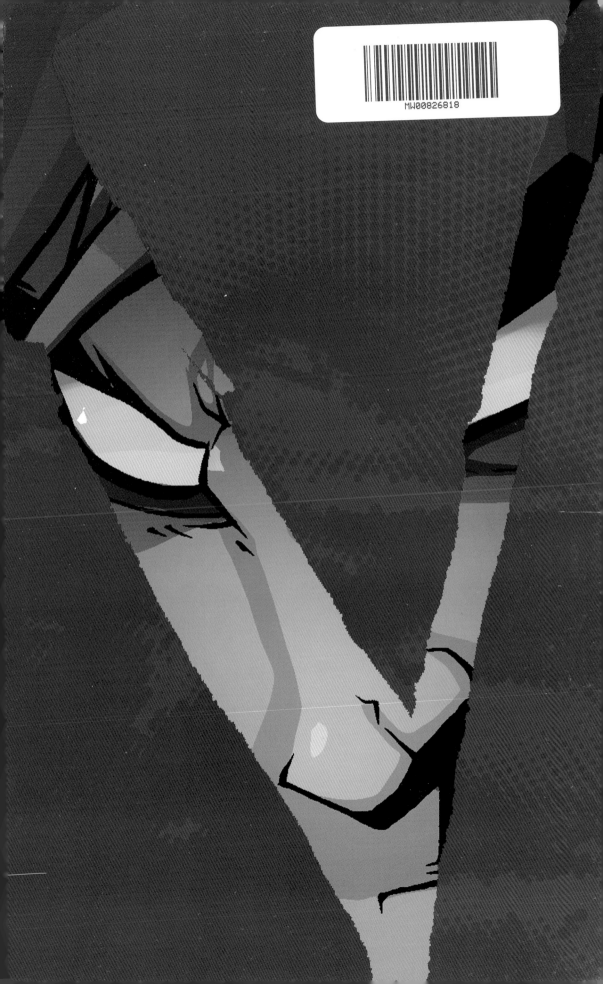

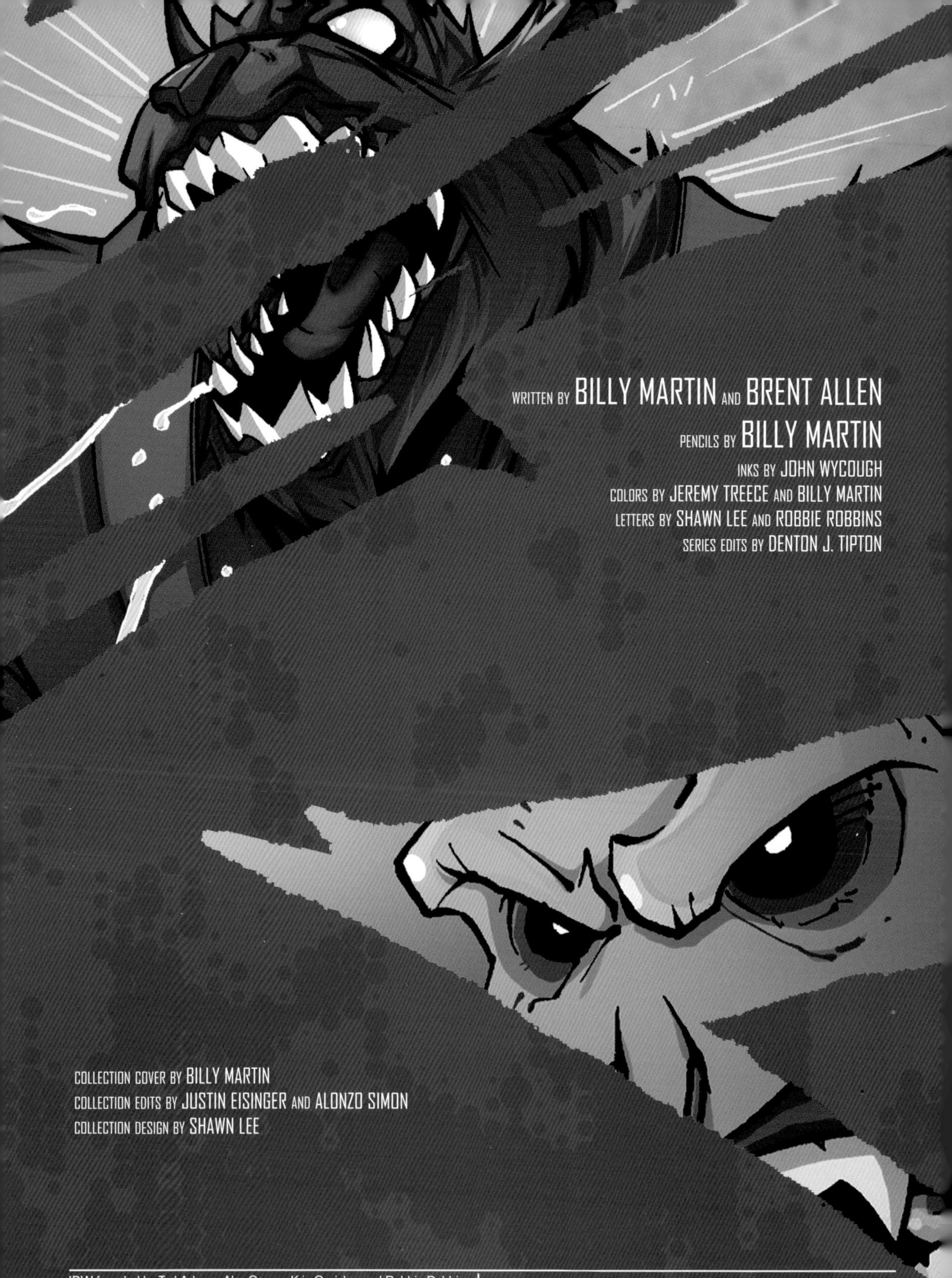

WRITTEN BY BILLY MARTIN AND BRENT ALLEN

PENCILS BY BILLY MARTIN

INKS BY JOHN WYCOUGH

COLORS BY JEREMY TREECE AND BILLY MARTIN

LETTERS BY SHAWN LEE AND ROBBIE ROBBINS

SERIES EDITS BY DENTON J. TIPTON

COLLECTION COVER BY BILLY MARTIN

COLLECTION EDITS BY JUSTIN EISINGER AND ALONZO SIMON

COLLECTION DESIGN BY SHAWN LEE

IDW founded by Ted Adams, Alex Garner, Kris Oprisko, and Robbie Robbins

ISBN: 978-1-61377-744-2

16 15 14 13 1 2 3 4

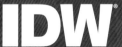

Ted Adams, CEO & Publisher
Greg Goldstein, President & COO
Robbie Robbins, EVP/Sr. Graphic Artist
Chris Ryall, Chief Creative Officer/Editor-in-Chief
Matthew Ruzicka, CPA, Chief Financial Officer
Alan Payne, VP of Sales
Dirk Wood, VP of Marketing
Lorelei Bunjes, VP of Digital Services

Originally published as VITRIOL THE HUNTER issues #1–6.

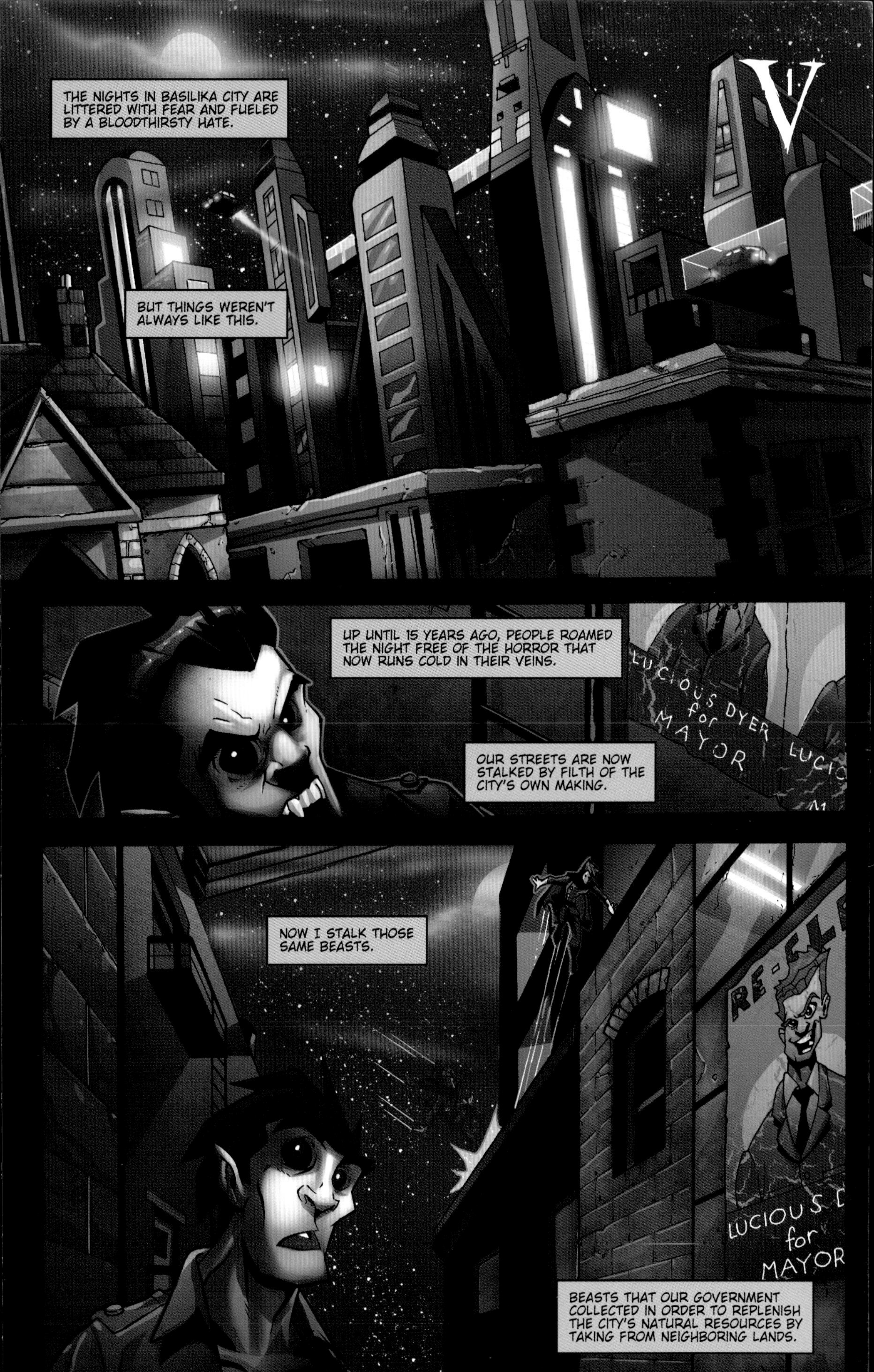
V1
THE NIGHTS IN BASILIKA CITY ARE LITTERED WITH FEAR AND FUELED BY A BLOODTHIRSTY HATE.
BUT THINGS WEREN'T ALWAYS LIKE THIS.
UP UNTIL 15 YEARS AGO, PEOPLE ROAMED THE NIGHT FREE OF THE HORROR THAT NOW RUNS COLD IN THEIR VEINS.
LUCIOUS DYER for MAYOR
OUR STREETS ARE NOW STALKED BY FILTH OF THE CITY'S OWN MAKING.
NOW I STALK THOSE SAME BEASTS.
LUCIOUS
for
MAYOR
BEASTS THAT OUR GOVERNMENT COLLECTED IN ORDER TO REPLENISH THE CITY'S NATURAL RESOURCES BY TAKING FROM NEIGHBORING LANDS.

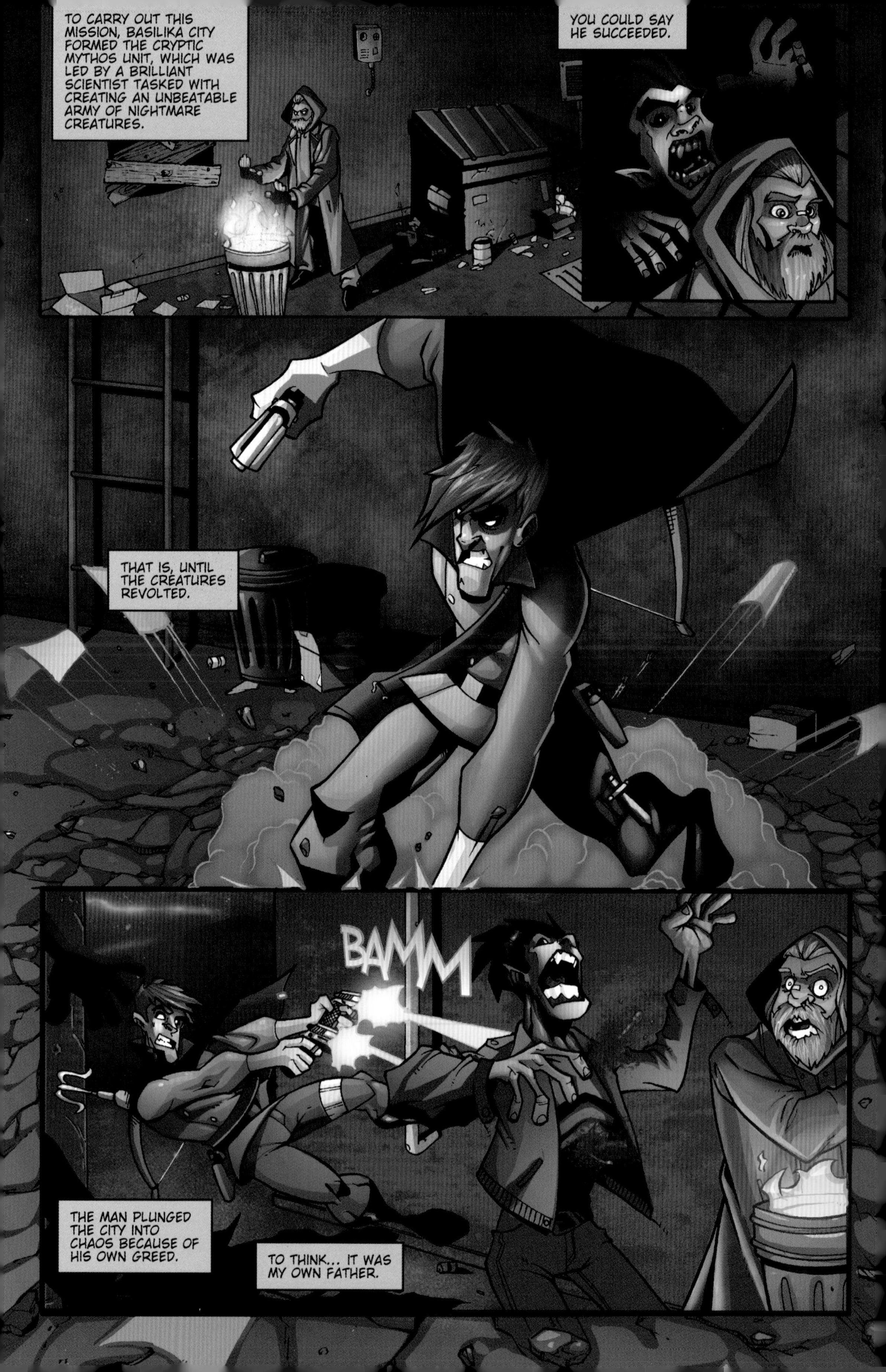
TO CARRY OUT THIS MISSION, BASILIKA CITY FORMED THE CRYPTIC MYTHOS UNIT, WHICH WAS LED BY A BRILLIANT SCIENTIST TASKED WITH CREATING AN UNBEATABLE ARMY OF NIGHTMARE CREATURES.
YOU COULD SAY HE SUCCEEDED.
THAT IS, UNTIL THE CREATURES REVOLTED.
BAMM
THE MAN PLUNGED THE CITY INTO CHAOS BECAUSE OF HIS OWN GREED.
TO THINK... IT WAS MY OWN FATHER.

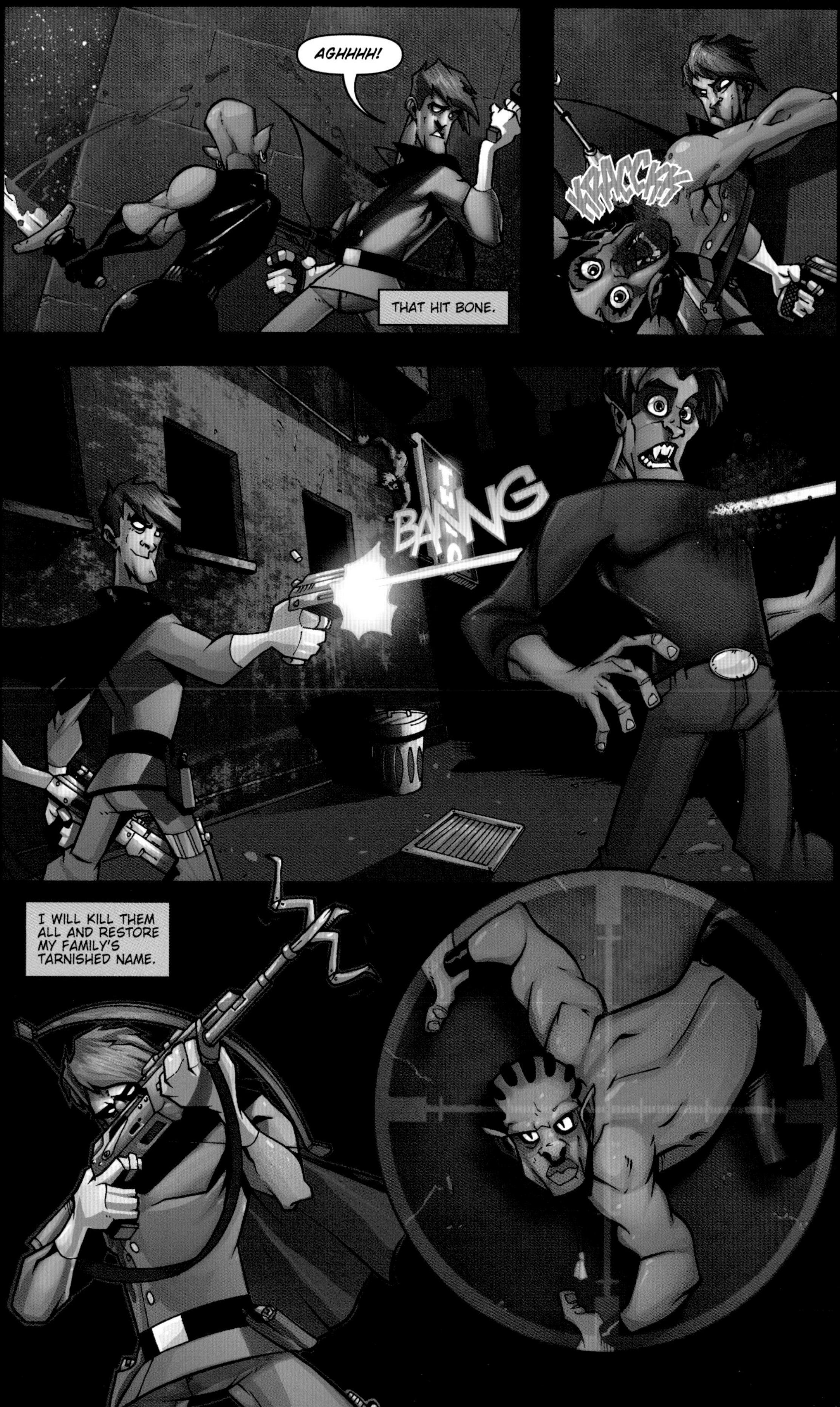
AGHHHH!
THAT HIT BONE.
KRACCKK
BANNG
I WILL KILL THEM ALL AND RESTORE MY FAMILY'S TARNISHED NAME.

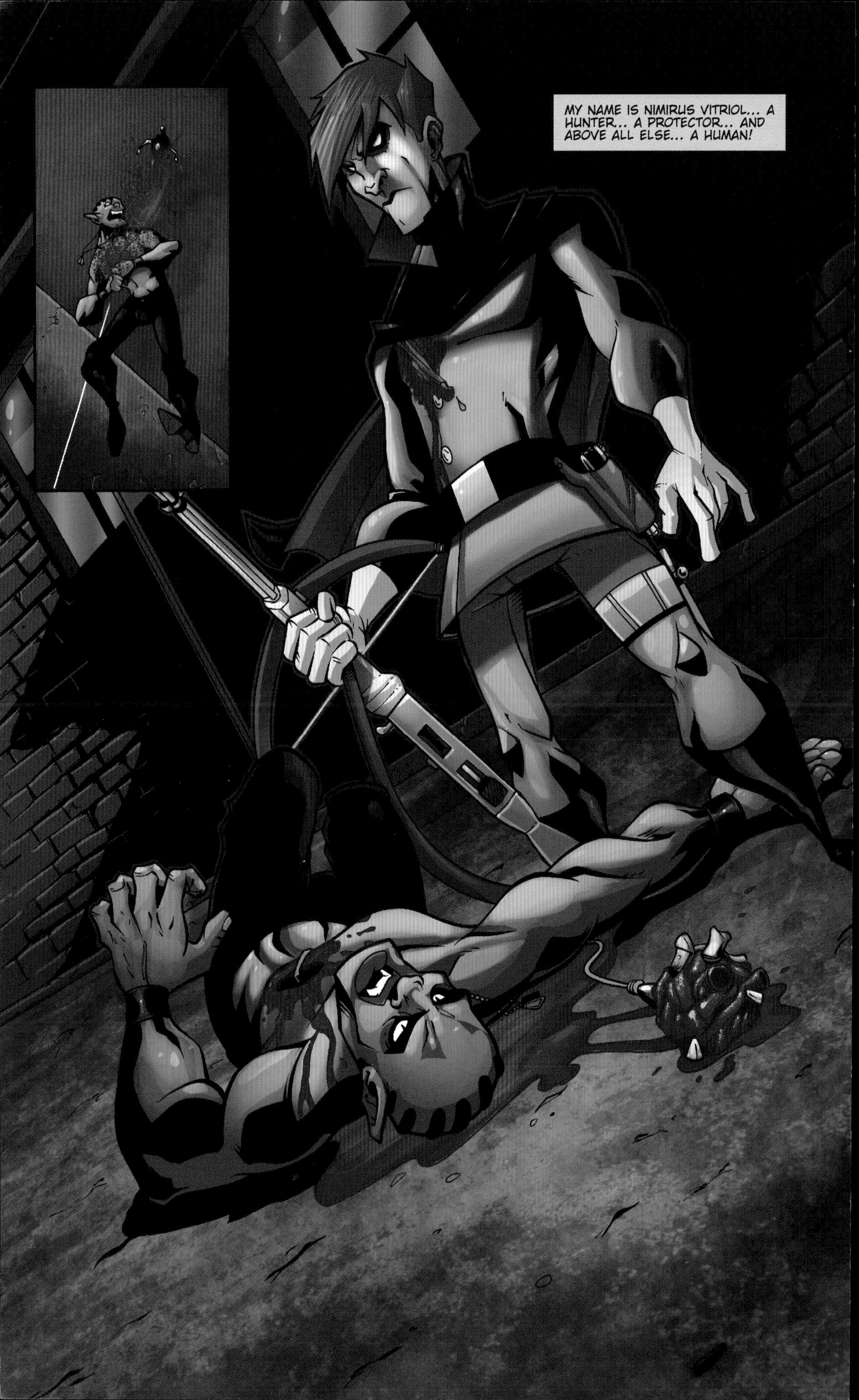
MY NAME IS NIMIRUS VITRIOL... A HUNTER... A PROTECTOR... AND ABOVE ALL ELSE... A HUMAN!

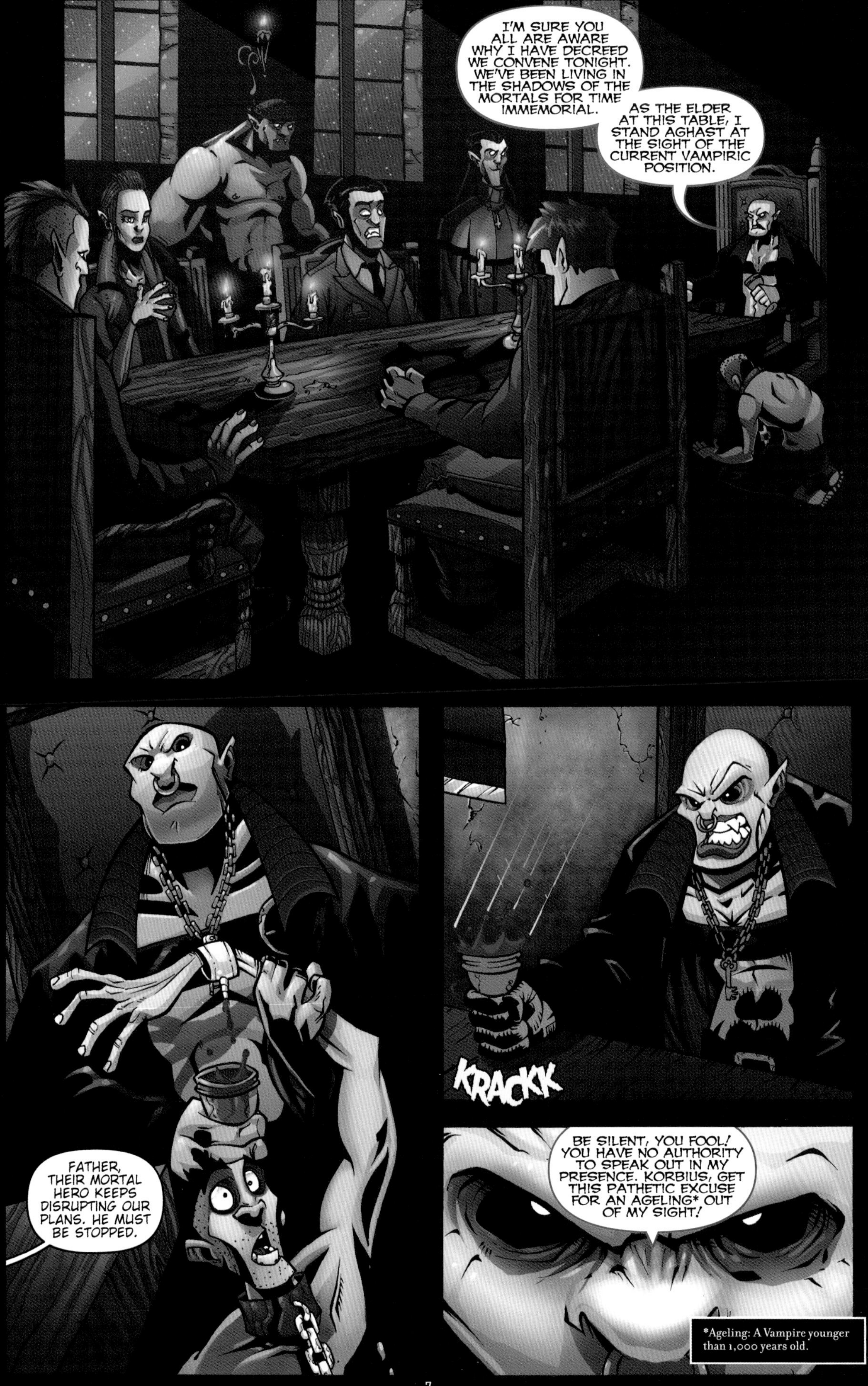
I'M SURE YOU ALL ARE AWARE WHY I HAVE DECREED WE CONVENE TONIGHT. WE'VE BEEN LIVING IN THE SHADOWS OF THE MORTALS FOR TIME IMMEMORIAL.
AS THE ELDER AT THIS TABLE, I STAND AGHAST AT THE SIGHT OF THE CURRENT VAMPIRIC POSITION.
FATHER, THEIR MORTAL HERO KEEPS DISRUPTING OUR PLANS. HE MUST BE STOPPED.
KRACKK
BE SILENT, YOU FOOL! YOU HAVE NO AUTHORITY TO SPEAK OUT IN MY PRESENCE. KORBIUS, GET THIS PATHETIC EXCUSE FOR AN AGELING* OUT OF MY SIGHT!

*Ageling: A Vampire younger than 1,000 years old.

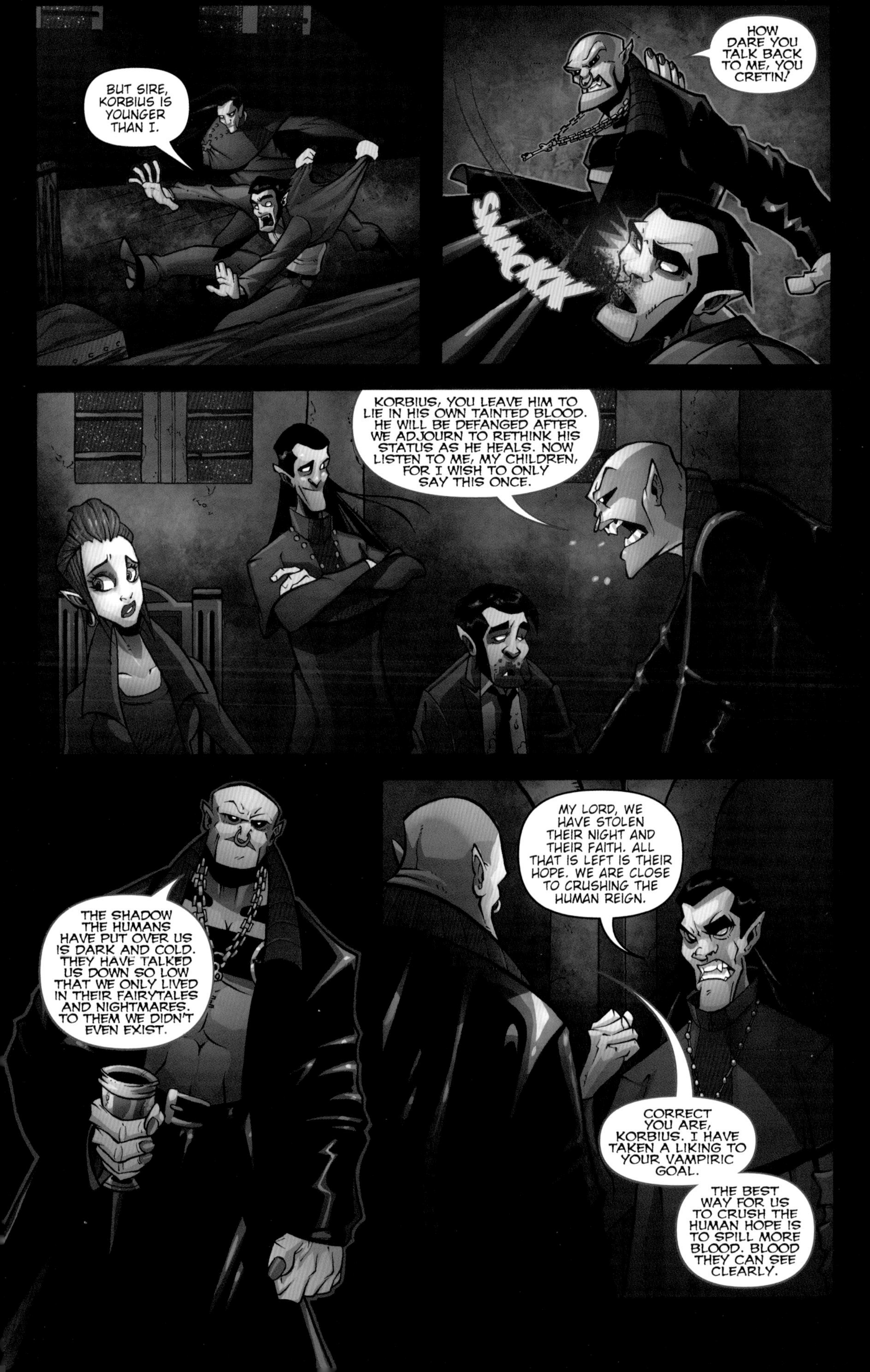
BUT SIRE, KORBIUS IS YOUNGER THAN I.
HOW DARE YOU TALK BACK TO ME, YOU CRETIN!
SMACK
KORBIUS, YOU LEAVE HIM TO LIE IN HIS OWN TAINTED BLOOD. HE WILL BE DEFANGED AFTER WE ADJOURN TO RETHINK HIS STATUS AS HE HEALS. NOW LISTEN TO ME, MY CHILDREN, FOR I WISH TO ONLY SAY THIS ONCE.
THE SHADOW THE HUMANS HAVE PUT OVER US IS DARK AND COLD. THEY HAVE TALKED US DOWN SO LOW THAT WE ONLY LIVED IN THEIR FAIRYTALES AND NIGHTMARES. TO THEM WE DIDN'T EVEN EXIST.
MY LORD, WE HAVE STOLEN THEIR NIGHT AND THEIR FAITH. ALL THAT IS LEFT IS THEIR HOPE. WE ARE CLOSE TO CRUSHING THE HUMAN REIGN.
CORRECT YOU ARE, KORBIUS. I HAVE TAKEN A LIKING TO YOUR VAMPIRIC GOAL.
THE BEST WAY FOR US TO CRUSH THE HUMAN HOPE IS TO SPILL MORE BLOOD. BLOOD THEY CAN SEE CLEARLY.

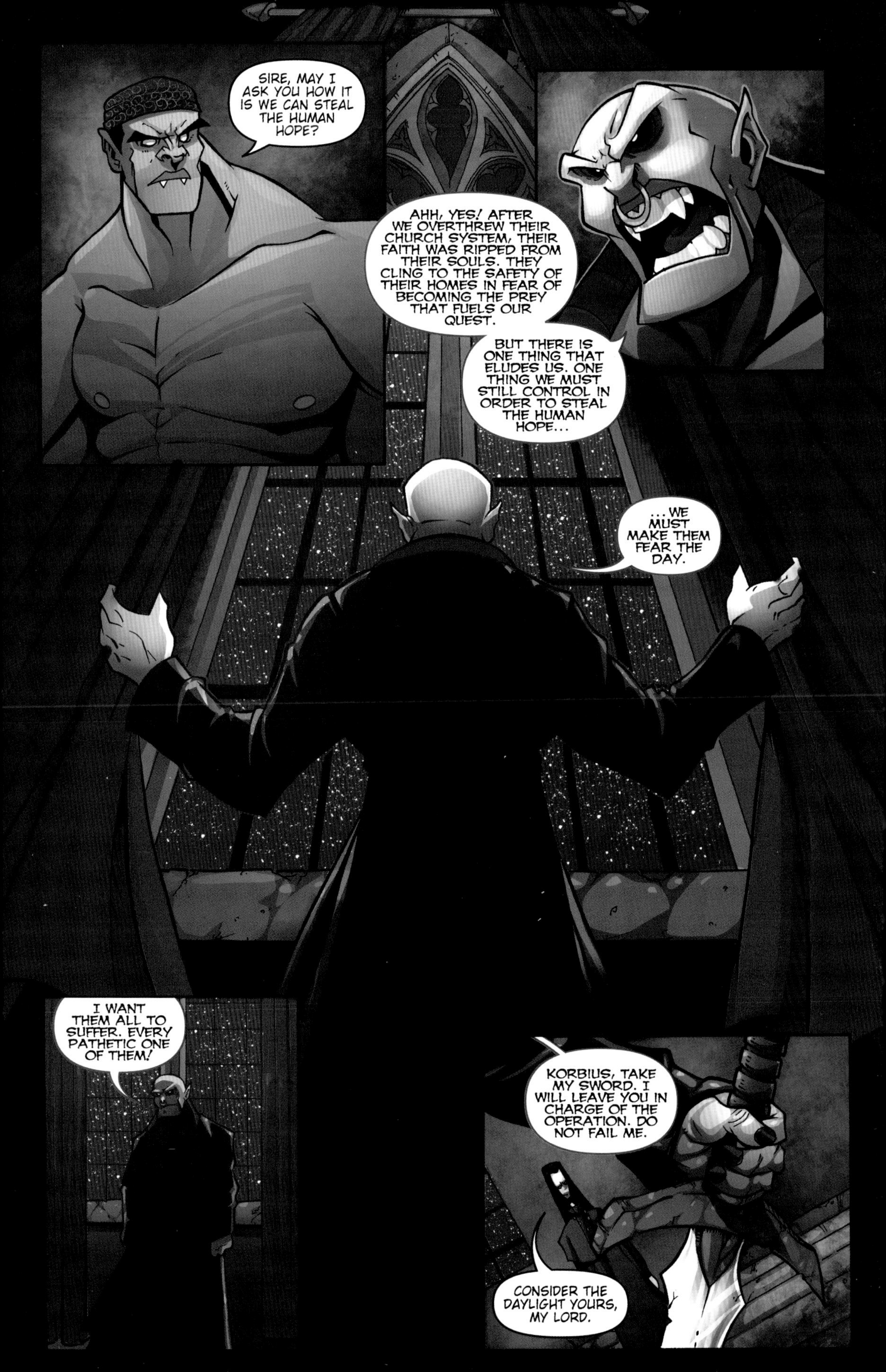
SIRE, MAY I ASK YOU HOW IT IS WE CAN STEAL THE HUMAN HOPE?
AHH, YES! AFTER WE OVERTHREW THEIR CHURCH SYSTEM, THEIR FAITH WAS RIPPED FROM THEIR SOULS. THEY CLING TO THE SAFETY OF THEIR HOMES IN FEAR OF BECOMING THE PREY THAT FUELS OUR QUEST.
BUT THERE IS ONE THING THAT ELUDES US. ONE THING WE MUST STILL CONTROL IN ORDER TO STEAL THE HUMAN HOPE...
...WE MUST MAKE THEM FEAR THE DAY.
I WANT THEM ALL TO SUFFER. EVERY PATHETIC ONE OF THEM!
KORBIUS, TAKE MY SWORD. I WILL LEAVE YOU IN CHARGE OF THE OPERATION. DO NOT FAIL ME.
CONSIDER THE DAYLIGHT YOURS, MY LORD.

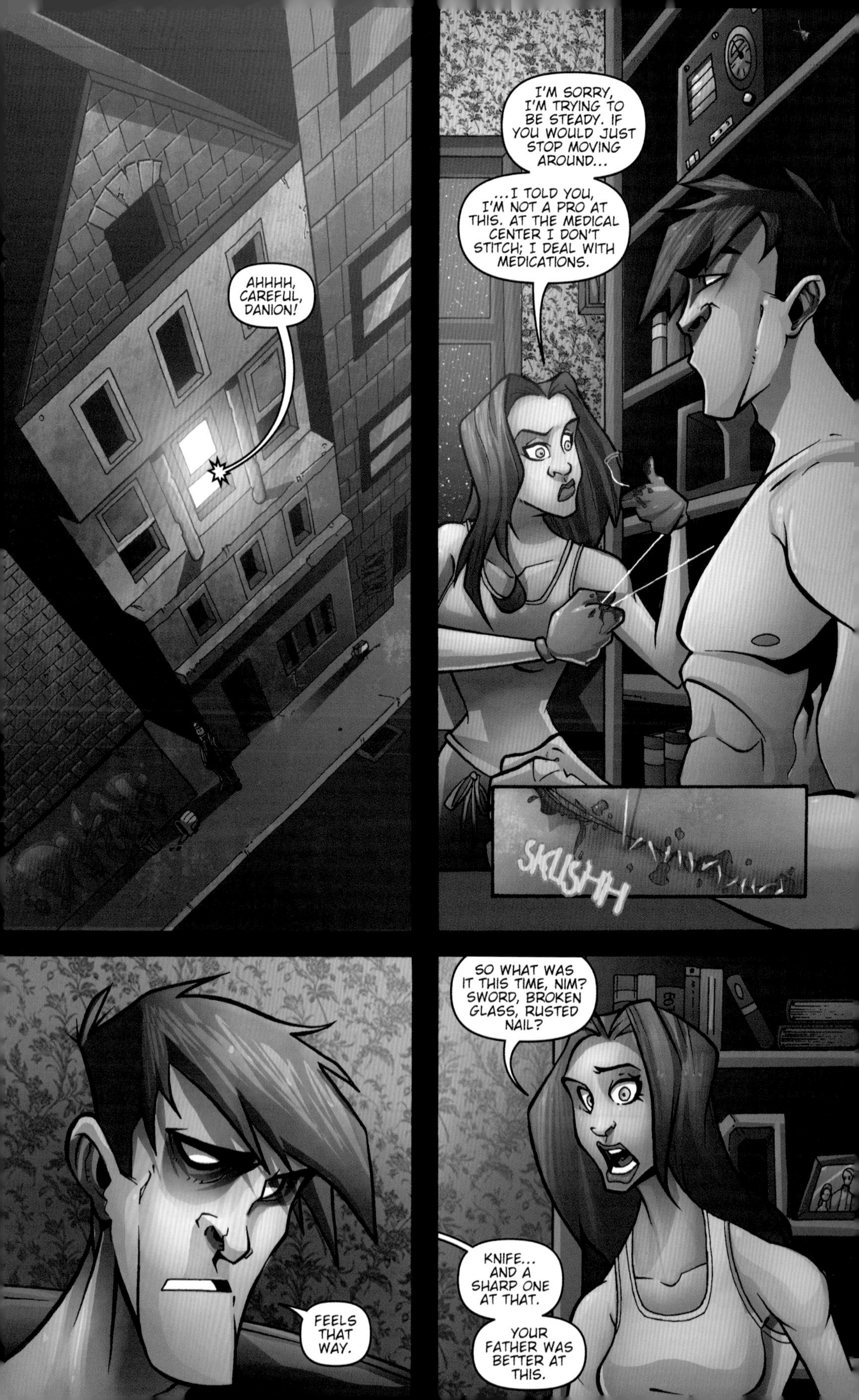
AHHHH, CAREFUL, DANION!
I'M SORRY, I'M TRYING TO BE STEADY. IF YOU WOULD JUST STOP MOVING AROUND...
...I TOLD YOU, I'M NOT A PRO AT THIS. AT THE MEDICAL CENTER I DON'T STITCH; I DEAL WITH MEDICATIONS.
SKLUSHHH
FEELS THAT WAY.
SO WHAT WAS IT THIS TIME, NIM? SWORD, BROKEN GLASS, RUSTED NAIL?
KNIFE... AND A SHARP ONE AT THAT.
YOUR FATHER WAS BETTER AT THIS.

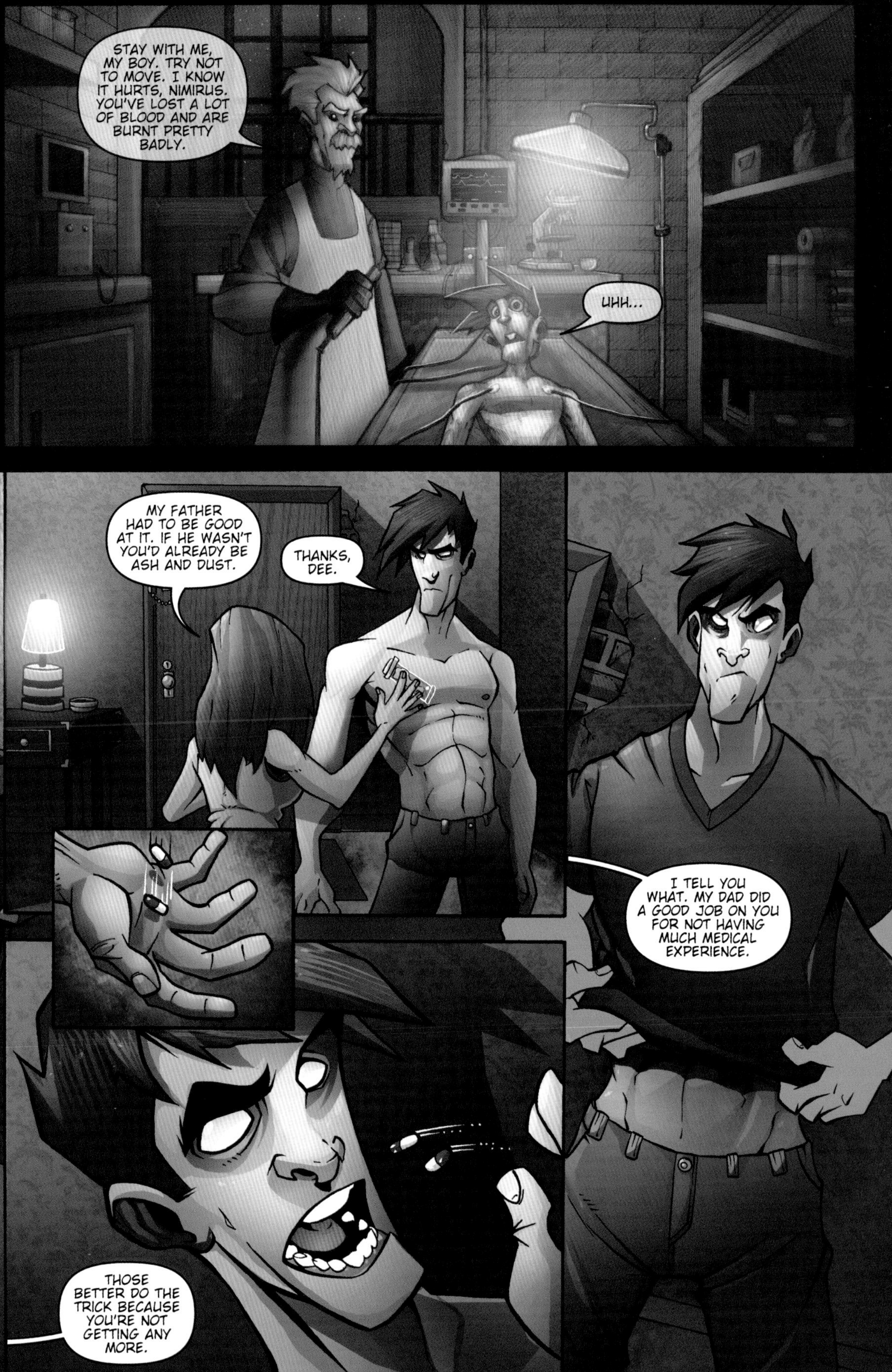
STAY WITH ME, MY BOY. TRY NOT TO MOVE. I KNOW IT HURTS, NIMIRUS. YOU'VE LOST A LOT OF BLOOD AND ARE BURNT PRETTY BADLY.
UHH...
MY FATHER HAD TO BE GOOD AT IT. IF HE WASN'T YOU'D ALREADY BE ASH AND DUST.
THANKS, DEE.
I TELL YOU WHAT. MY DAD DID A GOOD JOB ON YOU FOR NOT HAVING MUCH MEDICAL EXPERIENCE.
THOSE BETTER DO THE TRICK BECAUSE YOU'RE NOT GETTING ANY MORE.

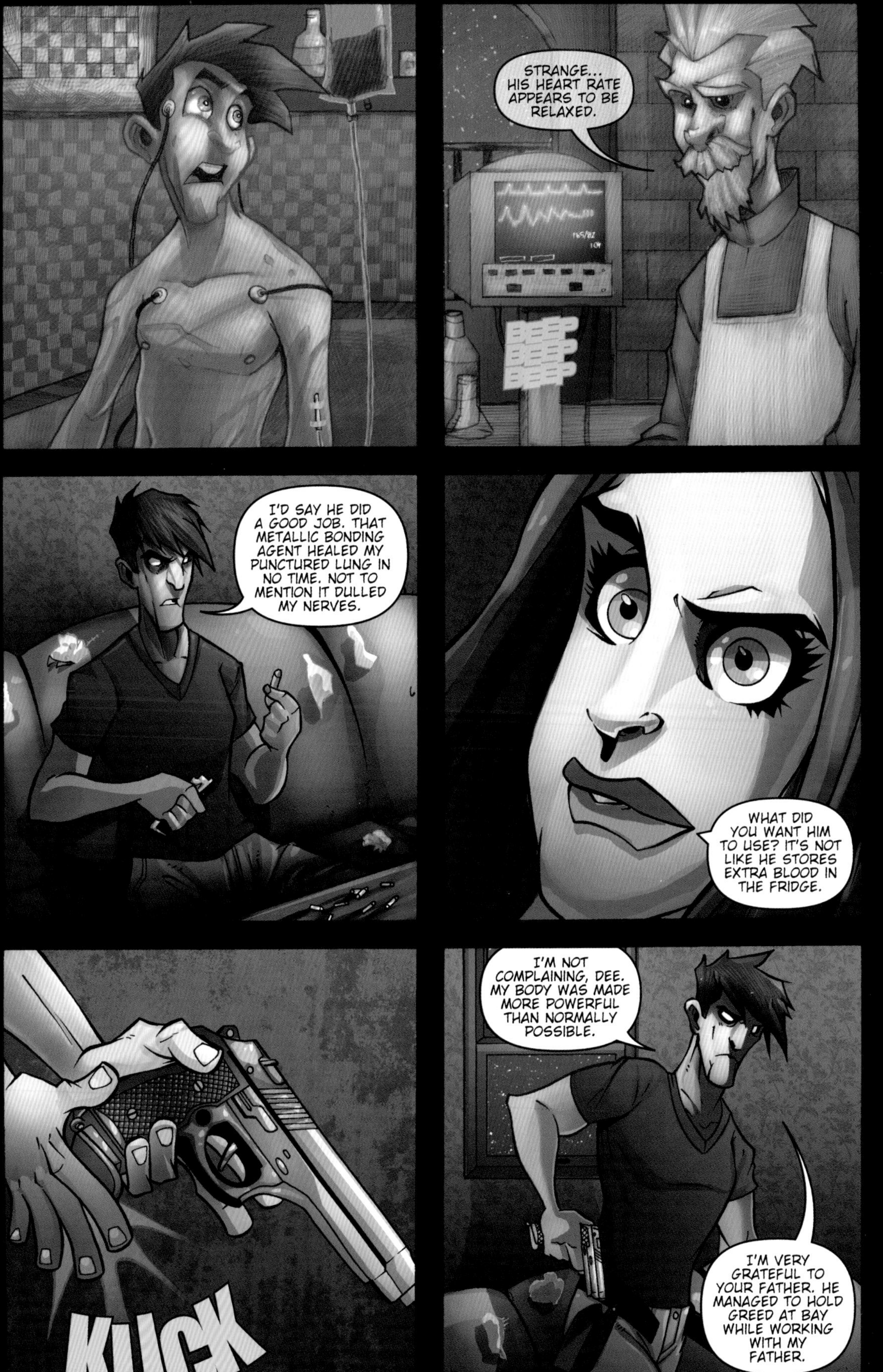
STRANGE... HIS HEART RATE APPEARS TO BE RELAXED.
BEEP BEEP BEEP
I'D SAY HE DID A GOOD JOB. THAT METALLIC BONDING AGENT HEALED MY PUNCTURED LUNG IN NO TIME. NOT TO MENTION IT DULLED MY NERVES.
WHAT DID YOU WANT HIM TO USE? IT'S NOT LIKE HE STORES EXTRA BLOOD IN THE FRIDGE.
KLICK
I'M NOT COMPLAINING, DEE. MY BODY WAS MADE MORE POWERFUL THAN NORMALLY POSSIBLE.
I'M VERY GRATEFUL TO YOUR FATHER. HE MANAGED TO HOLD GREED AT BAY WHILE WORKING WITH MY FATHER.

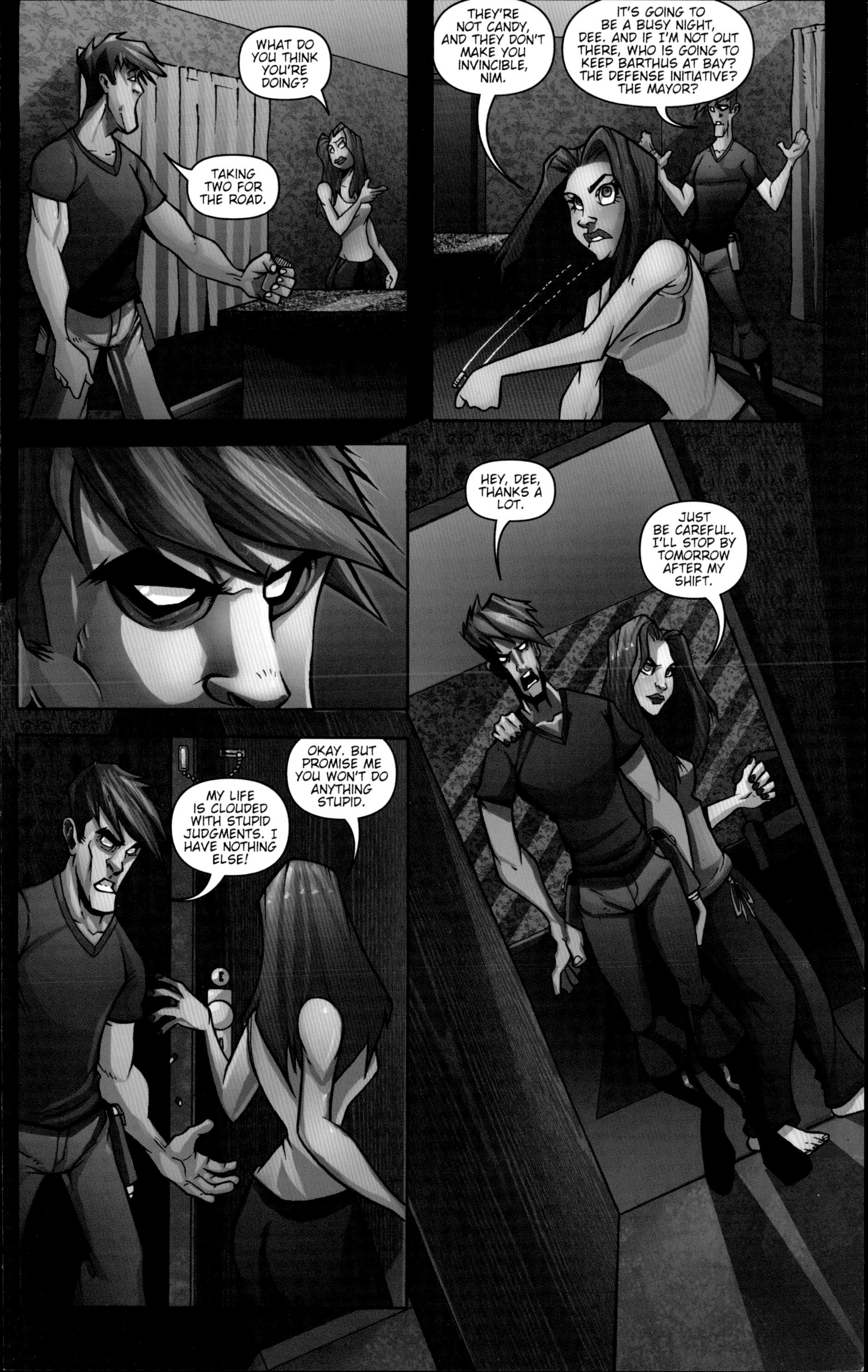
WHAT DO YOU THINK YOU'RE DOING?
TAKING TWO FOR THE ROAD.
THEY'RE NOT CANDY, AND THEY DON'T MAKE YOU INVINCIBLE, NIM.
IT'S GOING TO BE A BUSY NIGHT, DEE. AND IF I'M NOT OUT THERE, WHO IS GOING TO KEEP BARTHUS AT BAY? THE DEFENSE INITIATIVE? THE MAYOR?
HEY, DEE, THANKS A LOT.
JUST BE CAREFUL. I'LL STOP BY TOMORROW AFTER MY SHIFT.
MY LIFE IS CLOUDED WITH STUPID JUDGMENTS. I HAVE NOTHING ELSE!
OKAY. BUT PROMISE ME YOU WON'T DO ANYTHING STUPID.

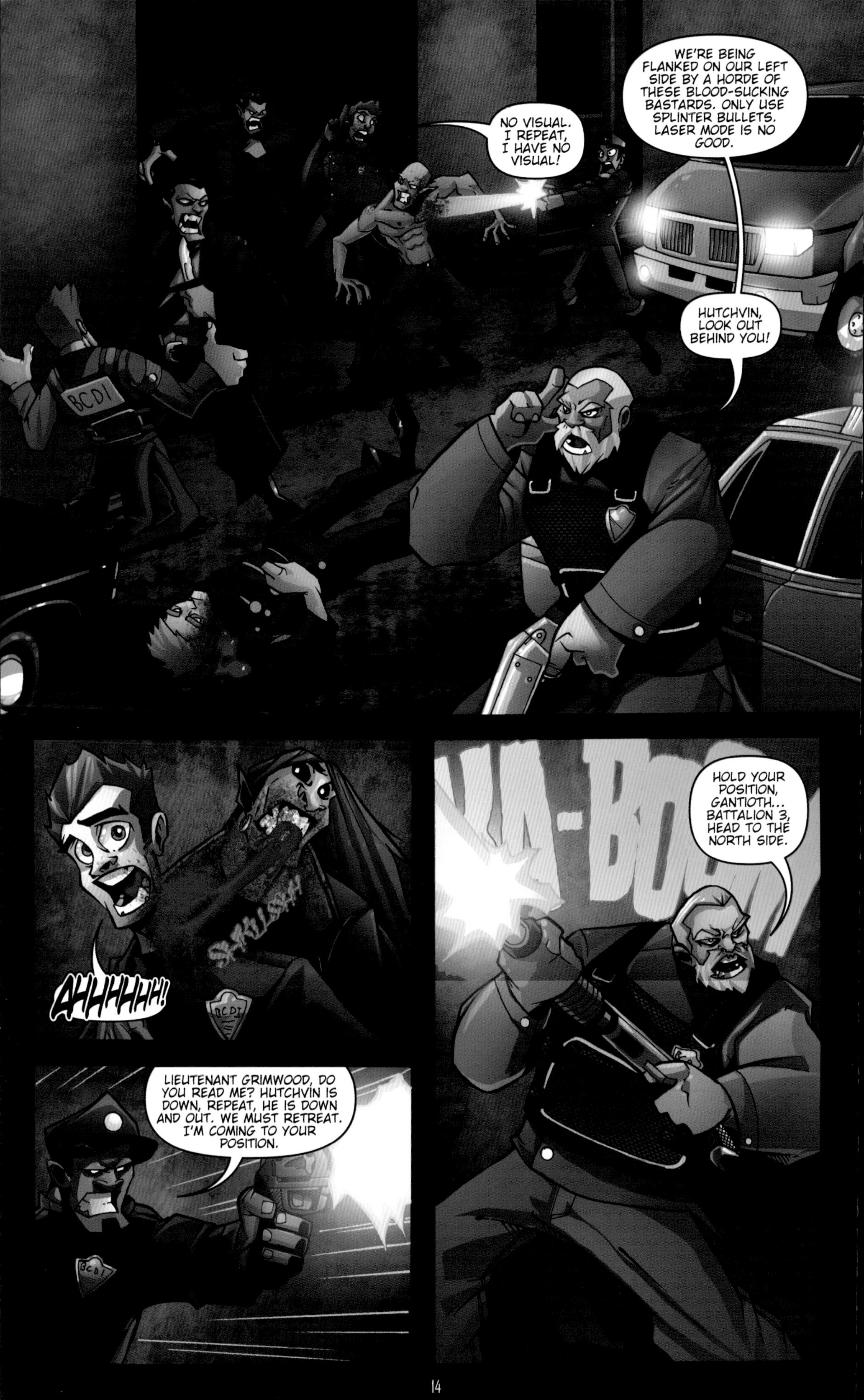
NO VISUAL. I REPEAT, I HAVE NO VISUAL!
WE'RE BEING FLANKED ON OUR LEFT SIDE BY A HORDE OF THESE BLOOD-SUCKING BASTARDS. ONLY USE SPLINTER BULLETS. LASER MODE IS NO GOOD.
HUTCHVIN, LOOK OUT BEHIND YOU!
BCDI
AHHHHHH!
HOLD YOUR POSITION, GANTIOTH... BATTALION 3, HEAD TO THE NORTH SIDE.
LIEUTENANT GRIMWOOD, DO YOU READ ME? HUTCHVIN IS DOWN, REPEAT, HE IS DOWN AND OUT. WE MUST RETREAT. I'M COMING TO YOUR POSITION.

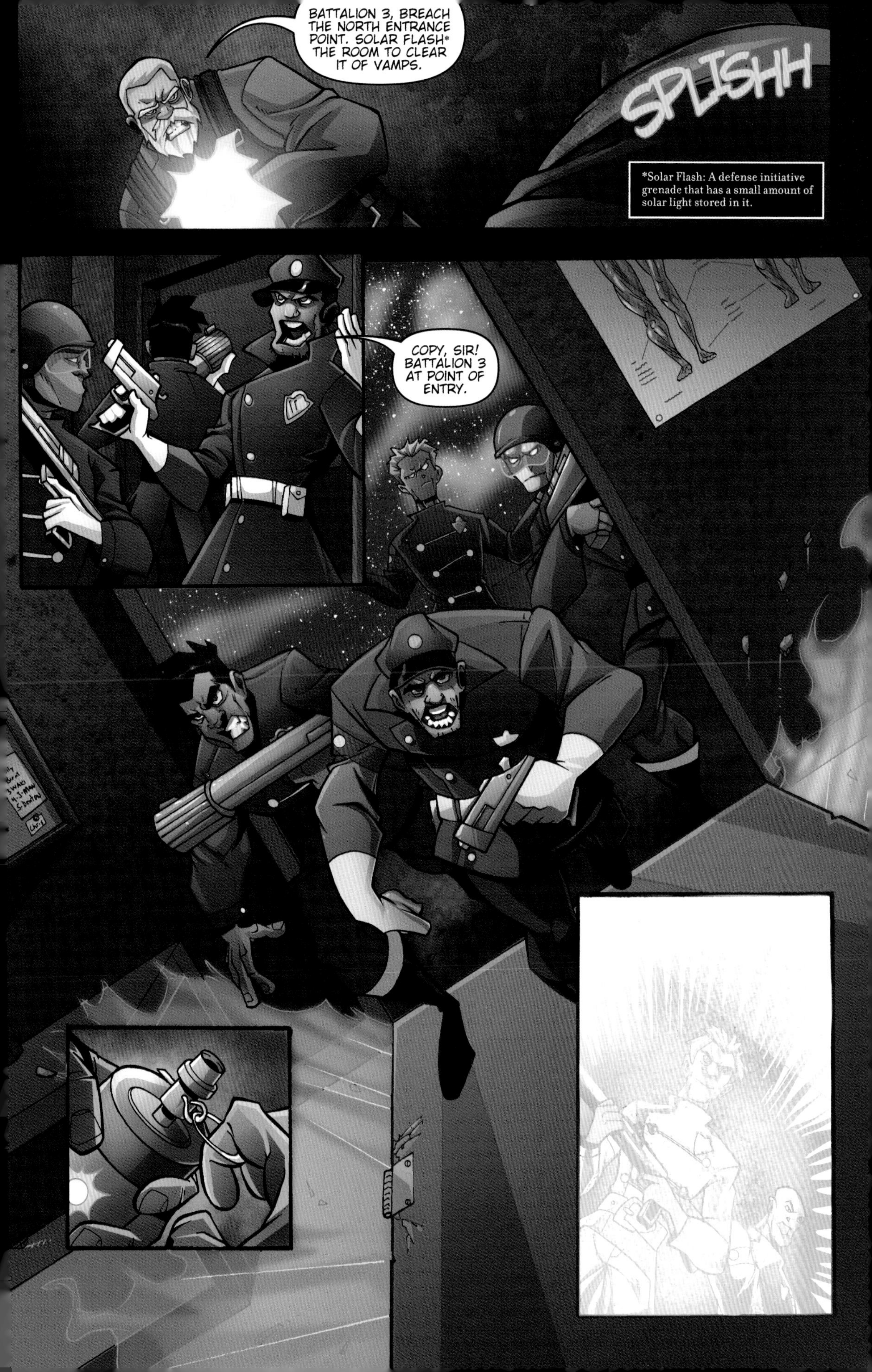
BATTALION 3, BREACH THE NORTH ENTRANCE POINT. SOLAR FLASH* THE ROOM TO CLEAR IT OF VAMPS.
SPLISHH
*Solar Flash: A defense initiative grenade that has a small amount of solar light stored in it.
COPY, SIR! BATTALION 3 AT POINT OF ENTRY.

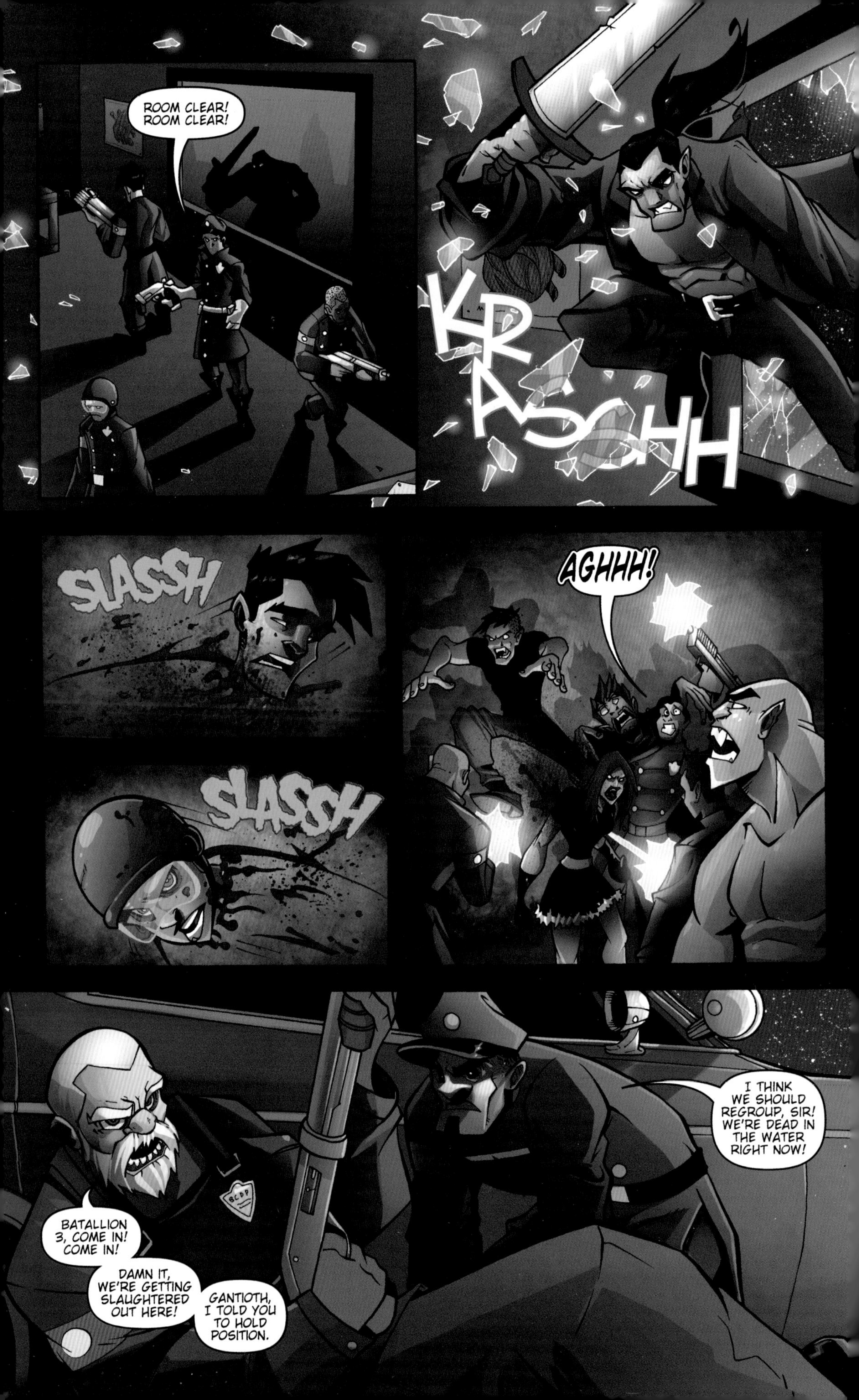

ROOM CLEAR! ROOM CLEAR!
KRASHH
SLASSH
SLASSH
AGHHH!
BATALLION 3, COME IN! COME IN!
DAMN IT, WE'RE GETTING SLAUGHTERED OUT HERE!
GANTIOTH, I TOLD YOU TO HOLD POSITION.
I THINK WE SHOULD REGROUP, SIR! WE'RE DEAD IN THE WATER RIGHT NOW!

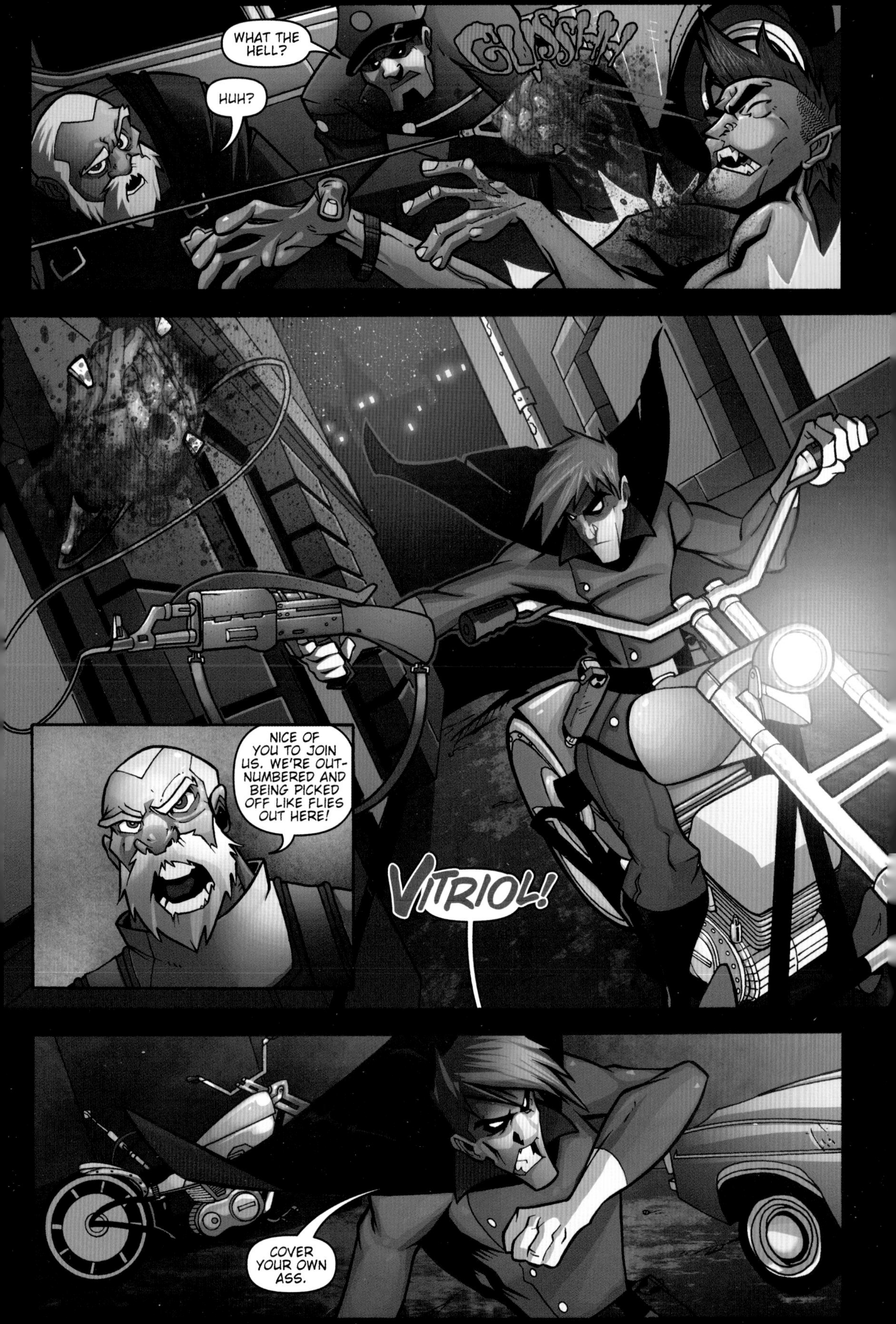
WHAT THE HELL?
HUH?
GUSSHH
NICE OF YOU TO JOIN US. WE'RE OUT-NUMBERED AND BEING PICKED OFF LIKE FLIES OUT HERE!
VITRIOL!
COVER YOUR OWN ASS.

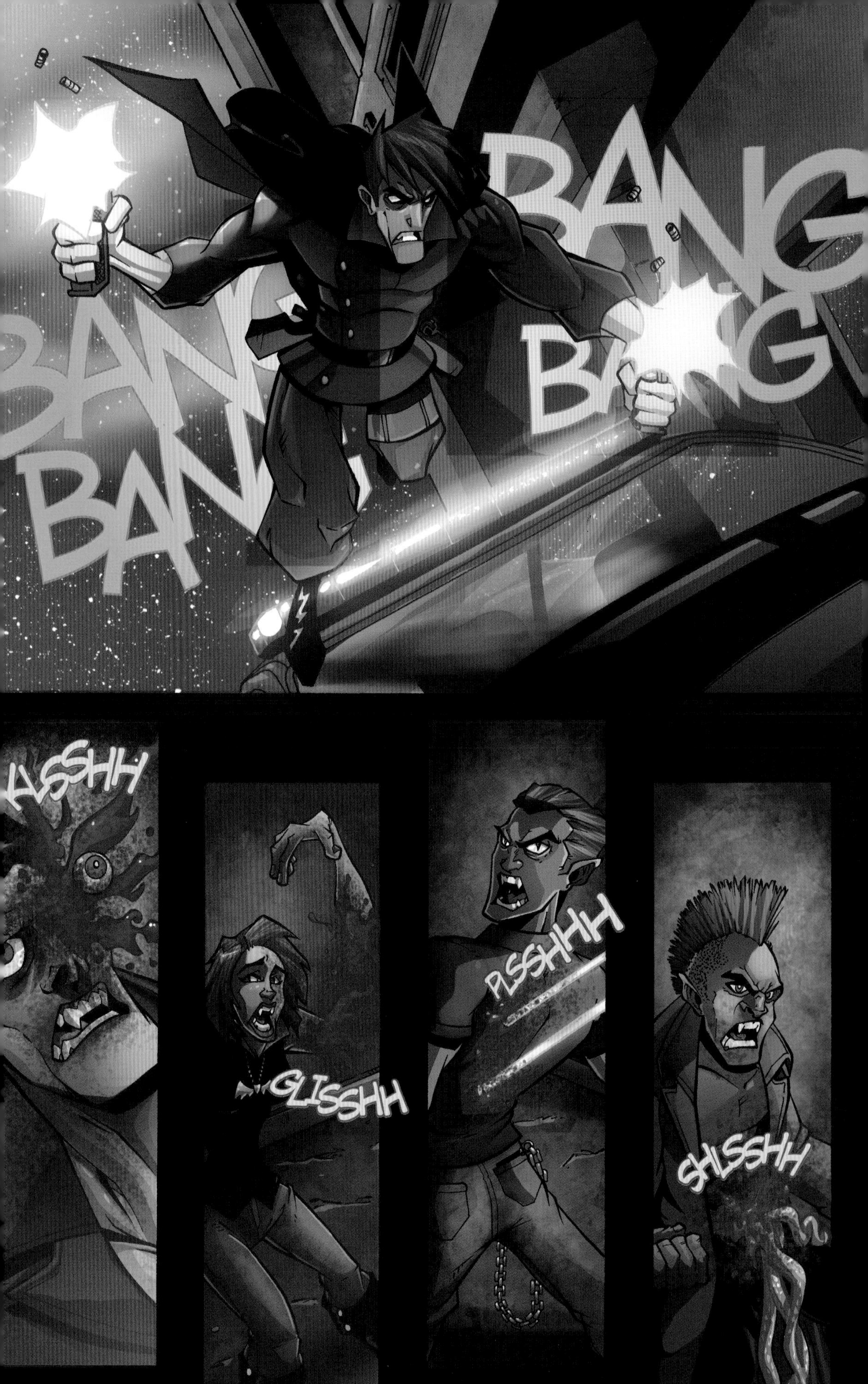
BANG
BANG
BANG
BANG
KLSSHH
GLISSHH
PLSSHHH
SHLSSHH

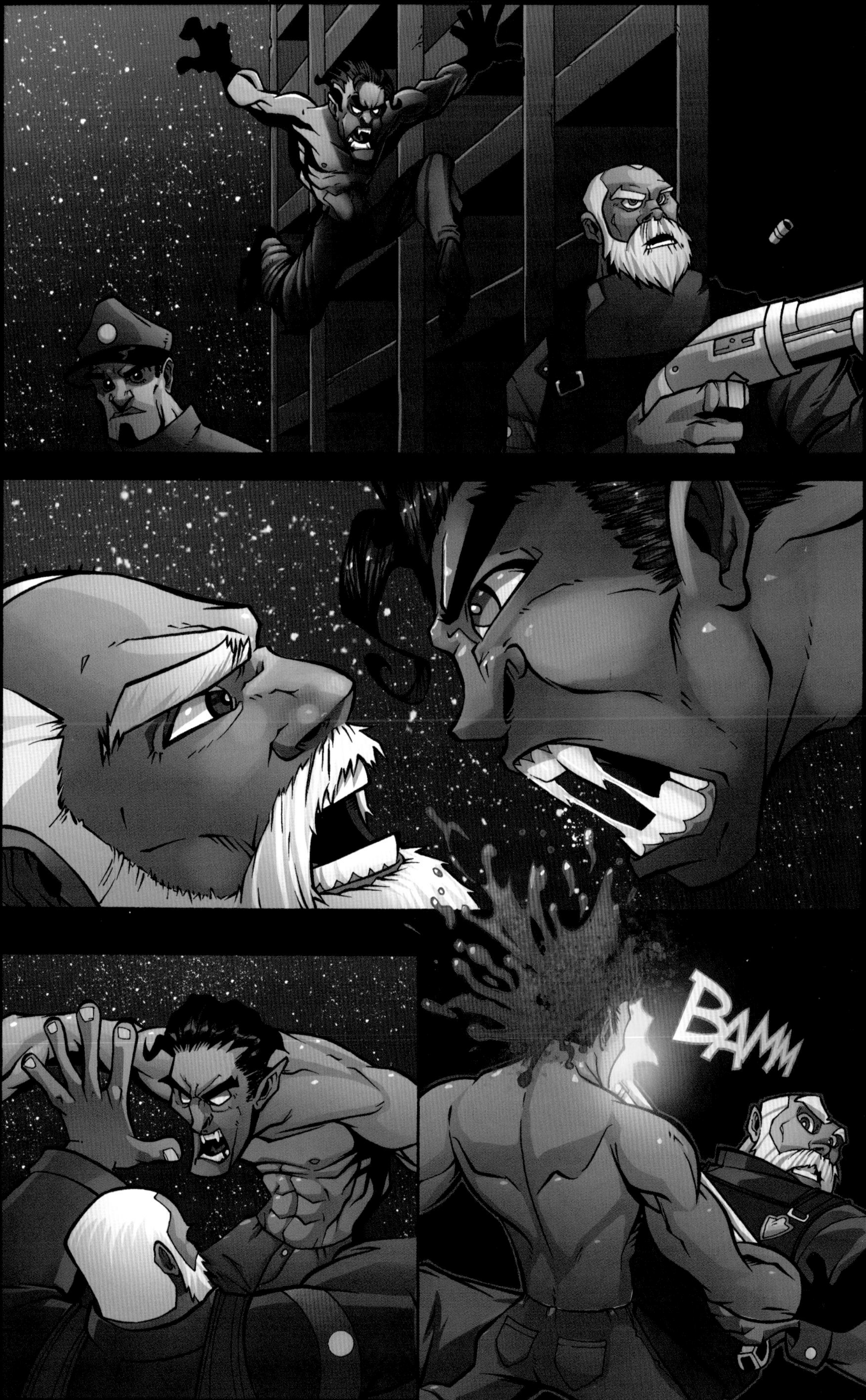
BAMM

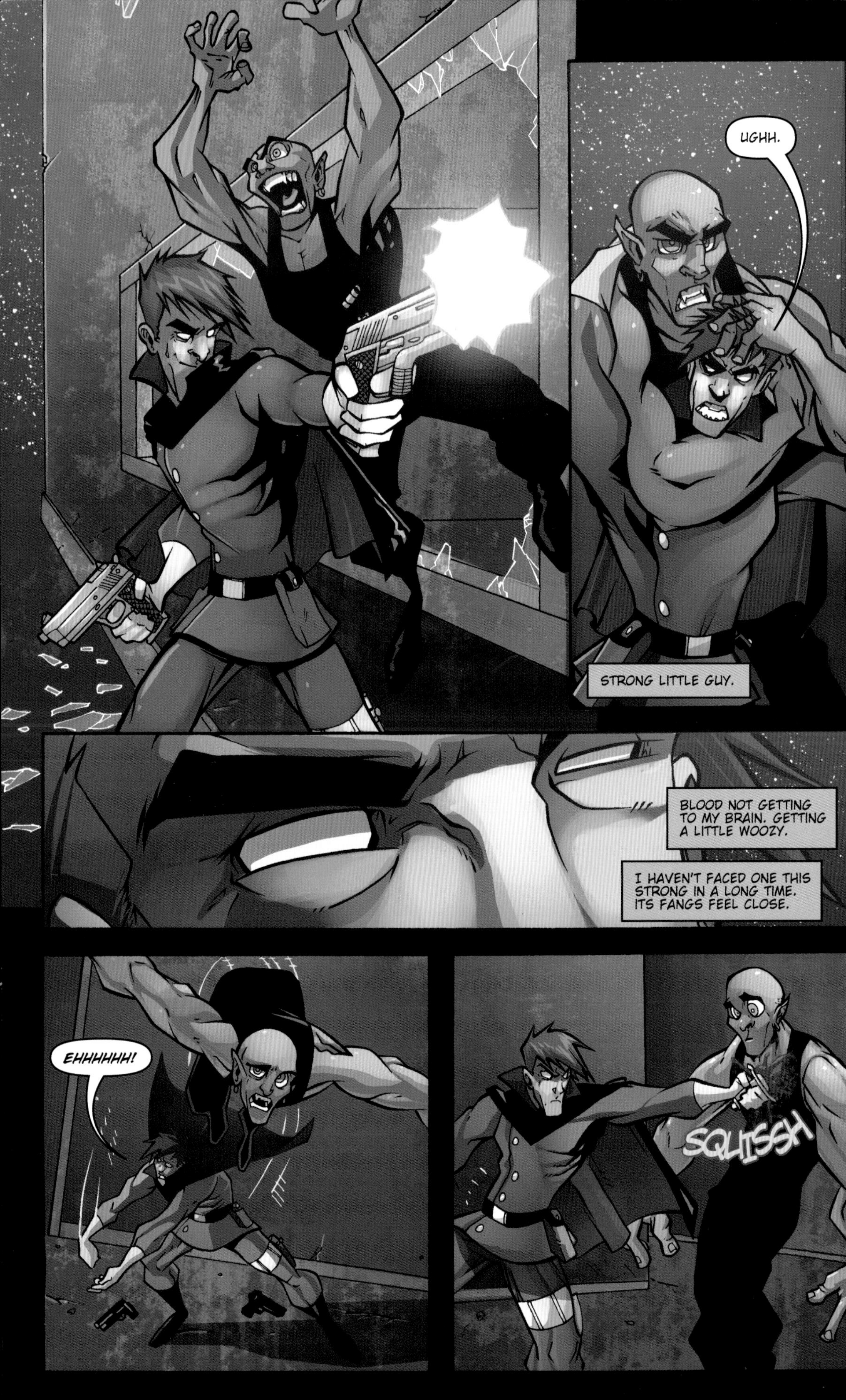
UGHH.
STRONG LITTLE GUY.
BLOOD NOT GETTING TO MY BRAIN. GETTING A LITTLE WOOZY.
I HAVEN'T FACED ONE THIS STRONG IN A LONG TIME. ITS FANGS FEEL CLOSE.
EHHHHHH!
SQUISSH

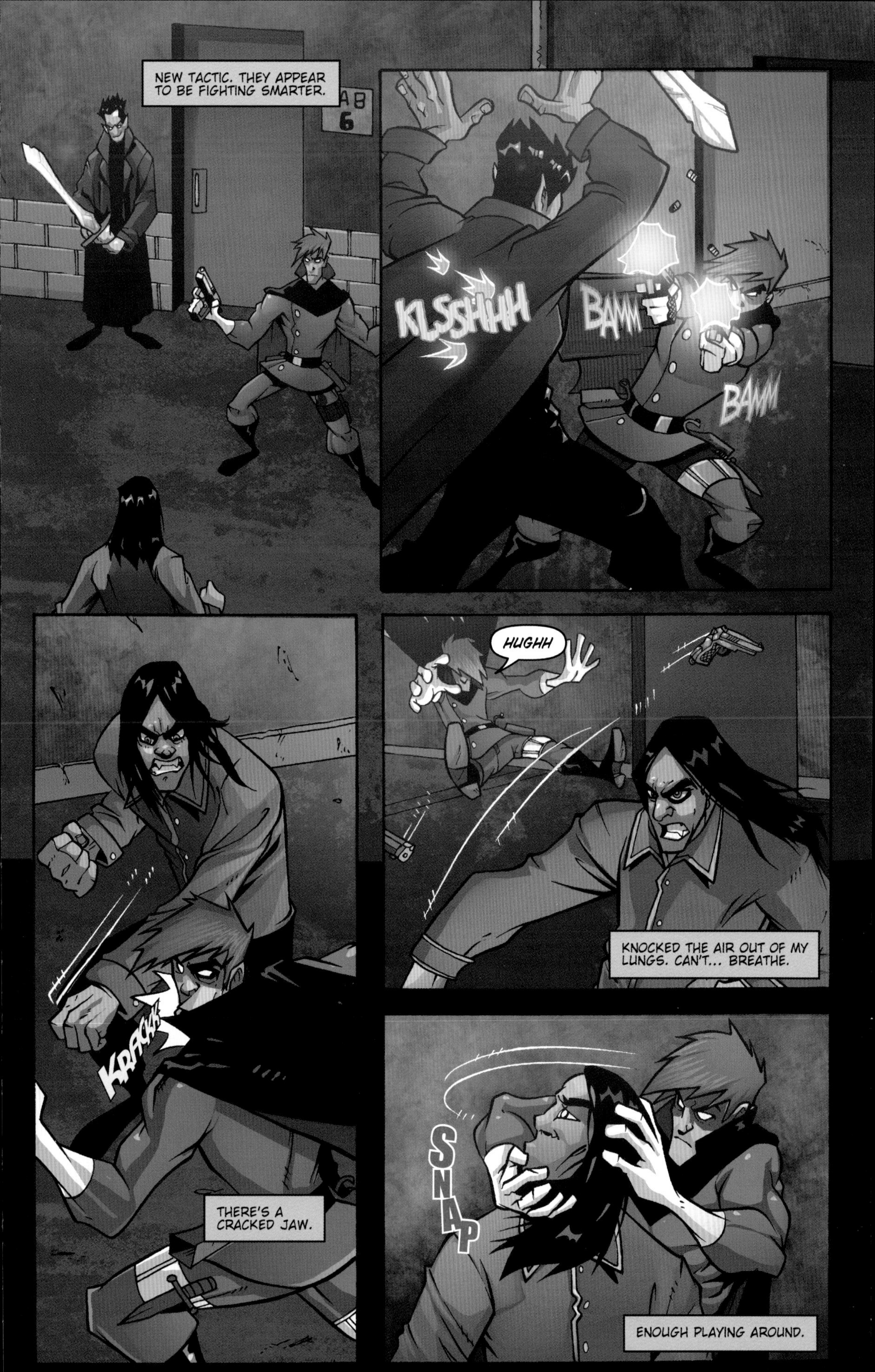
NEW TACTIC. THEY APPEAR TO BE FIGHTING SMARTER.
AB 6
KLSSHHH
BAMM
BAMM
KRACKK
THERE'S A CRACKED JAW.
HUGHH
KNOCKED THE AIR OUT OF MY LUNGS. CAN'T... BREATHE.
SNAP
ENOUGH PLAYING AROUND.

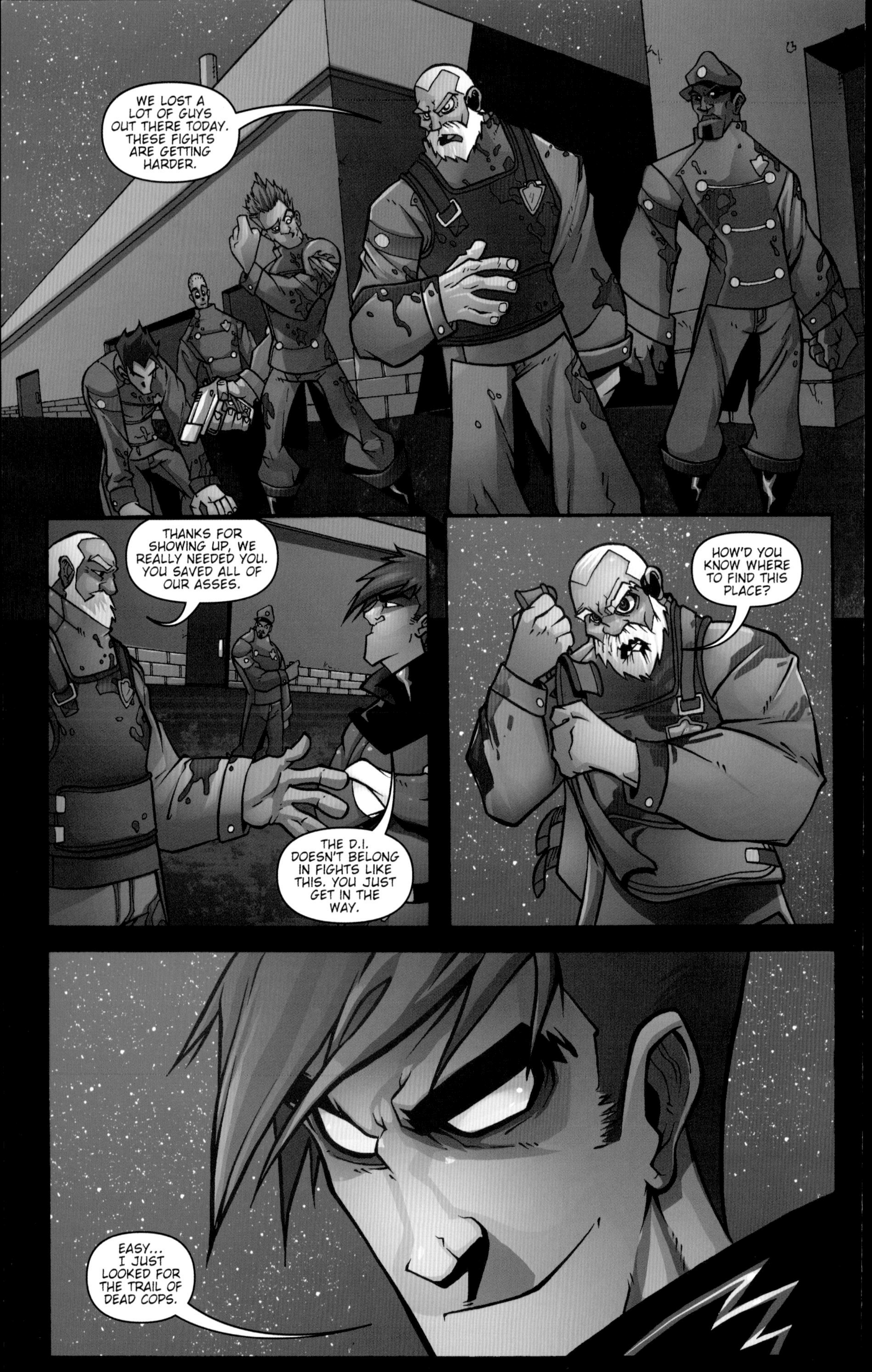
WE LOST A LOT OF GUYS OUT THERE TODAY. THESE FIGHTS ARE GETTING HARDER.
THANKS FOR SHOWING UP, WE REALLY NEEDED YOU. YOU SAVED ALL OF OUR ASSES.
THE D.I. DOESN'T BELONG IN FIGHTS LIKE THIS. YOU JUST GET IN THE WAY.
HOW'D YOU KNOW WHERE TO FIND THIS PLACE?
EASY... I JUST LOOKED FOR THE TRAIL OF DEAD COPS.

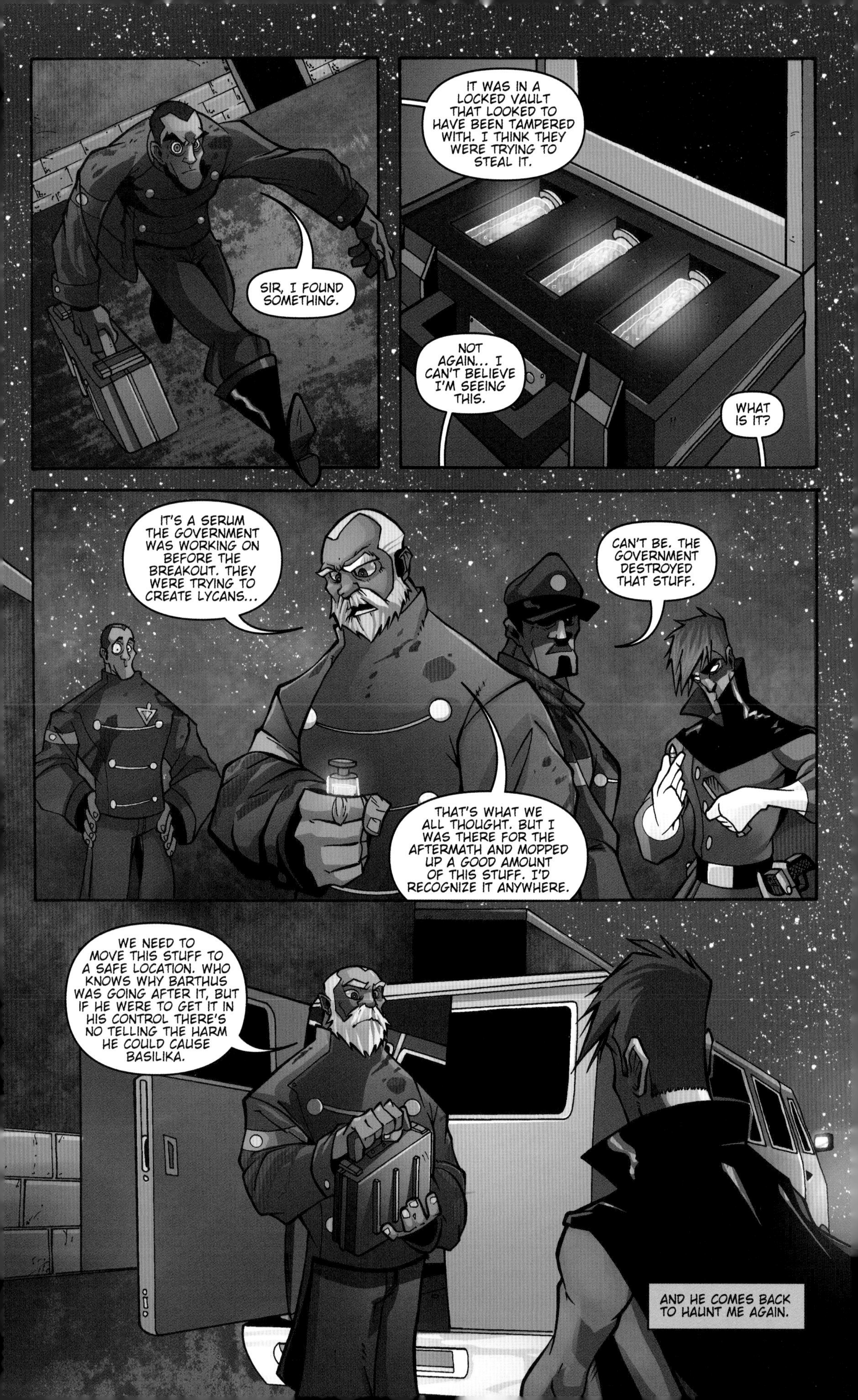
SIR, I FOUND SOMETHING.
IT WAS IN A LOCKED VAULT THAT LOOKED TO HAVE BEEN TAMPERED WITH. I THINK THEY WERE TRYING TO STEAL IT.
NOT AGAIN... I CAN'T BELIEVE I'M SEEING THIS.
WHAT IS IT?
IT'S A SERUM THE GOVERNMENT WAS WORKING ON BEFORE THE BREAKOUT. THEY WERE TRYING TO CREATE LYCANS...
CAN'T BE. THE GOVERNMENT DESTROYED THAT STUFF.
THAT'S WHAT WE ALL THOUGHT. BUT I WAS THERE FOR THE AFTERMATH AND MOPPED UP A GOOD AMOUNT OF THIS STUFF. I'D RECOGNIZE IT ANYWHERE.
WE NEED TO MOVE THIS STUFF TO A SAFE LOCATION. WHO KNOWS WHY BARTHUS WAS GOING AFTER IT, BUT IF HE WERE TO GET IT IN HIS CONTROL THERE'S NO TELLING THE HARM HE COULD CAUSE BASILIKA.
AND HE COMES BACK TO HAUNT ME AGAIN.

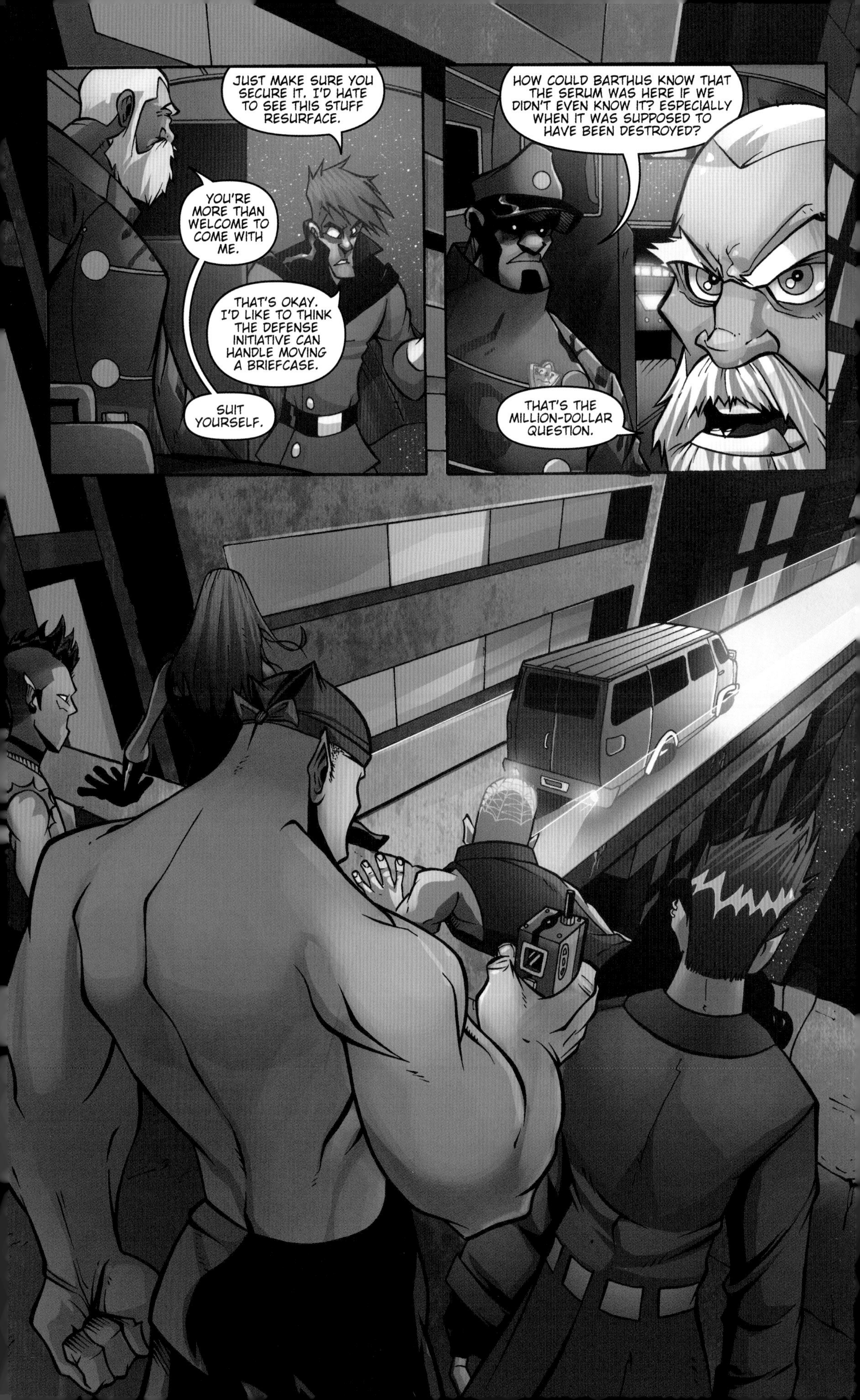
JUST MAKE SURE YOU SECURE IT. I'D HATE TO SEE THIS STUFF RESURFACE.
YOU'RE MORE THAN WELCOME TO COME WITH ME.
THAT'S OKAY. I'D LIKE TO THINK THE DEFENSE INITIATIVE CAN HANDLE MOVING A BRIEFCASE.
SUIT YOURSELF.
HOW COULD BARTHUS KNOW THAT THE SERUM WAS HERE IF WE DIDN'T EVEN KNOW IT? ESPECIALLY WHEN IT WAS SUPPOSED TO HAVE BEEN DESTROYED?
THAT'S THE MILLION-DOLLAR QUESTION.

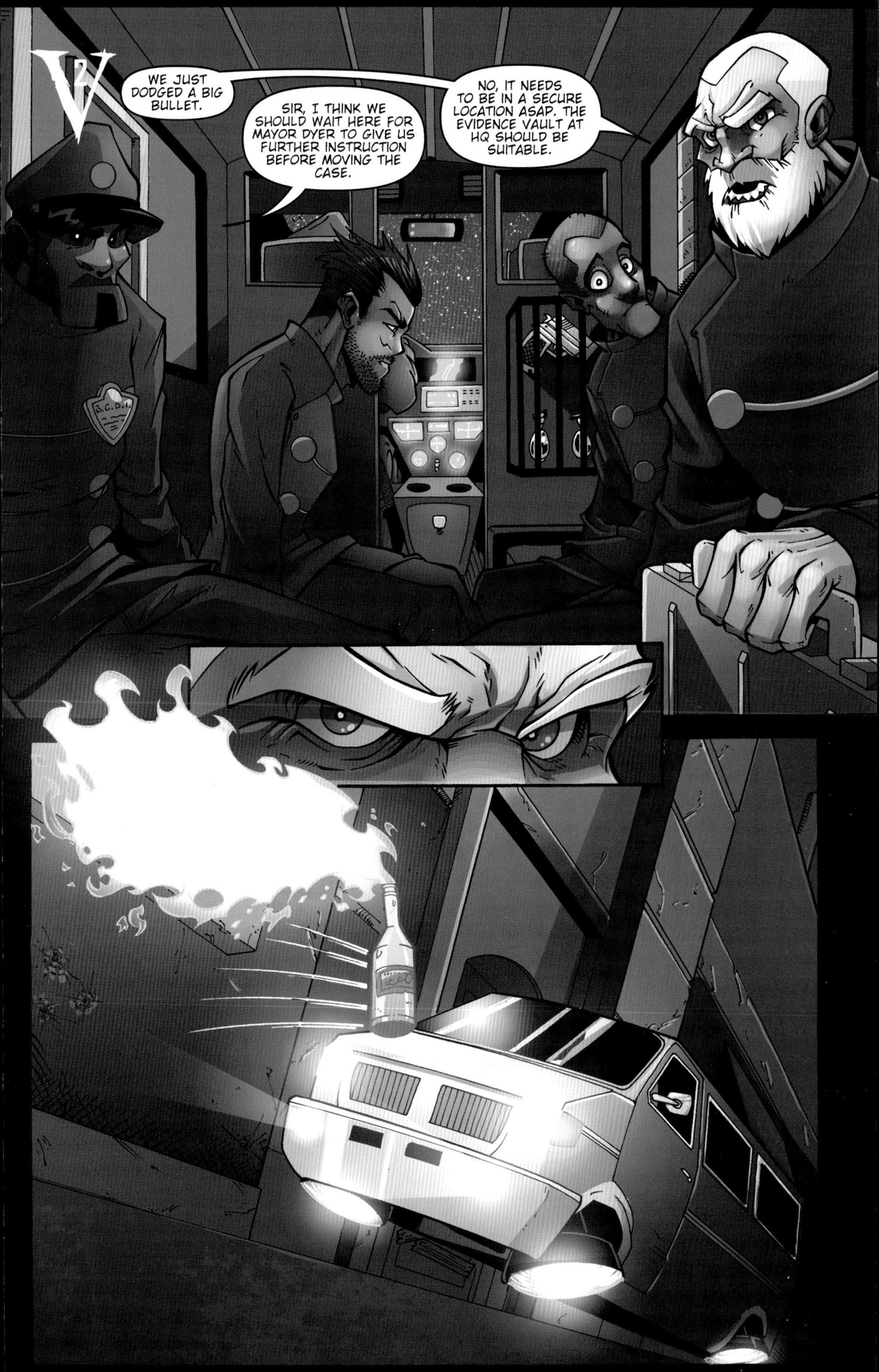
V2
WE JUST DODGED A BIG BULLET.
SIR, I THINK WE SHOULD WAIT HERE FOR MAYOR DYER TO GIVE US FURTHER INSTRUCTION BEFORE MOVING THE CASE.
NO, IT NEEDS TO BE IN A SECURE LOCATION ASAP. THE EVIDENCE VAULT AT HQ SHOULD BE SUITABLE.

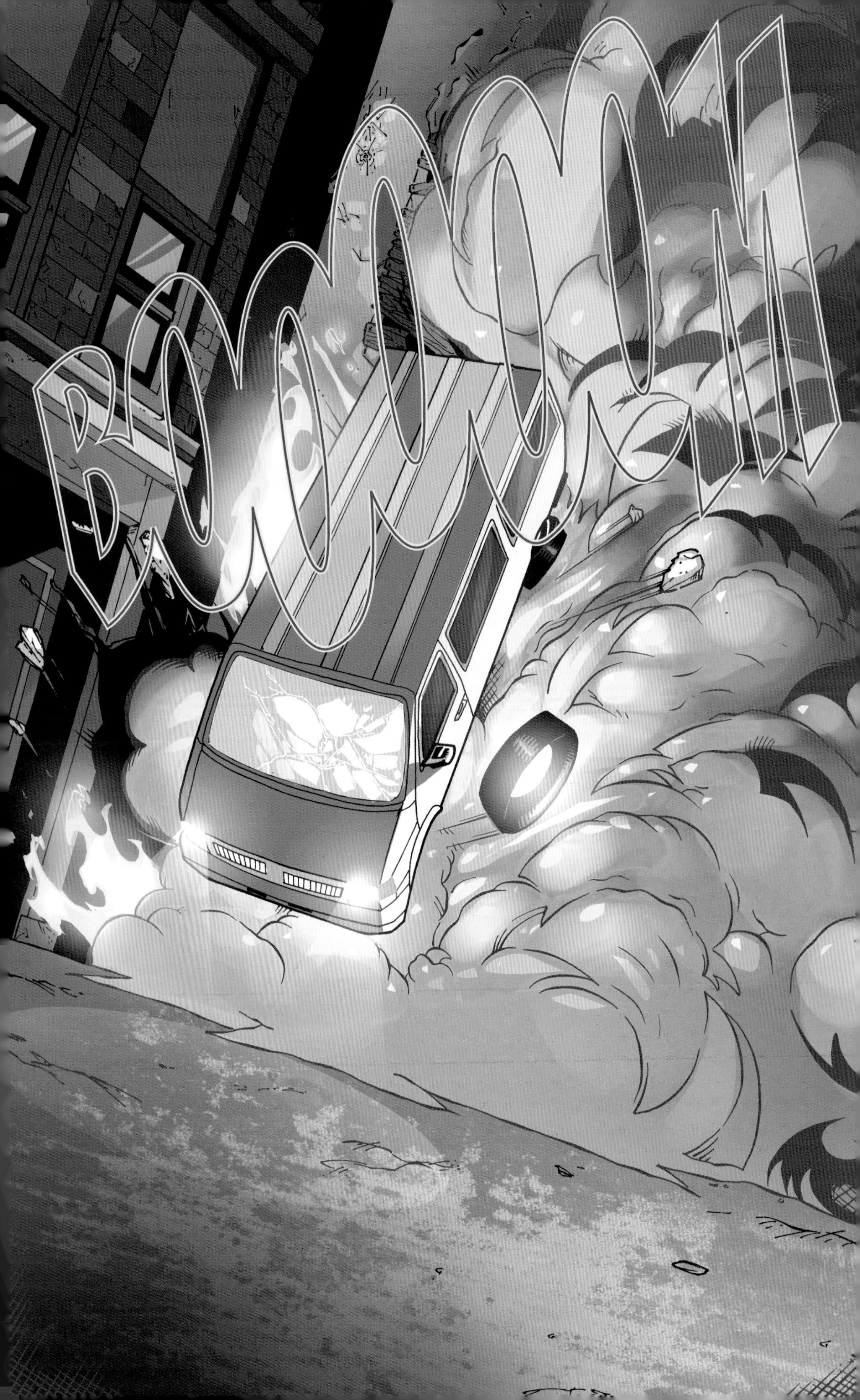
BOOOOOOM

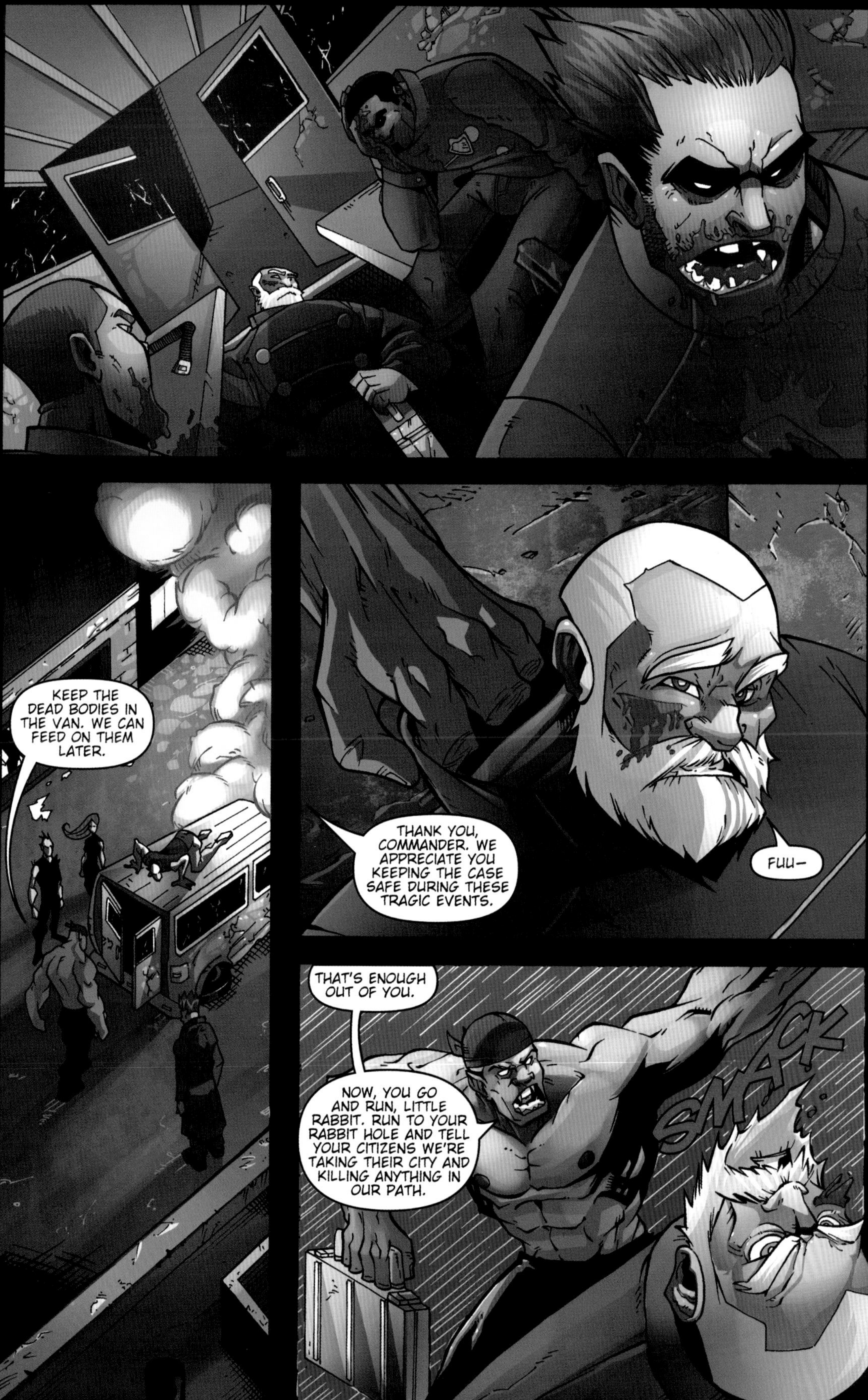
KEEP THE DEAD BODIES IN THE VAN. WE CAN FEED ON THEM LATER.
THANK YOU, COMMANDER. WE APPRECIATE YOU KEEPING THE CASE SAFE DURING THESE TRAGIC EVENTS.
FUU–
THAT'S ENOUGH OUT OF YOU.
NOW, YOU GO AND RUN, LITTLE RABBIT. RUN TO YOUR RABBIT HOLE AND TELL YOUR CITIZENS WE'RE TAKING THEIR CITY AND KILLING ANYTHING IN OUR PATH.
SMACK

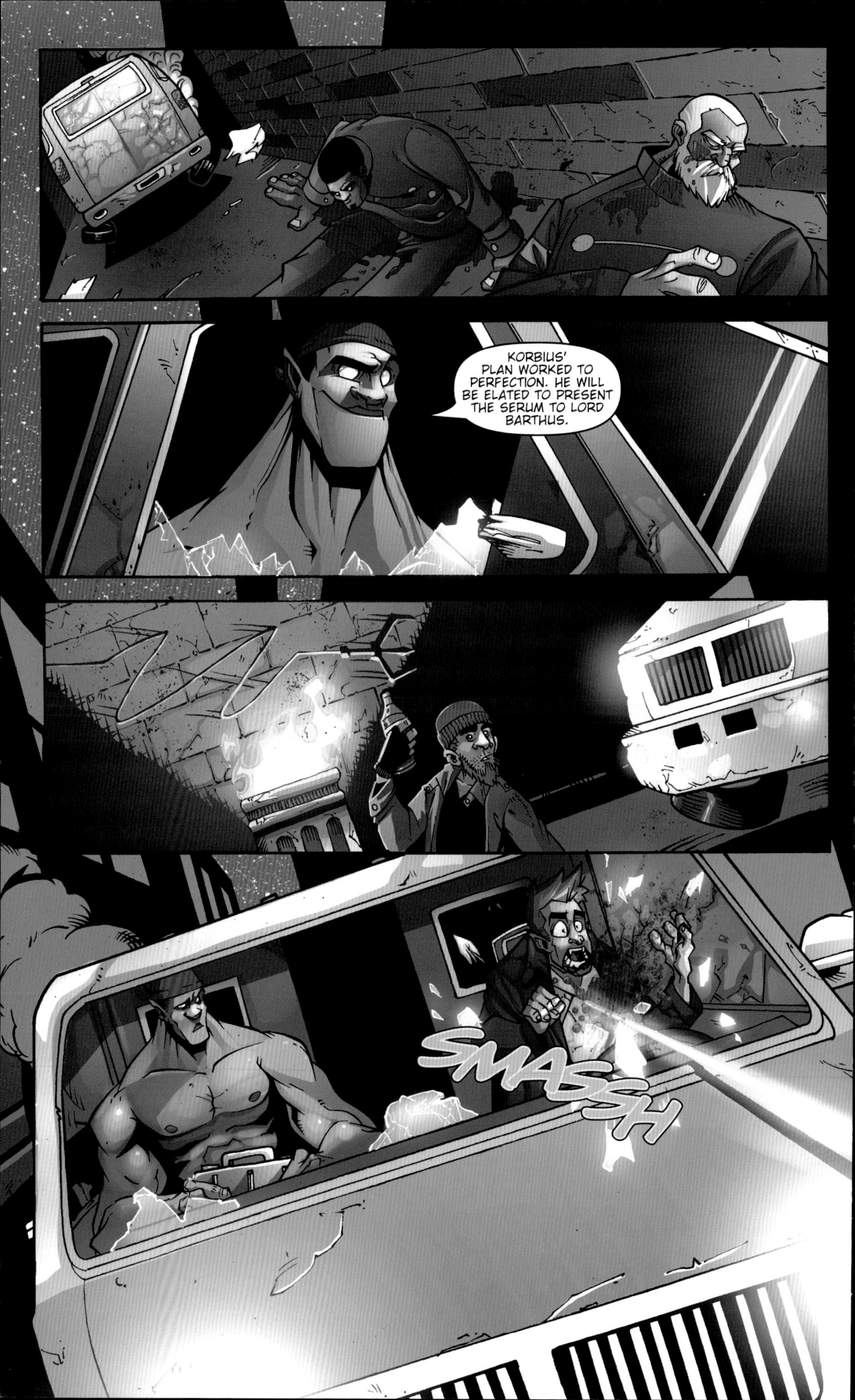
KORBIUS' PLAN WORKED TO PERFECTION. HE WILL BE ELATED TO PRESENT THE SERUM TO LORD BARTHUS.
SMASSH

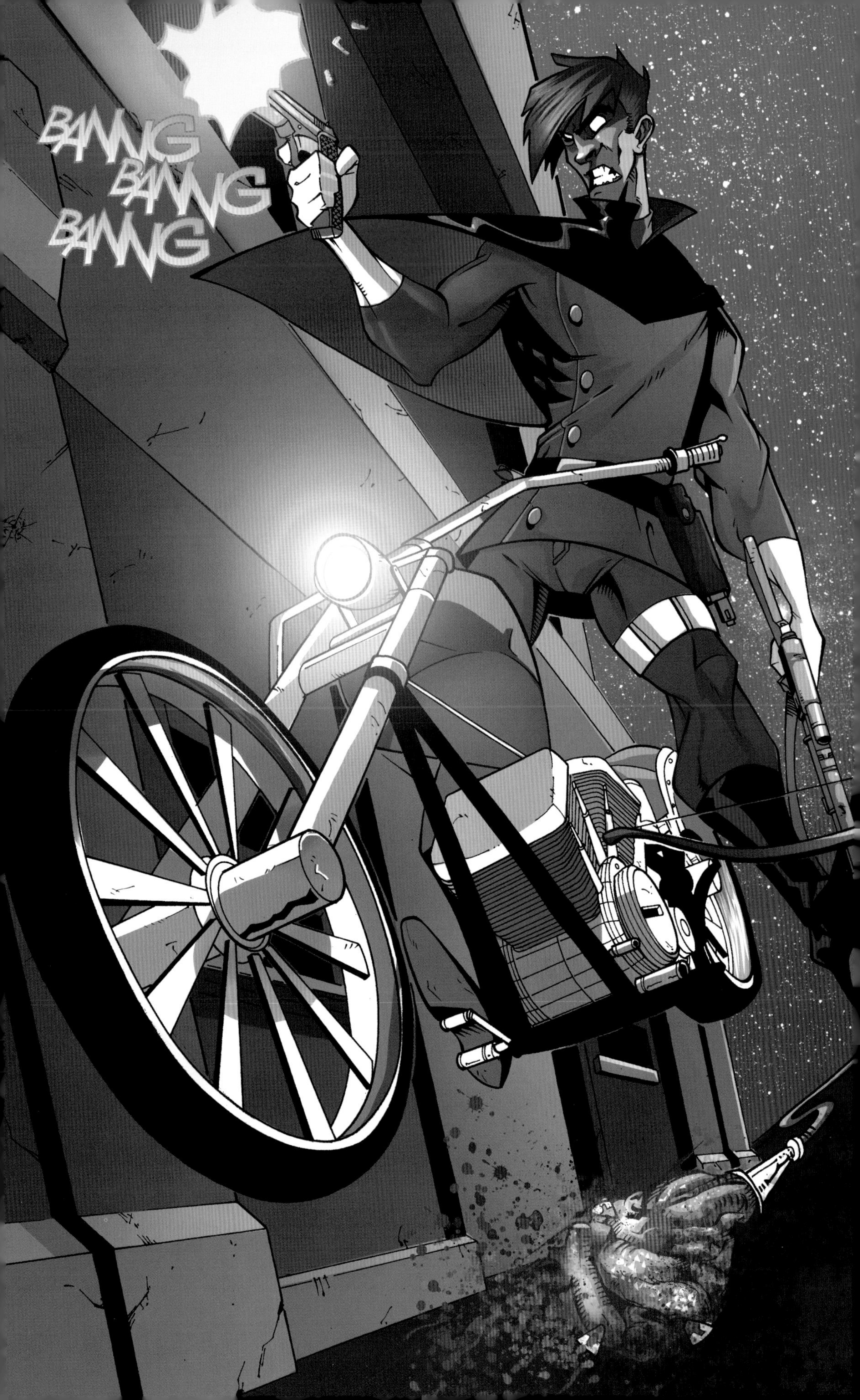
BANNG
BANNG
BANNG

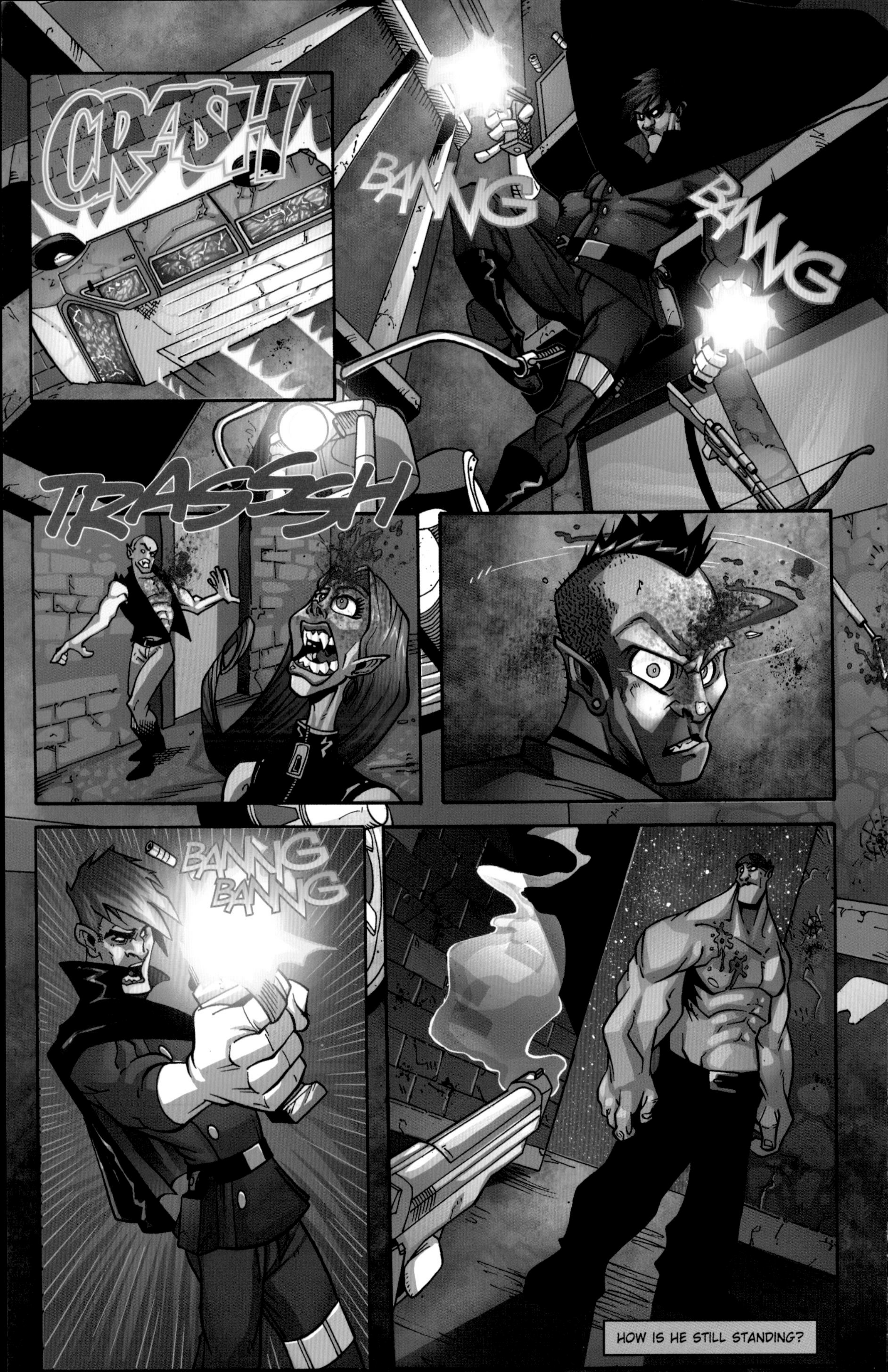
CRASH!
BANNG
BANNG
TRASSSH
BANNG
BANNG
HOW IS HE STILL STANDING?

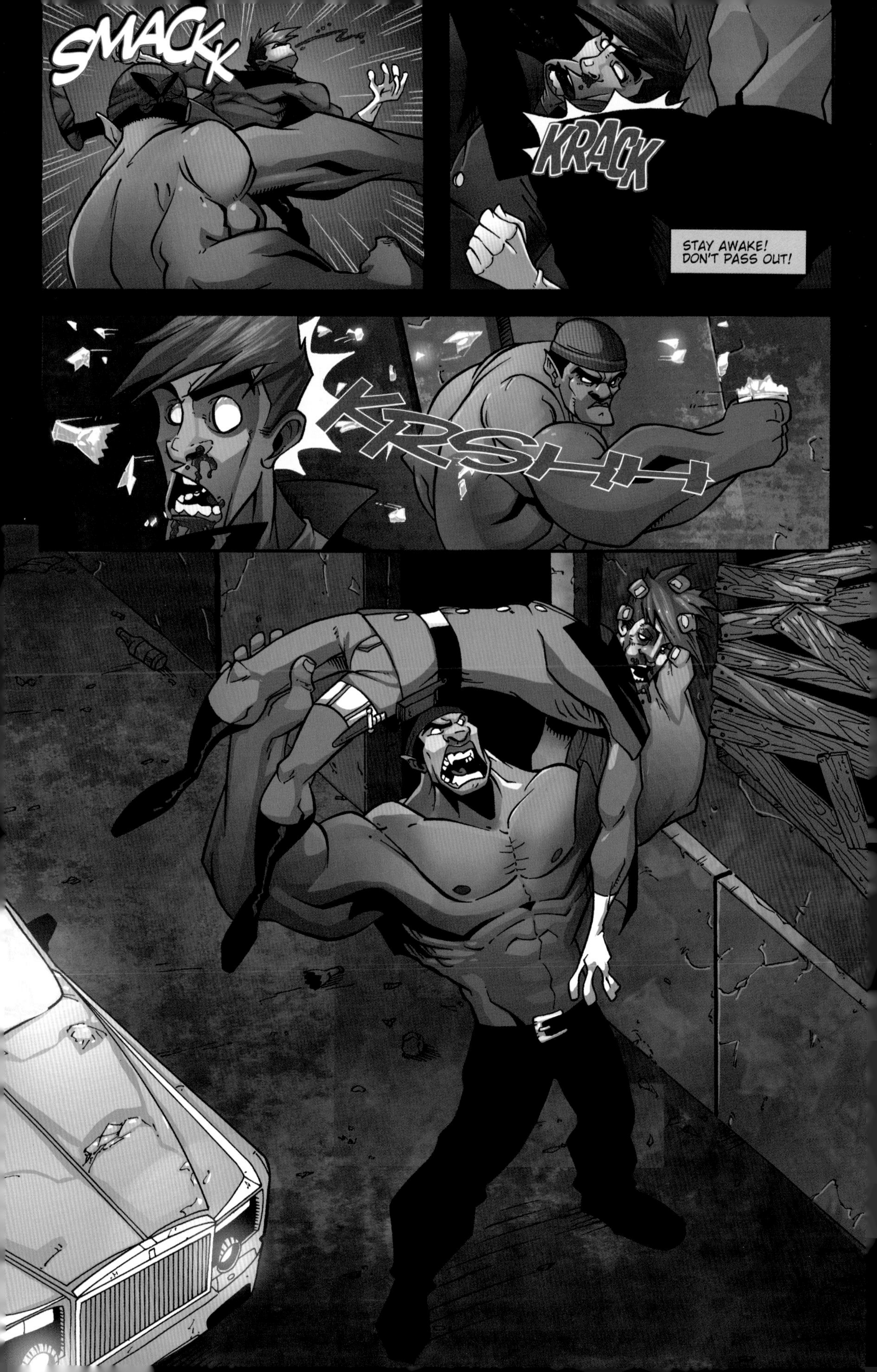
SMACKK
KRACK
STAY AWAKE! DON'T PASS OUT!
KRSHH

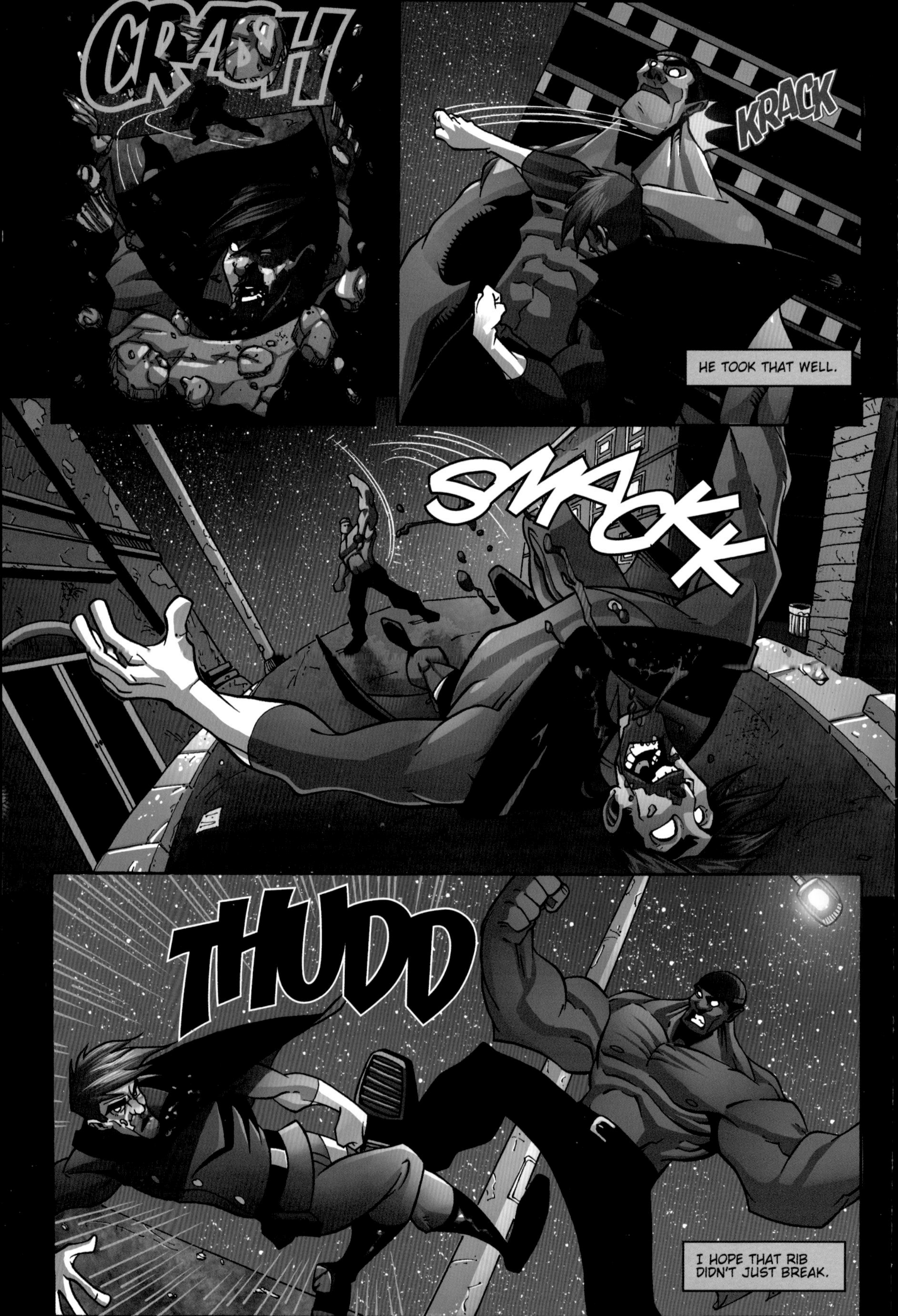
CRASH
KRACK
HE TOOK THAT WELL.
SMACKK
THUDD
I HOPE THAT RIB
DIDN'T JUST BREAK.

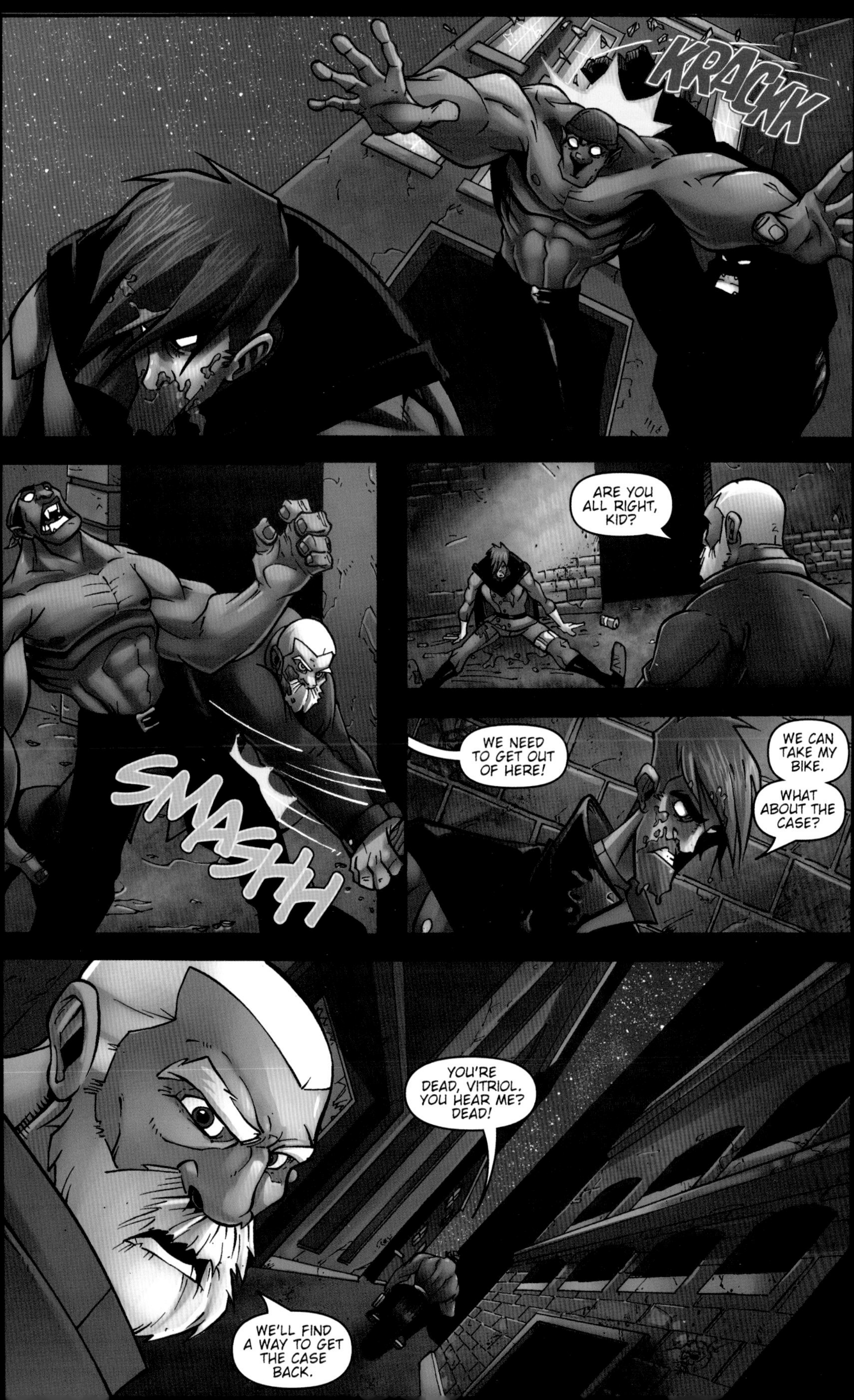
KRACKK
SMASHH
ARE YOU ALL RIGHT, KID?
WE NEED TO GET OUT OF HERE!
WE CAN TAKE MY BIKE.
WHAT ABOUT THE CASE?
YOU'RE DEAD, VITRIOL. YOU HEAR ME? DEAD!
WE'LL FIND A WAY TO GET THE CASE BACK.

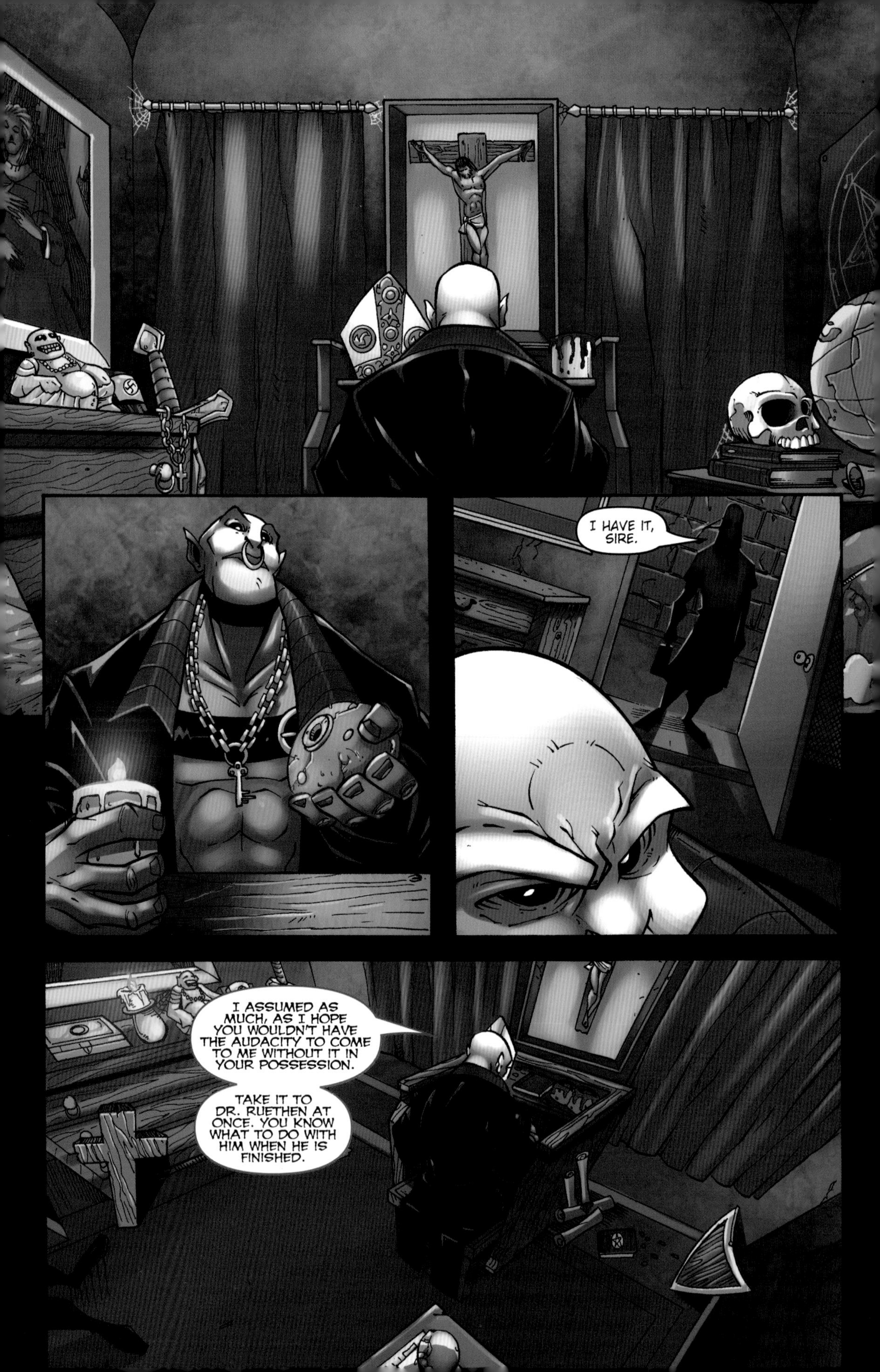
I HAVE IT, SIRE.
I ASSUMED AS MUCH, AS I HOPE YOU WOULDN'T HAVE THE AUDACITY TO COME TO ME WITHOUT IT IN YOUR POSSESSION.
TAKE IT TO DR. RUETHEN AT ONCE. YOU KNOW WHAT TO DO WITH HIM WHEN HE IS FINISHED.

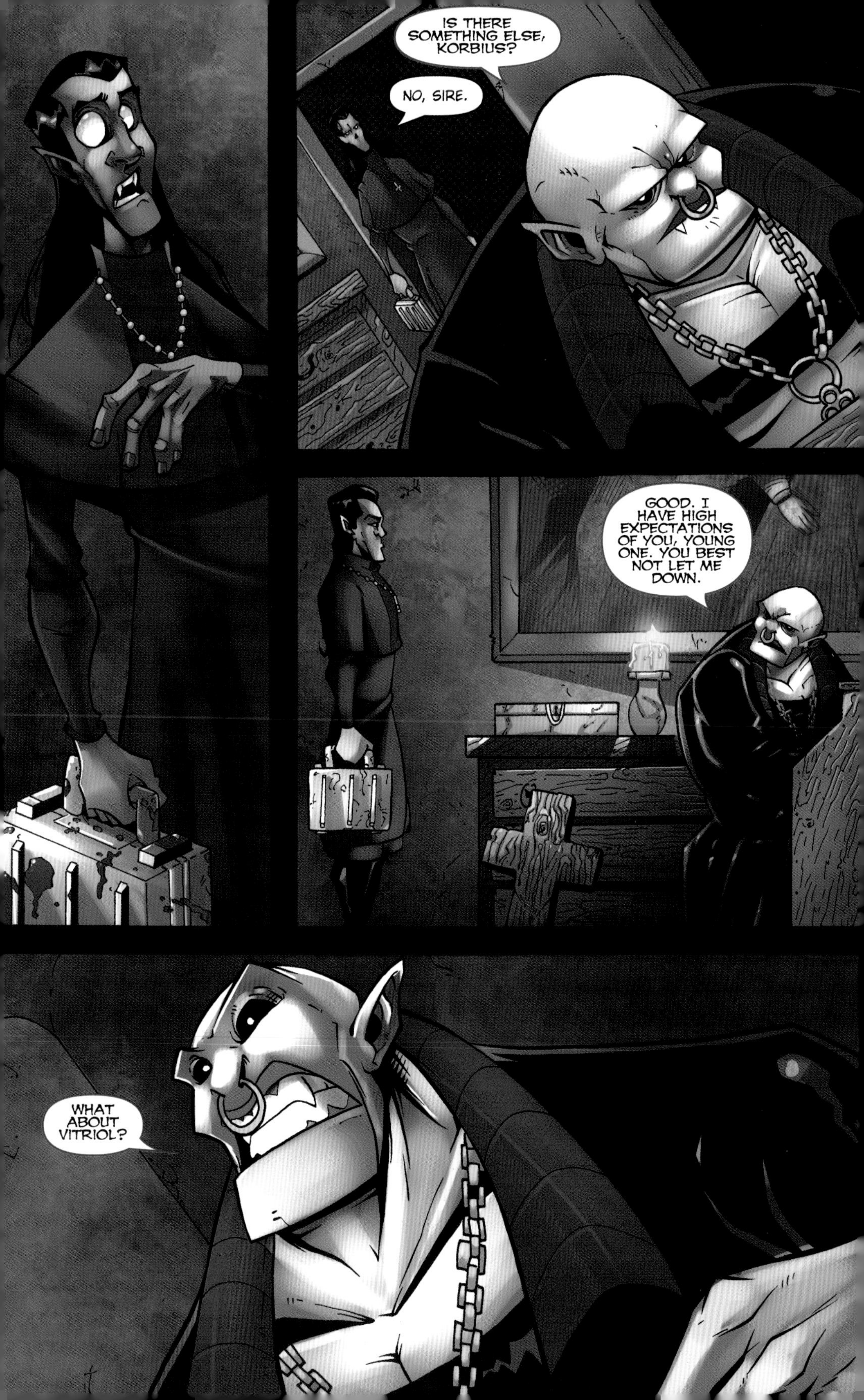
IS THERE SOMETHING ELSE, KORBIUS?
NO, SIRE.
GOOD. I HAVE HIGH EXPECTATIONS OF YOU, YOUNG ONE. YOU BEST NOT LET ME DOWN.
WHAT ABOUT VITRIOL?

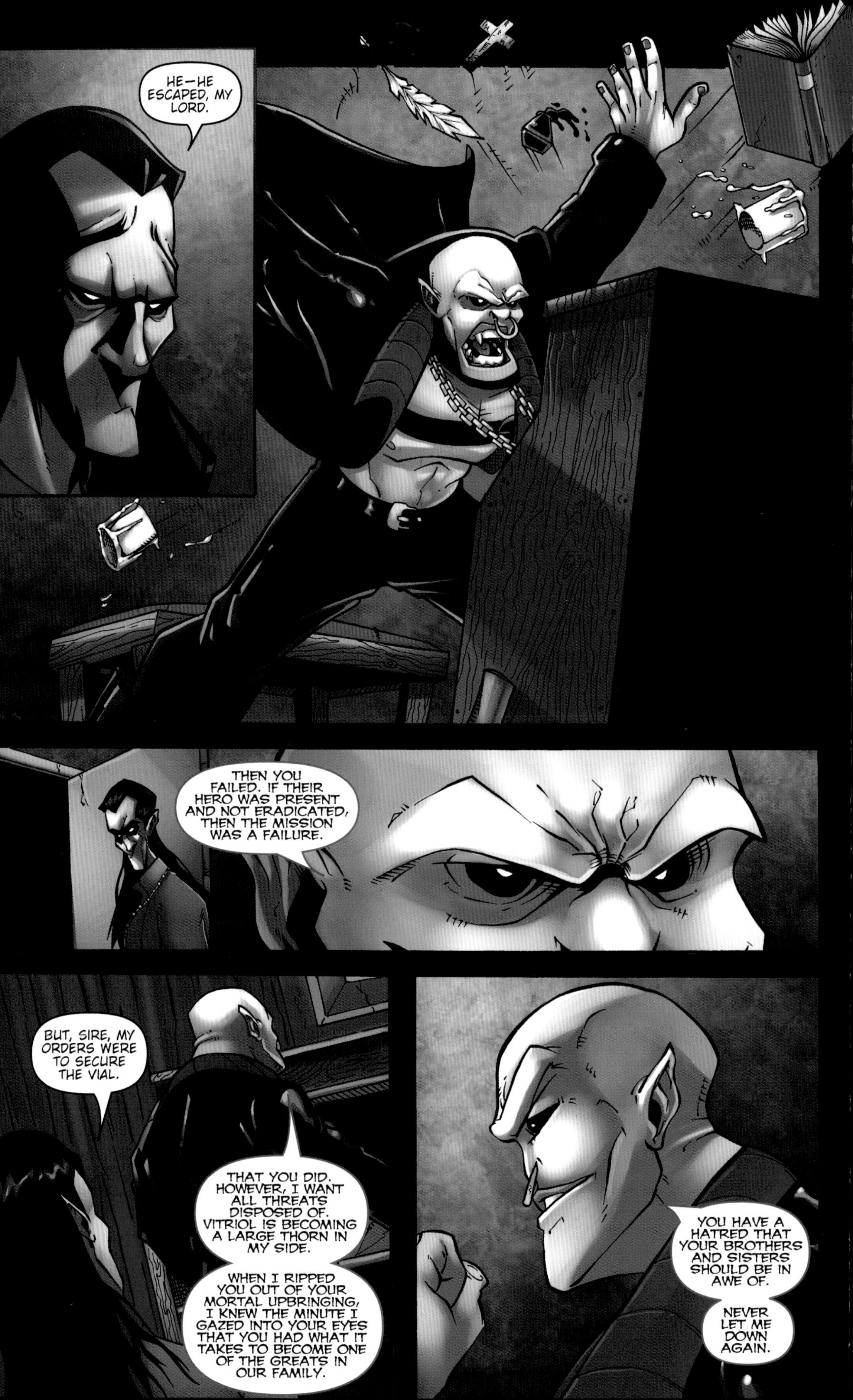
HE—HE ESCAPED, MY LORD.
THEN YOU FAILED. IF THEIR HERO WAS PRESENT AND NOT ERADICATED, THEN THE MISSION WAS A FAILURE.
BUT, SIRE, MY ORDERS WERE TO SECURE THE VIAL.
THAT YOU DID. HOWEVER, I WANT ALL THREATS DISPOSED OF. VITRIOL IS BECOMING A LARGE THORN IN MY SIDE.
WHEN I RIPPED YOU OUT OF YOUR MORTAL UPBRINGING, I KNEW THE MINUTE I GAZED INTO YOUR EYES THAT YOU HAD WHAT IT TAKES TO BECOME ONE OF THE GREATS IN OUR FAMILY.
YOU HAVE A HATRED THAT YOUR BROTHERS AND SISTERS SHOULD BE IN AWE OF.
NEVER LET ME DOWN AGAIN.

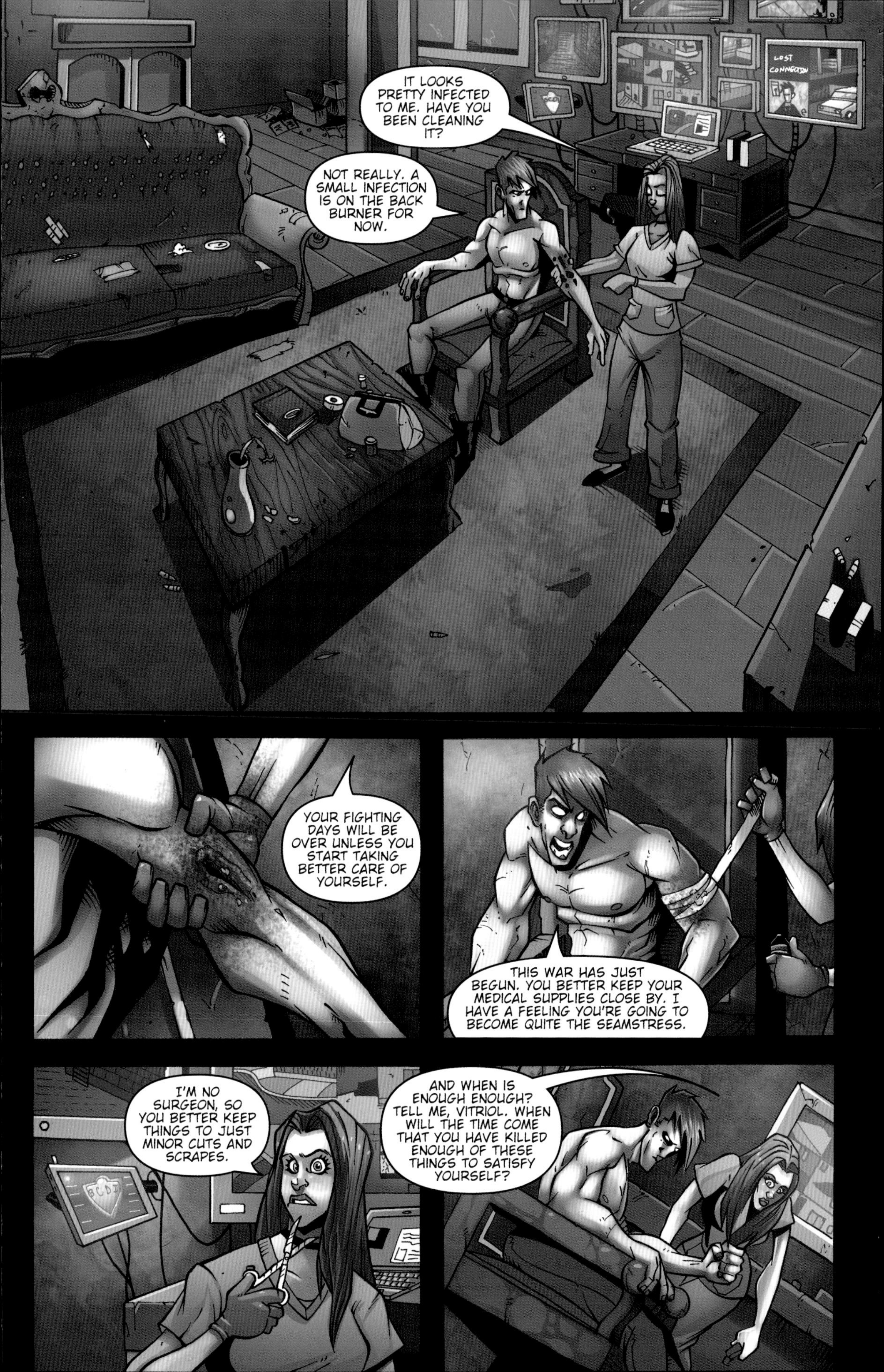
LOST CONNECTION
IT LOOKS PRETTY INFECTED TO ME. HAVE YOU BEEN CLEANING IT?
NOT REALLY. A SMALL INFECTION IS ON THE BACK BURNER FOR NOW.
YOUR FIGHTING DAYS WILL BE OVER UNLESS YOU START TAKING BETTER CARE OF YOURSELF.
THIS WAR HAS JUST BEGUN. YOU BETTER KEEP YOUR MEDICAL SUPPLIES CLOSE BY. I HAVE A FEELING YOU'RE GOING TO BECOME QUITE THE SEAMSTRESS.
I'M NO SURGEON, SO YOU BETTER KEEP THINGS TO JUST MINOR CUTS AND SCRAPES.
AND WHEN IS ENOUGH ENOUGH? TELL ME, VITRIOL. WHEN WILL THE TIME COME THAT YOU HAVE KILLED ENOUGH OF THESE THINGS TO SATISFY YOURSELF?

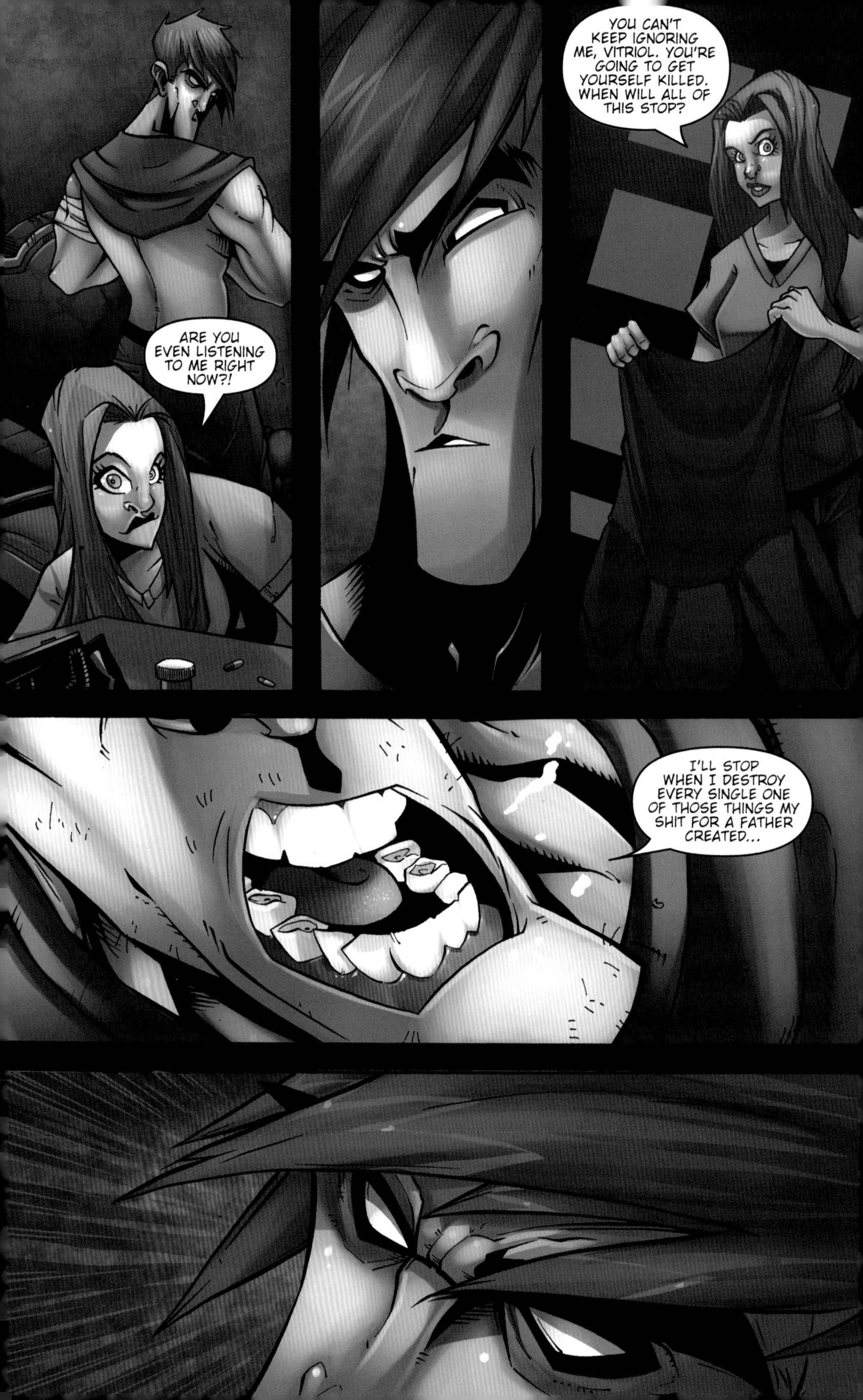
ARE YOU EVEN LISTENING TO ME RIGHT NOW?!
YOU CAN'T KEEP IGNORING ME, VITRIOL. YOU'RE GOING TO GET YOURSELF KILLED. WHEN WILL ALL OF THIS STOP?
I'LL STOP WHEN I DESTROY EVERY SINGLE ONE OF THOSE THINGS MY SHIT FOR A FATHER CREATED...

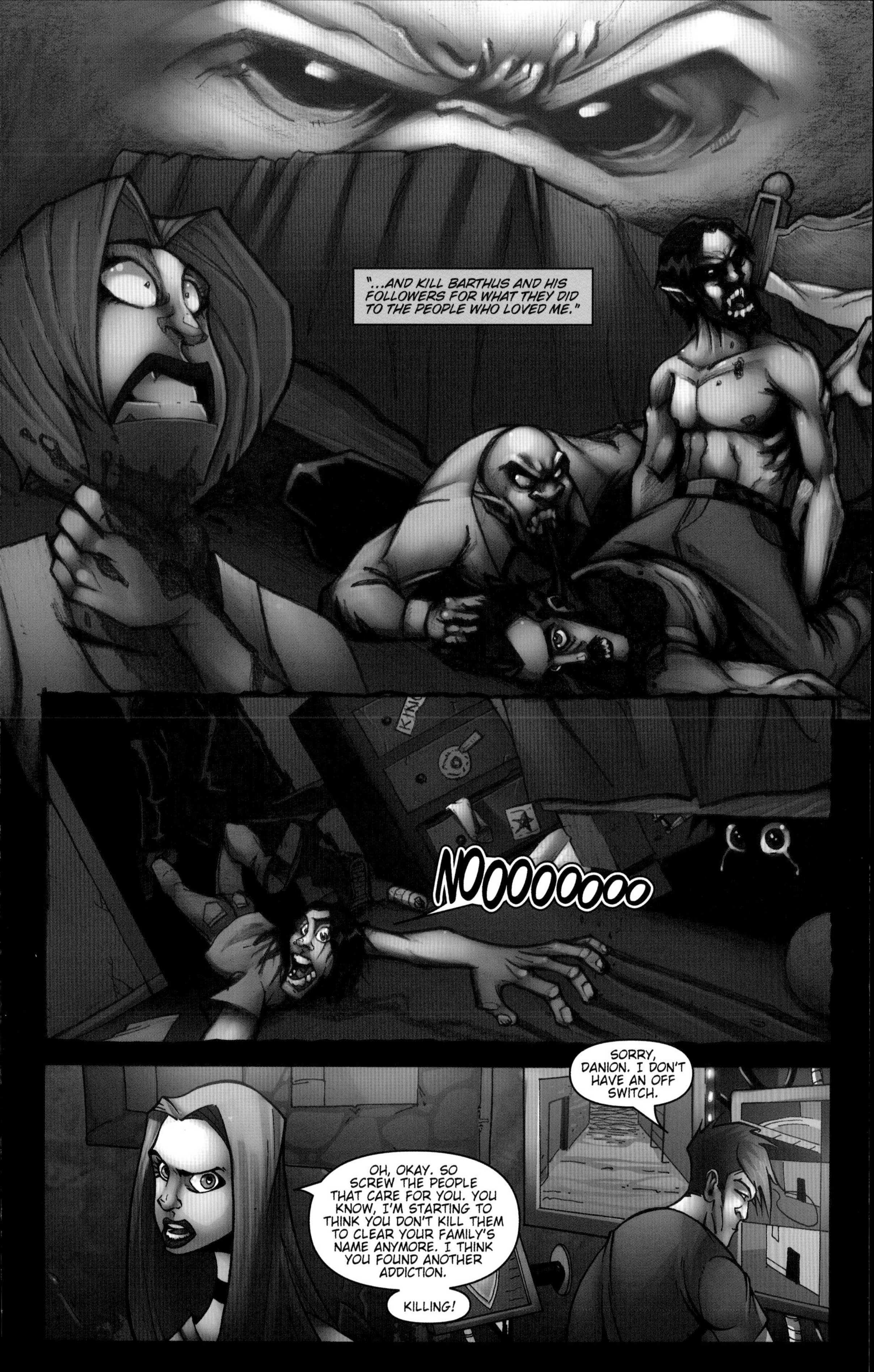
"...AND KILL BARTHUS AND HIS FOLLOWERS FOR WHAT THEY DID TO THE PEOPLE WHO LOVED ME."
NOOOOOOOO
SORRY, DANION. I DON'T HAVE AN OFF SWITCH.
OH, OKAY. SO SCREW THE PEOPLE THAT CARE FOR YOU. YOU KNOW, I'M STARTING TO THINK YOU DON'T KILL THEM TO CLEAR YOUR FAMILY'S NAME ANYMORE. I THINK YOU FOUND ANOTHER ADDICTION.
KILLING!

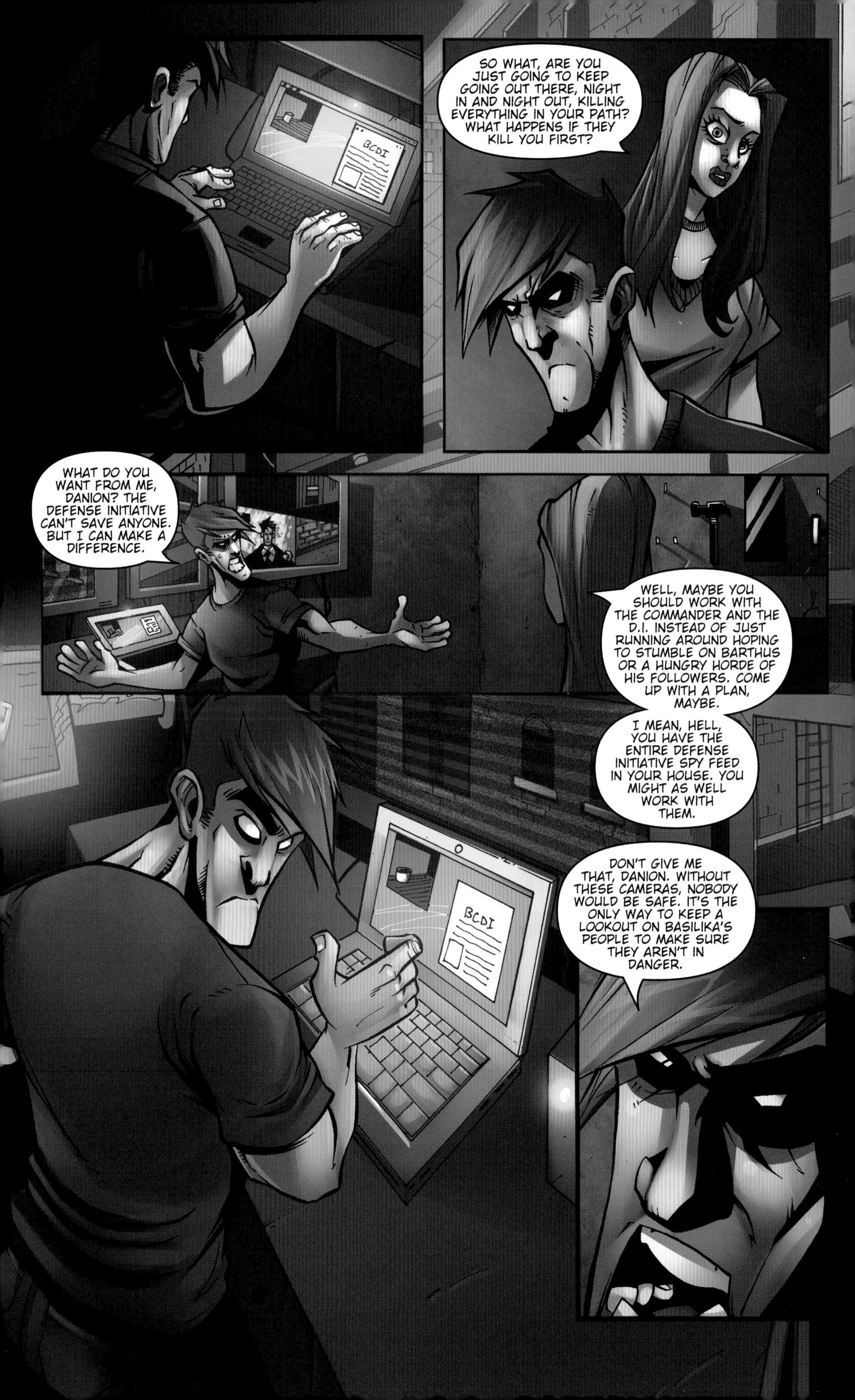
SO WHAT, ARE YOU JUST GOING TO KEEP GOING OUT THERE, NIGHT IN AND NIGHT OUT, KILLING EVERYTHING IN YOUR PATH? WHAT HAPPENS IF THEY KILL YOU FIRST?
BCDI
WHAT DO YOU WANT FROM ME, DANION? THE DEFENSE INITIATIVE CAN'T SAVE ANYONE. BUT I CAN MAKE A DIFFERENCE.
WELL, MAYBE YOU SHOULD WORK WITH THE COMMANDER AND THE D.I. INSTEAD OF JUST RUNNING AROUND HOPING TO STUMBLE ON BARTHUS OR A HUNGRY HORDE OF HIS FOLLOWERS. COME UP WITH A PLAN, MAYBE.
I MEAN, HELL, YOU HAVE THE ENTIRE DEFENSE INITIATIVE SPY FEED IN YOUR HOUSE. YOU MIGHT AS WELL WORK WITH THEM.
BCDI
DON'T GIVE ME THAT, DANION. WITHOUT THESE CAMERAS, NOBODY WOULD BE SAFE. IT'S THE ONLY WAY TO KEEP A LOOKOUT ON BASILIKA'S PEOPLE TO MAKE SURE THEY AREN'T IN DANGER.

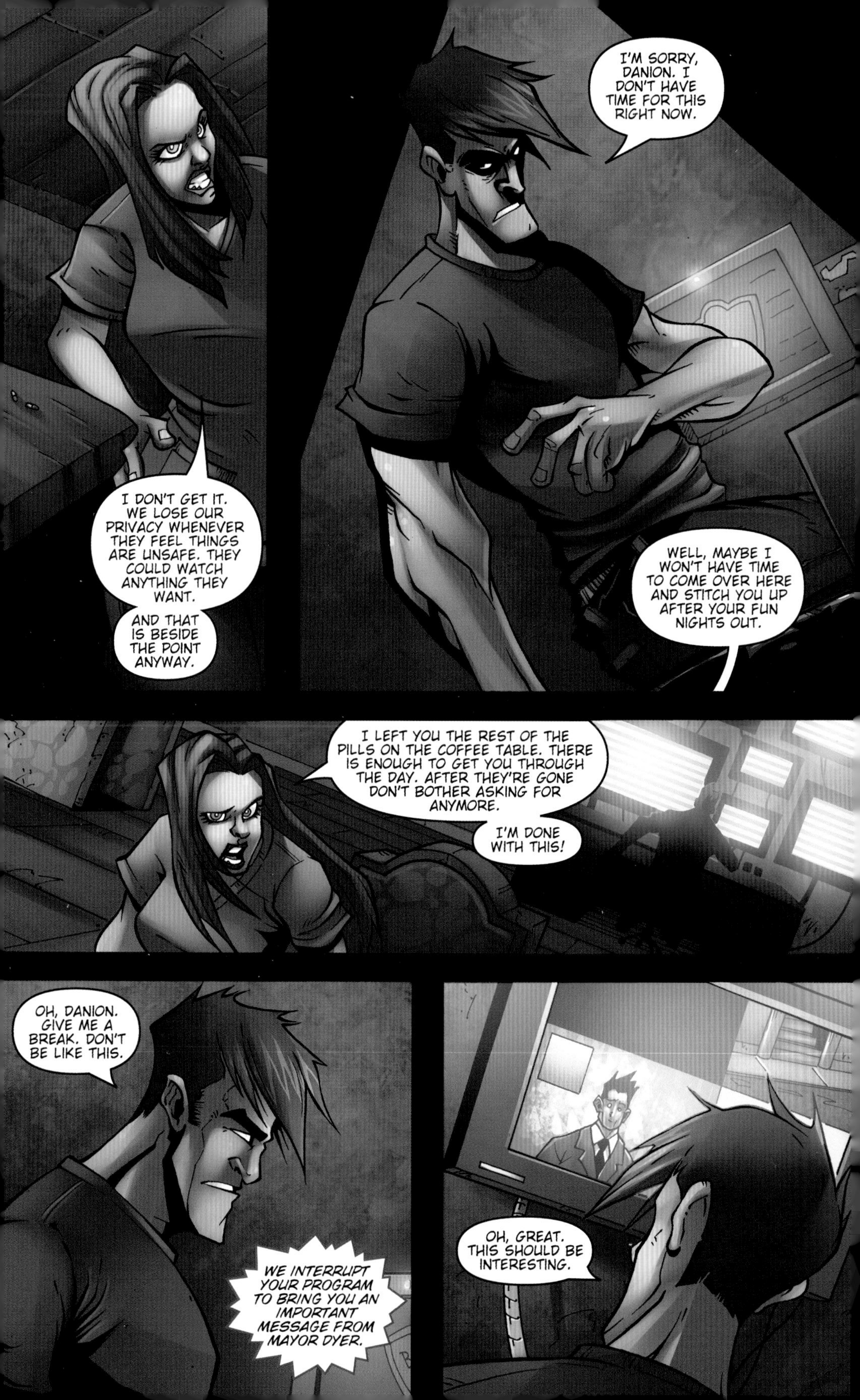
I'M SORRY, DANION. I DON'T HAVE TIME FOR THIS RIGHT NOW.
I DON'T GET IT. WE LOSE OUR PRIVACY WHENEVER THEY FEEL THINGS ARE UNSAFE. THEY COULD WATCH ANYTHING THEY WANT.
AND THAT IS BESIDE THE POINT ANYWAY.
WELL, MAYBE I WON'T HAVE TIME TO COME OVER HERE AND STITCH YOU UP AFTER YOUR FUN NIGHTS OUT.
I LEFT YOU THE REST OF THE PILLS ON THE COFFEE TABLE. THERE IS ENOUGH TO GET YOU THROUGH THE DAY. AFTER THEY'RE GONE DON'T BOTHER ASKING FOR ANYMORE.
I'M DONE WITH THIS!
OH, DANION. GIVE ME A BREAK. DON'T BE LIKE THIS.
WE INTERRUPT YOUR PROGRAM TO BRING YOU AN IMPORTANT MESSAGE FROM MAYOR DYER.
OH, GREAT. THIS SHOULD BE INTERESTING.

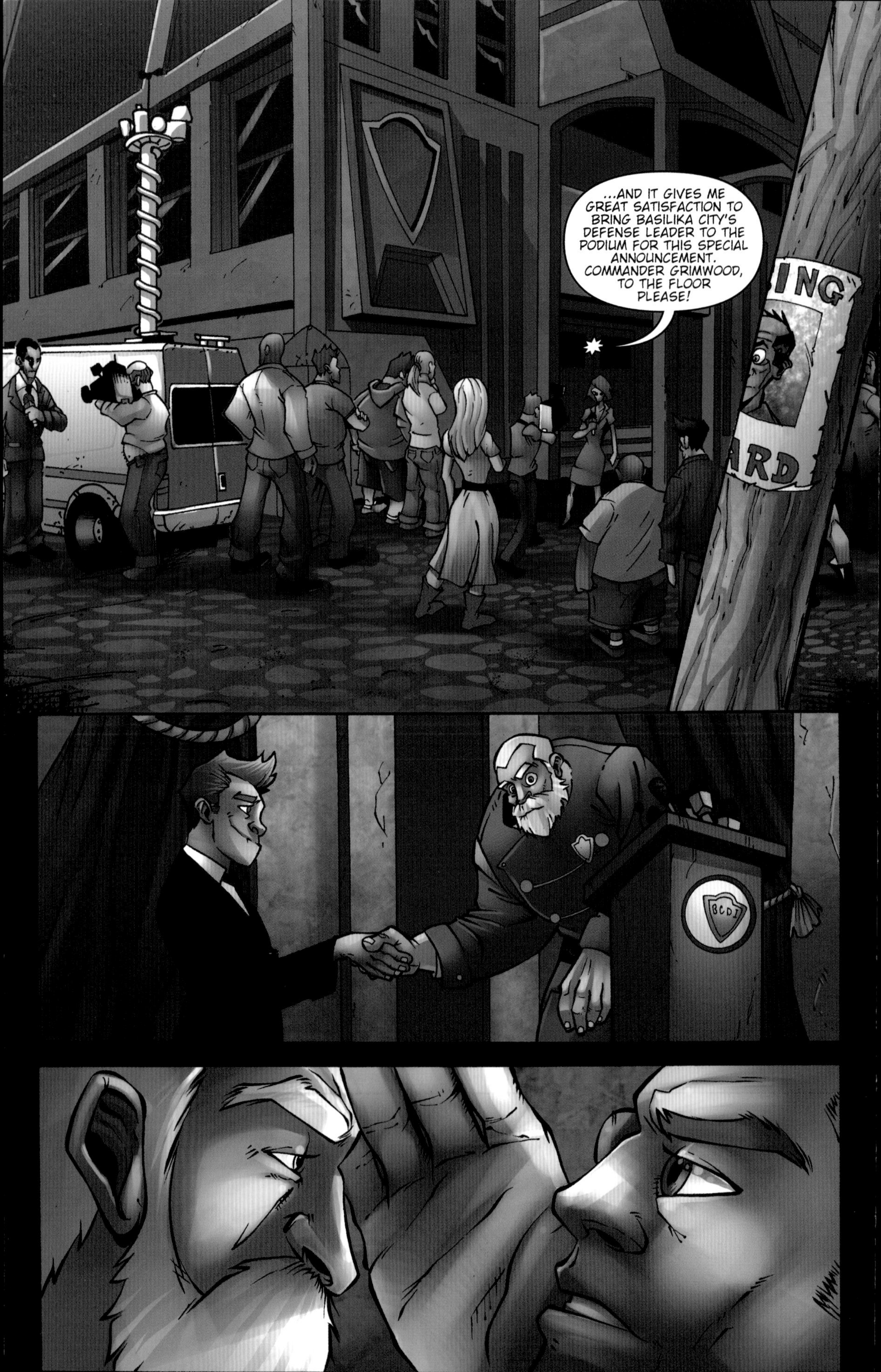
...AND IT GIVES ME GREAT SATISFACTION TO BRING BASILIKA CITY'S DEFENSE LEADER TO THE PODIUM FOR THIS SPECIAL ANNOUNCEMENT. COMMANDER GRIMWOOD, TO THE FLOOR PLEASE!

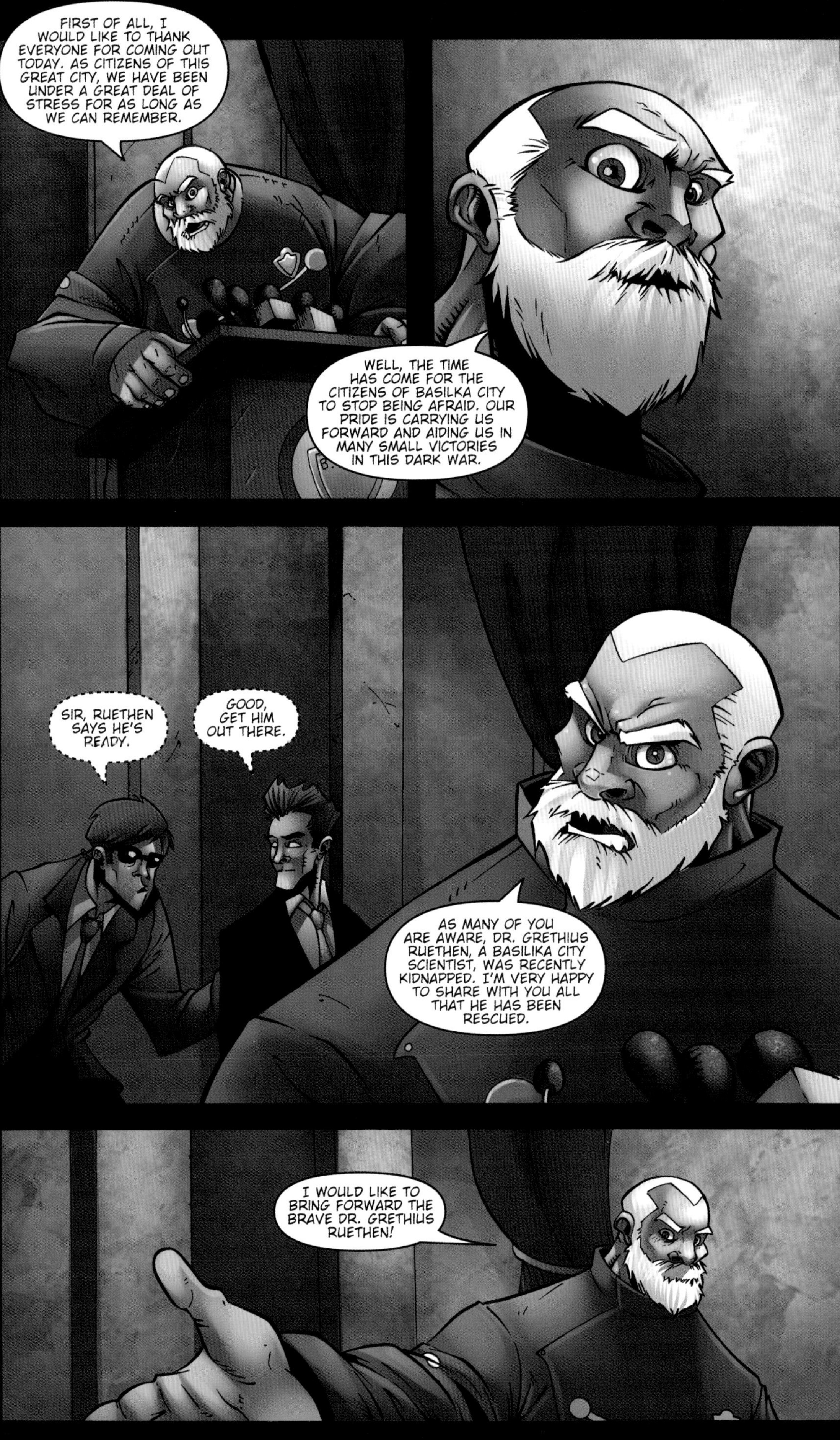
FIRST OF ALL, I WOULD LIKE TO THANK EVERYONE FOR COMING OUT TODAY. AS CITIZENS OF THIS GREAT CITY, WE HAVE BEEN UNDER A GREAT DEAL OF STRESS FOR AS LONG AS WE CAN REMEMBER.
WELL, THE TIME HAS COME FOR THE CITIZENS OF BASILKA CITY TO STOP BEING AFRAID. OUR PRIDE IS CARRYING US FORWARD AND AIDING US IN MANY SMALL VICTORIES IN THIS DARK WAR.
SIR, RUETHEN SAYS HE'S READY.
GOOD, GET HIM OUT THERE.
AS MANY OF YOU ARE AWARE, DR. GRETHIUS RUETHEN, A BASILIKA CITY SCIENTIST, WAS RECENTLY KIDNAPPED. I'M VERY HAPPY TO SHARE WITH YOU ALL THAT HE HAS BEEN RESCUED.
I WOULD LIKE TO BRING FORWARD THE BRAVE DR. GRETHIUS RUETHEN!

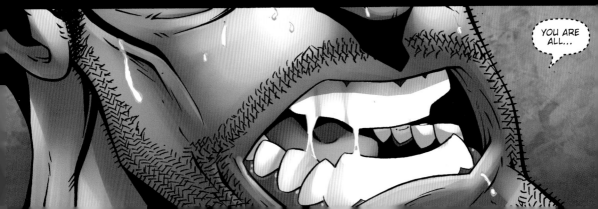

YOU ARE
ALL...

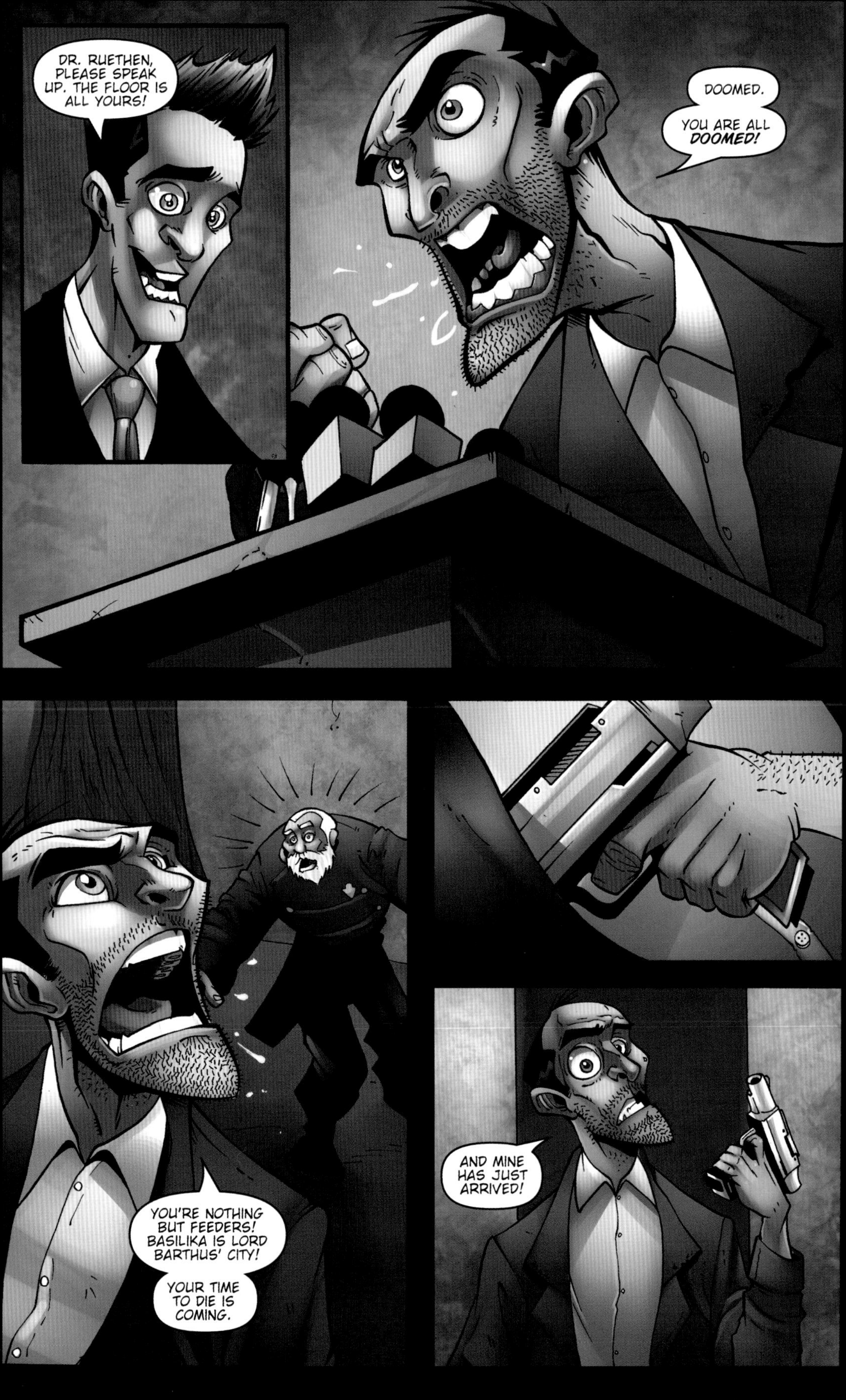

DR. RUETHEN, PLEASE SPEAK UP. THE FLOOR IS ALL YOURS!
DOOMED.
YOU ARE ALL **DOOMED!**
YOU'RE NOTHING BUT FEEDERS! BASILIKA IS LORD BARTHUS' CITY!
YOUR TIME TO DIE IS COMING.
AND MINE HAS JUST ARRIVED!

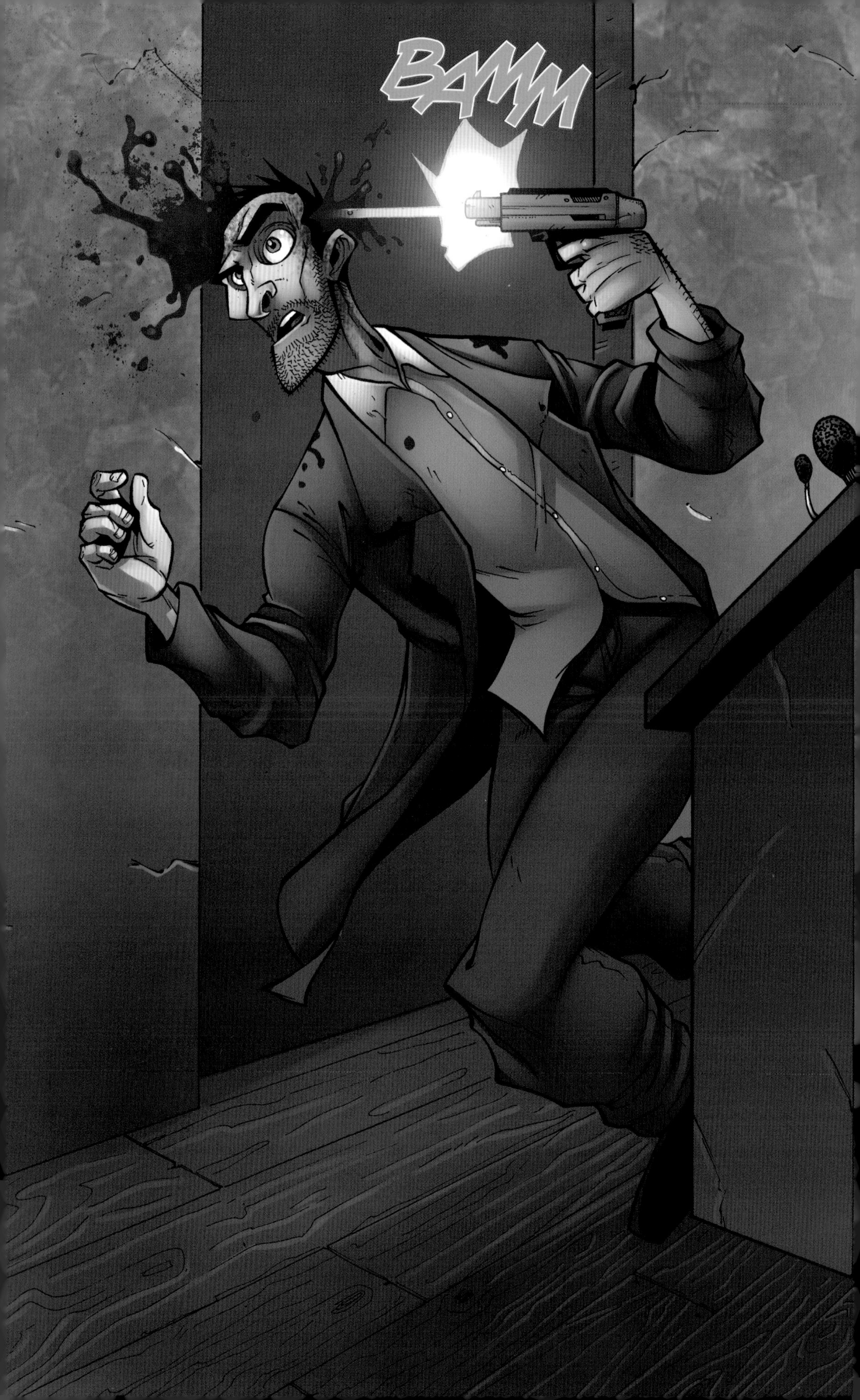
BAMM

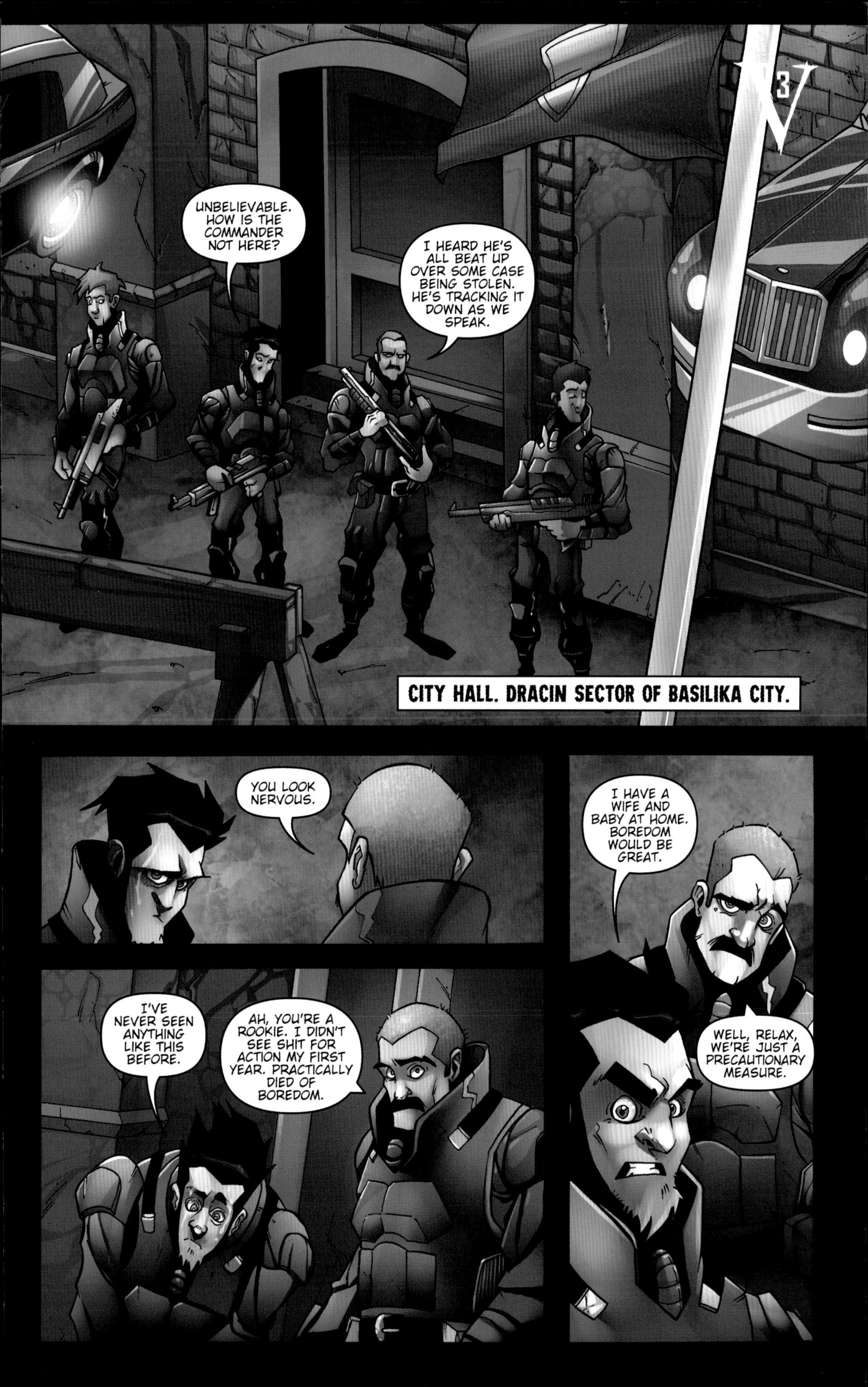
UNBELIEVABLE. HOW IS THE COMMANDER NOT HERE?
I HEARD HE'S ALL BEAT UP OVER SOME CASE BEING STOLEN. HE'S TRACKING IT DOWN AS WE SPEAK.
CITY HALL. DRACIN SECTOR OF BASILIKA CITY.
YOU LOOK NERVOUS.
I'VE NEVER SEEN ANYTHING LIKE THIS BEFORE.
AH, YOU'RE A ROOKIE. I DIDN'T SEE SHIT FOR ACTION MY FIRST YEAR. PRACTICALLY DIED OF BOREDOM.
I HAVE A WIFE AND BABY AT HOME. BOREDOM WOULD BE GREAT.
WELL, RELAX, WE'RE JUST A PRECAUTIONARY MEASURE.

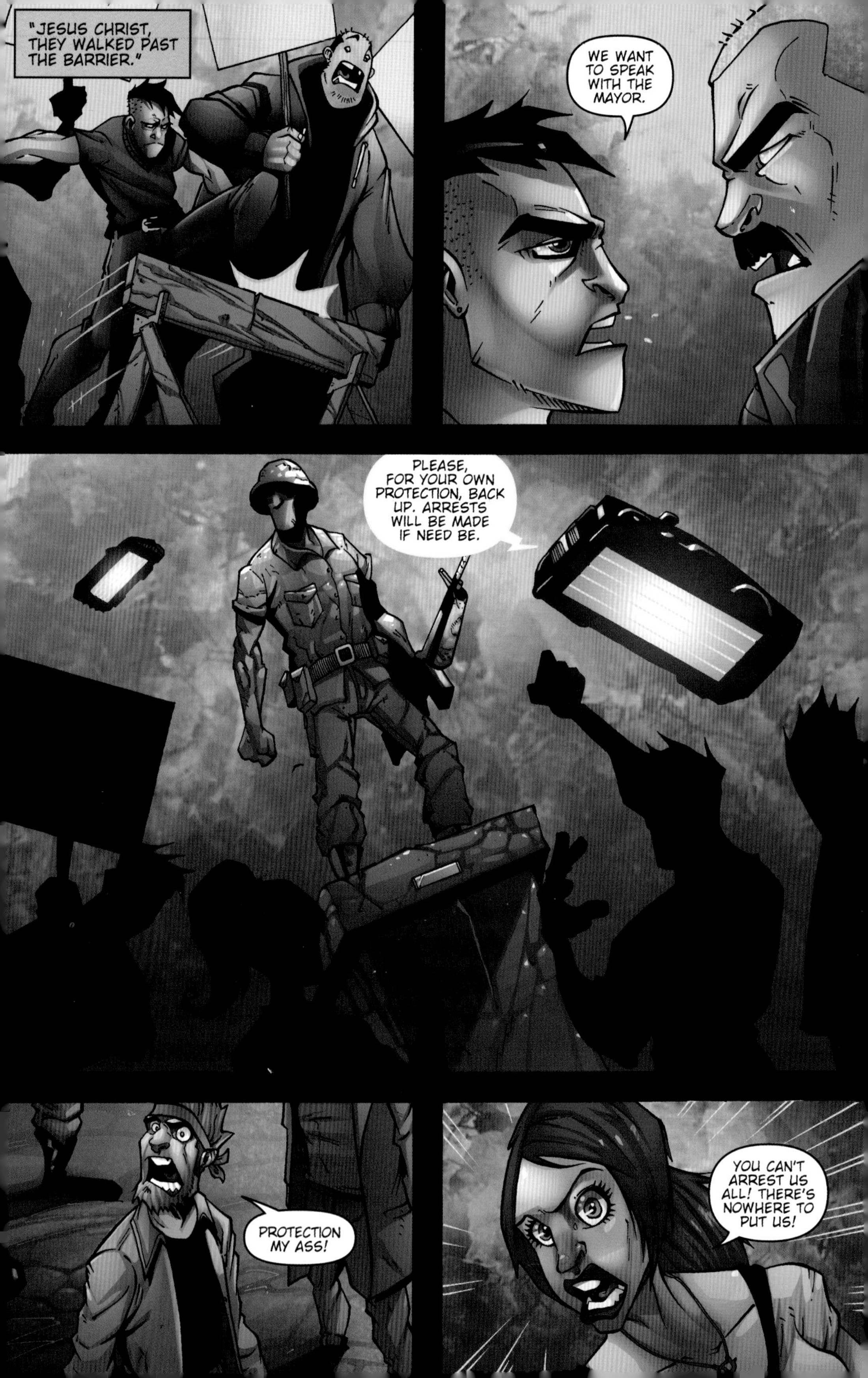
"JESUS CHRIST, THEY WALKED PAST THE BARRIER."
WE WANT TO SPEAK WITH THE MAYOR.
PLEASE, FOR YOUR OWN PROTECTION, BACK UP. ARRESTS WILL BE MADE IF NEED BE.
PROTECTION MY ASS!
YOU CAN'T ARREST US ALL! THERE'S NOWHERE TO PUT US!

BEST STEP BACK BEFORE I MOVE YOU MYSELF, SON.

GET OUT OF MY FACE, YOU PRICK!

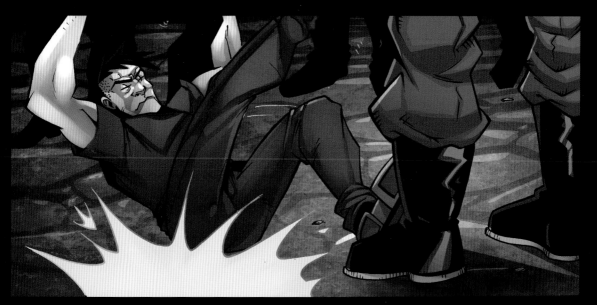

BRING IT, MAN.

SCREW YOU, ASSHOLE!

HOLD IT. THE MAYOR WILL HAVE YOUR BADGE IF YOU'RE SEEN HITTING A DEFENSELESS CIVILIAN.

HIS WORD AGAINST MINE!

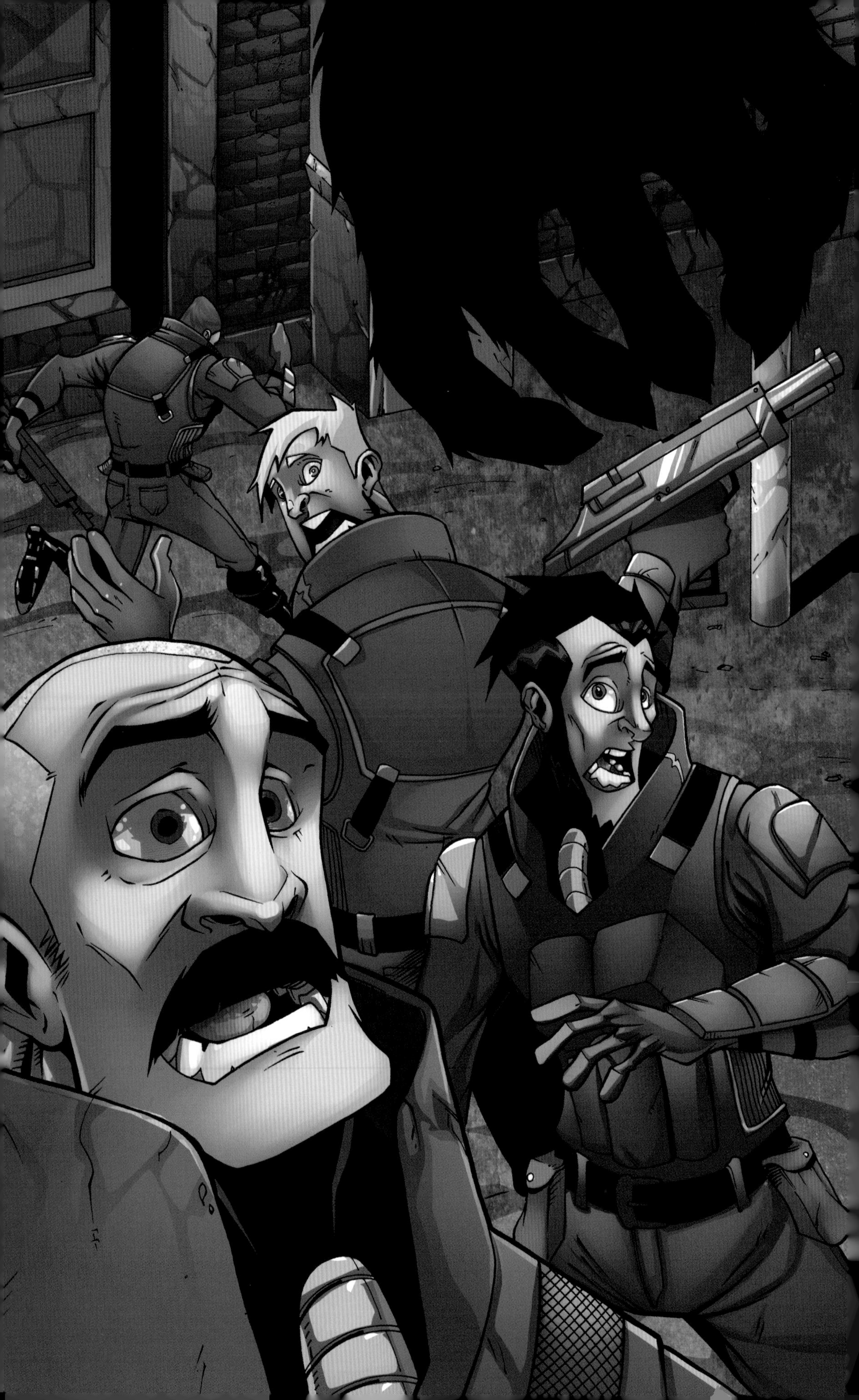

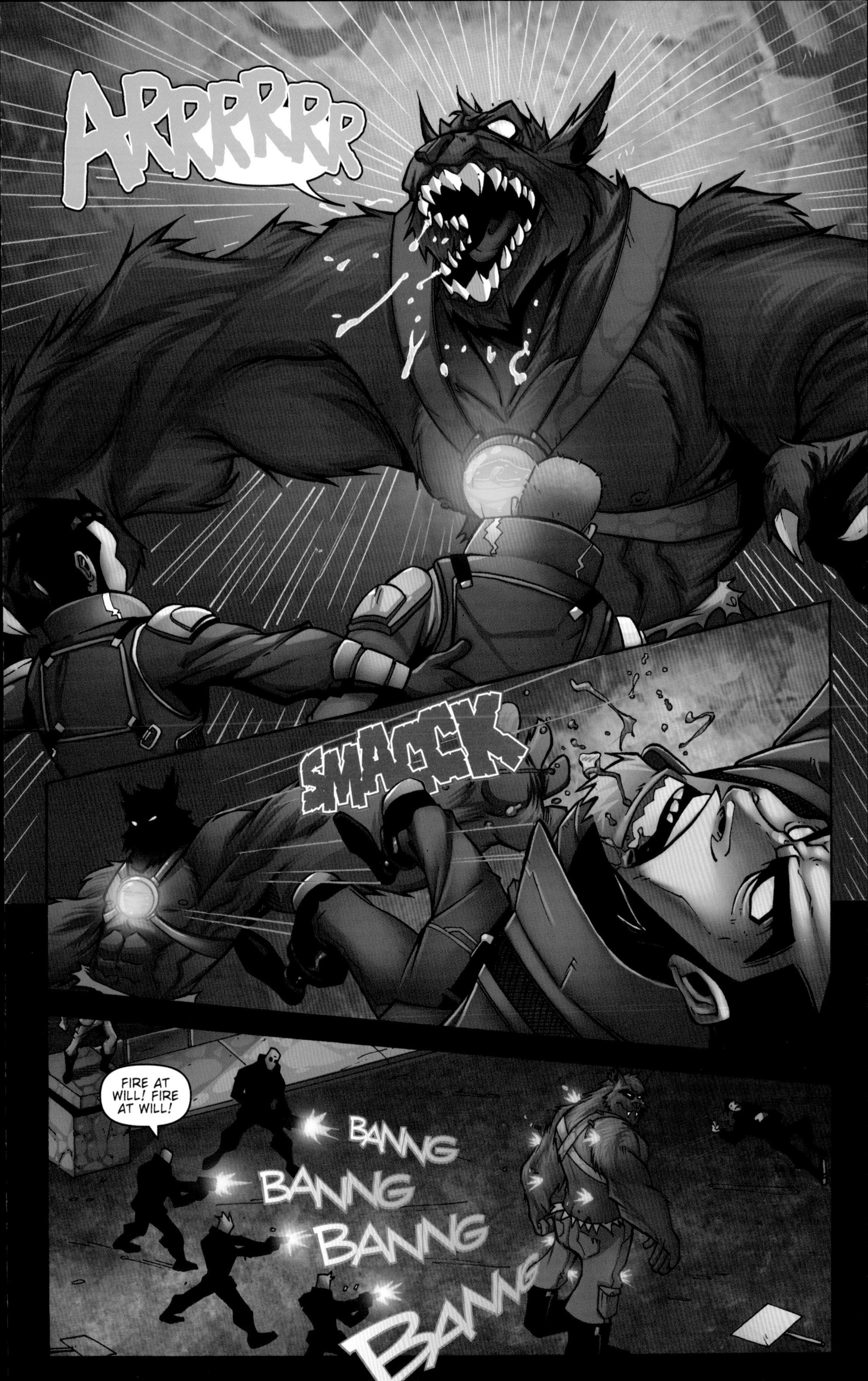
ARRRRRR
SMACCK
FIRE AT WILL! FIRE AT WILL!
BANNG
BANNG
BANNG
BANNG

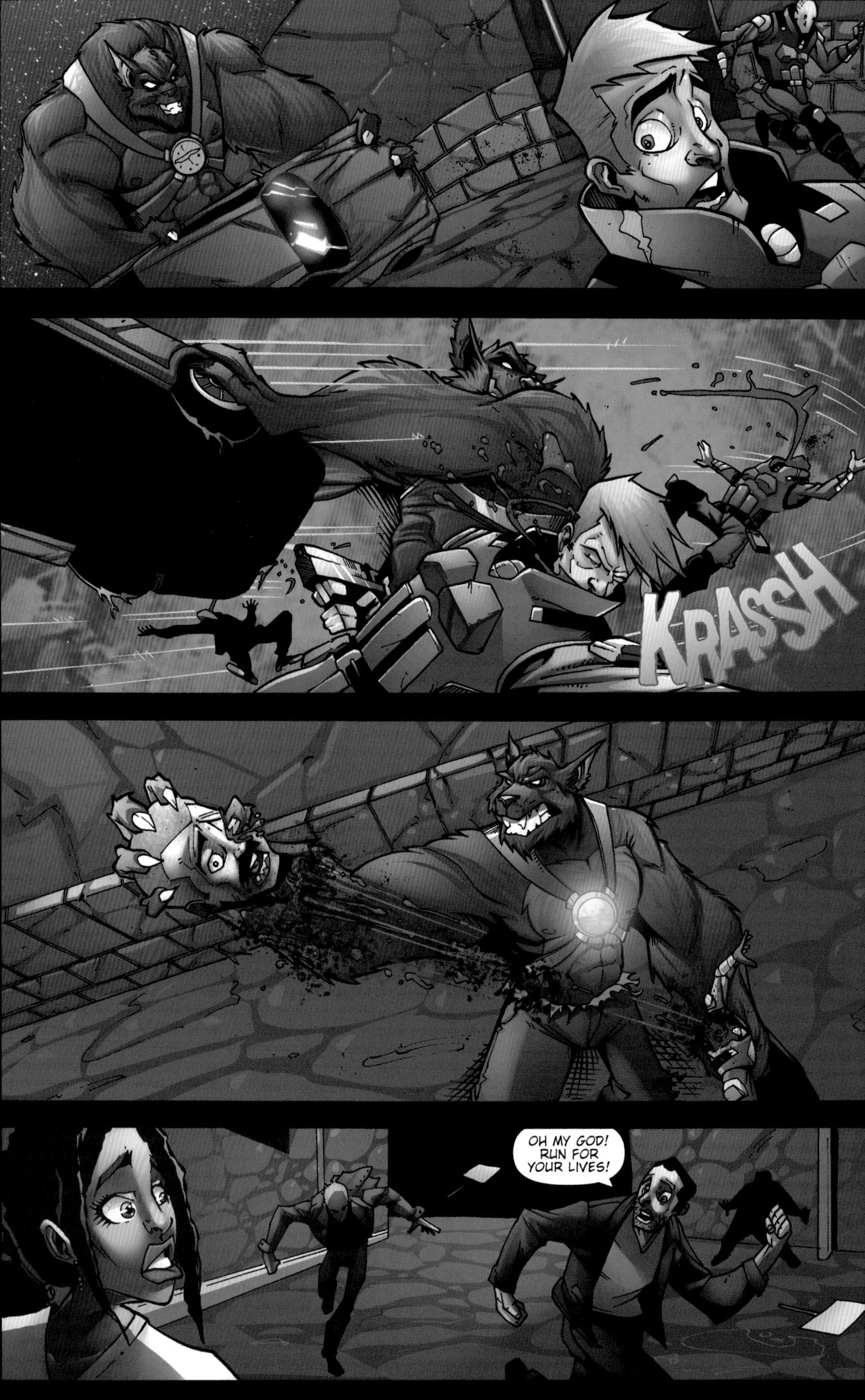
KRASSH
OH MY GOD! RUN FOR YOUR LIVES!

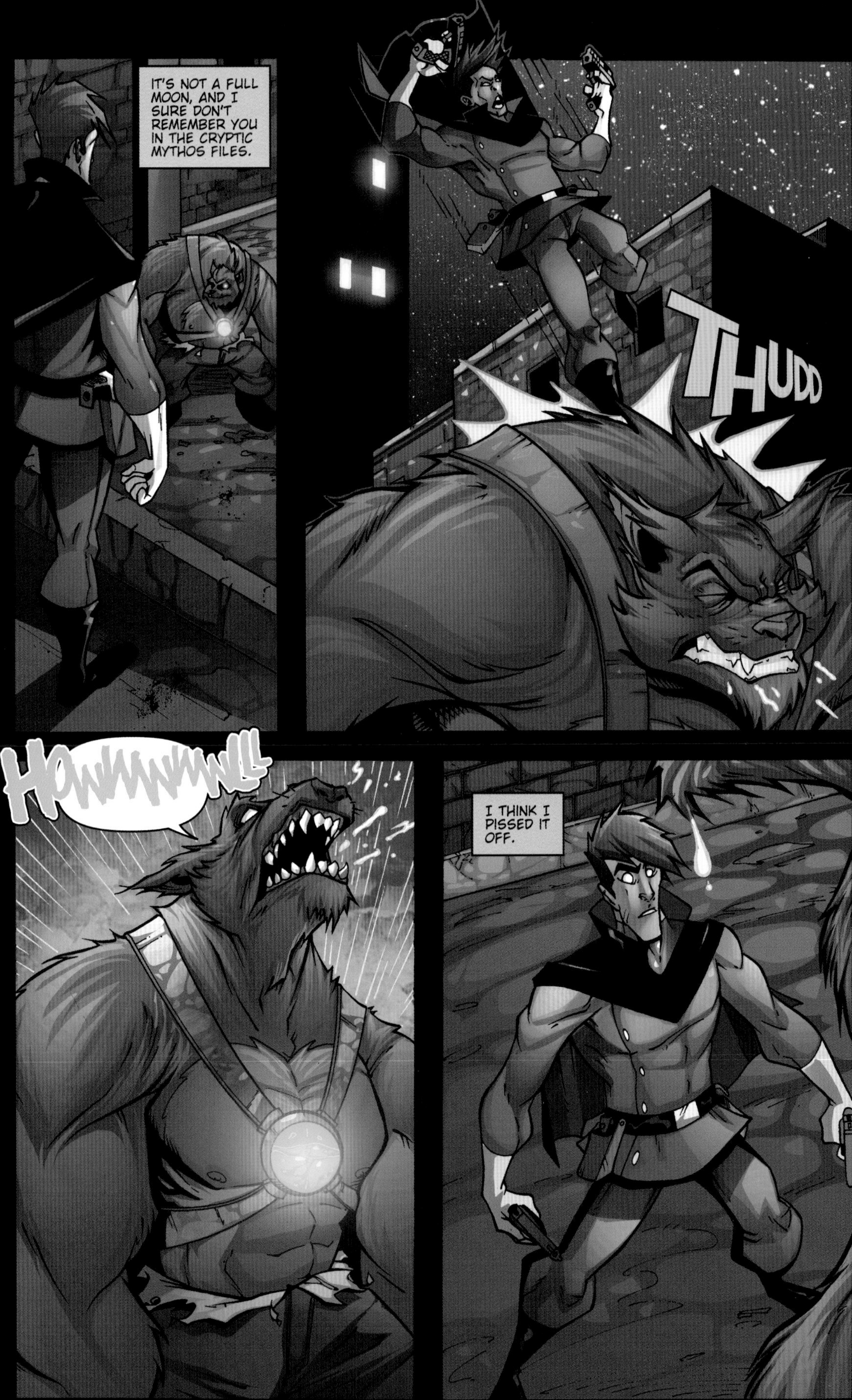
IT'S NOT A FULL MOON, AND I SURE DON'T REMEMBER YOU IN THE CRYPTIC MYTHOS FILES.
THUDD
HOWWWWWLLL
I THINK I PISSED IT OFF.

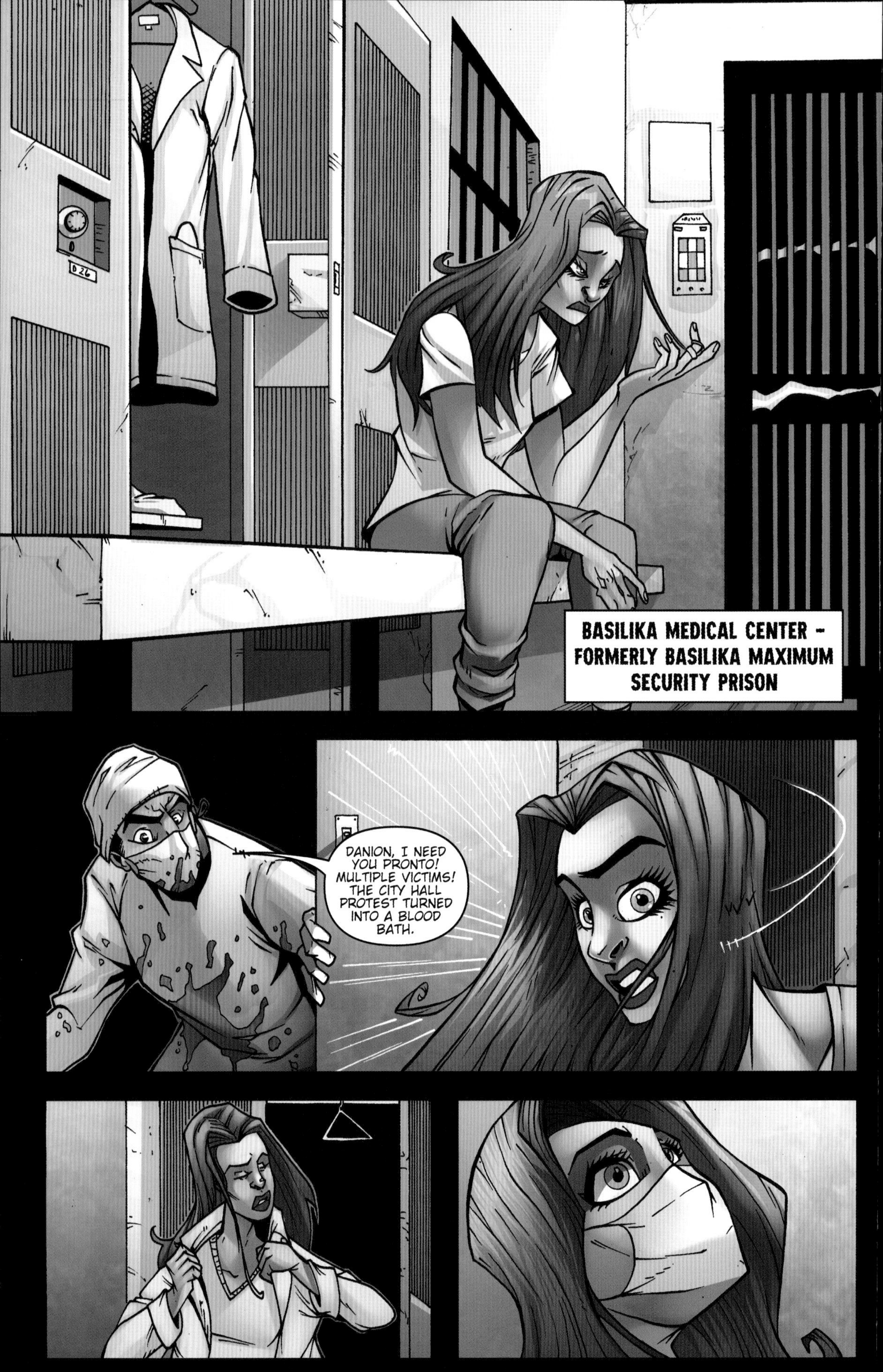
BASILIKA MEDICAL CENTER - FORMERLY BASILIKA MAXIMUM SECURITY PRISON
DANION, I NEED YOU PRONTO! MULTIPLE VICTIMS! THE CITY HALL PROTEST TURNED INTO A BLOOD BATH.

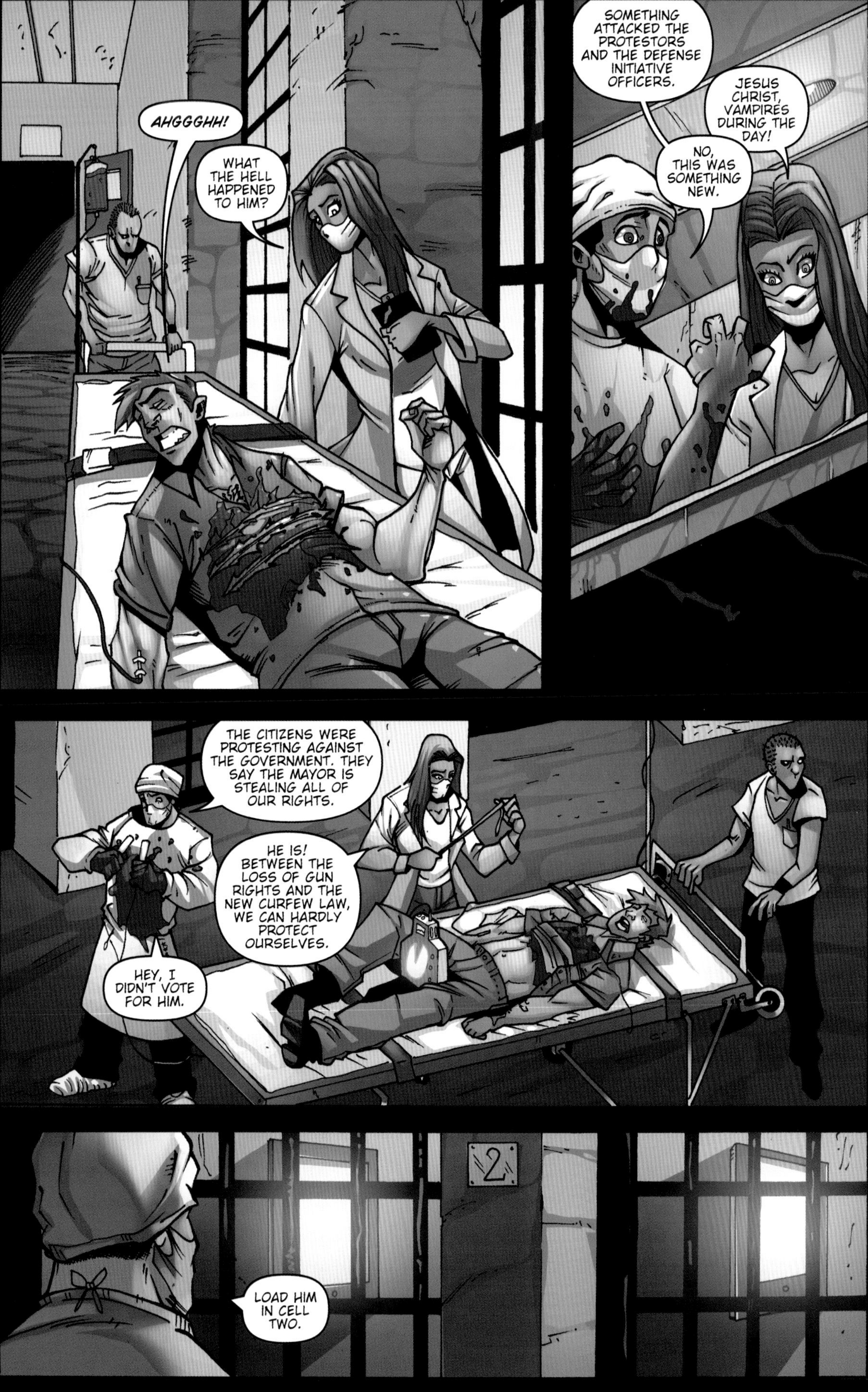
AHGGGHH!
WHAT THE HELL HAPPENED TO HIM?
SOMETHING ATTACKED THE PROTESTORS AND THE DEFENSE INITIATIVE OFFICERS.
JESUS CHRIST, VAMPIRES DURING THE DAY!
NO, THIS WAS SOMETHING NEW.
THE CITIZENS WERE PROTESTING AGAINST THE GOVERNMENT. THEY SAY THE MAYOR IS STEALING ALL OF OUR RIGHTS.
HE IS! BETWEEN THE LOSS OF GUN RIGHTS AND THE NEW CURFEW LAW, WE CAN HARDLY PROTECT OURSELVES.
HEY, I DIDN'T VOTE FOR HIM.
2
LOAD HIM IN CELL TWO.

ARTERY CLAMP.

DANION! ARTERY CLAMP, NOW!

OH, SORRY.

I'VE GOT THIS. DANION, GO GET SOME WATER OR SOMETHING.

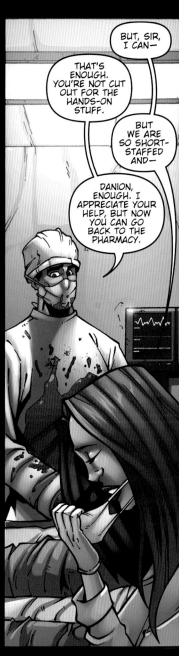

BUT, SIR, I CAN—

THAT'S ENOUGH. YOU'RE NOT CUT OUT FOR THE HANDS-ON STUFF.

BUT WE ARE SO SHORT-STAFFED AND—

DANION, ENOUGH. I APPRECIATE YOUR HELP, BUT NOW YOU CAN GO BACK TO THE PHARMACY.

DANION. GOOD JOB TODAY.

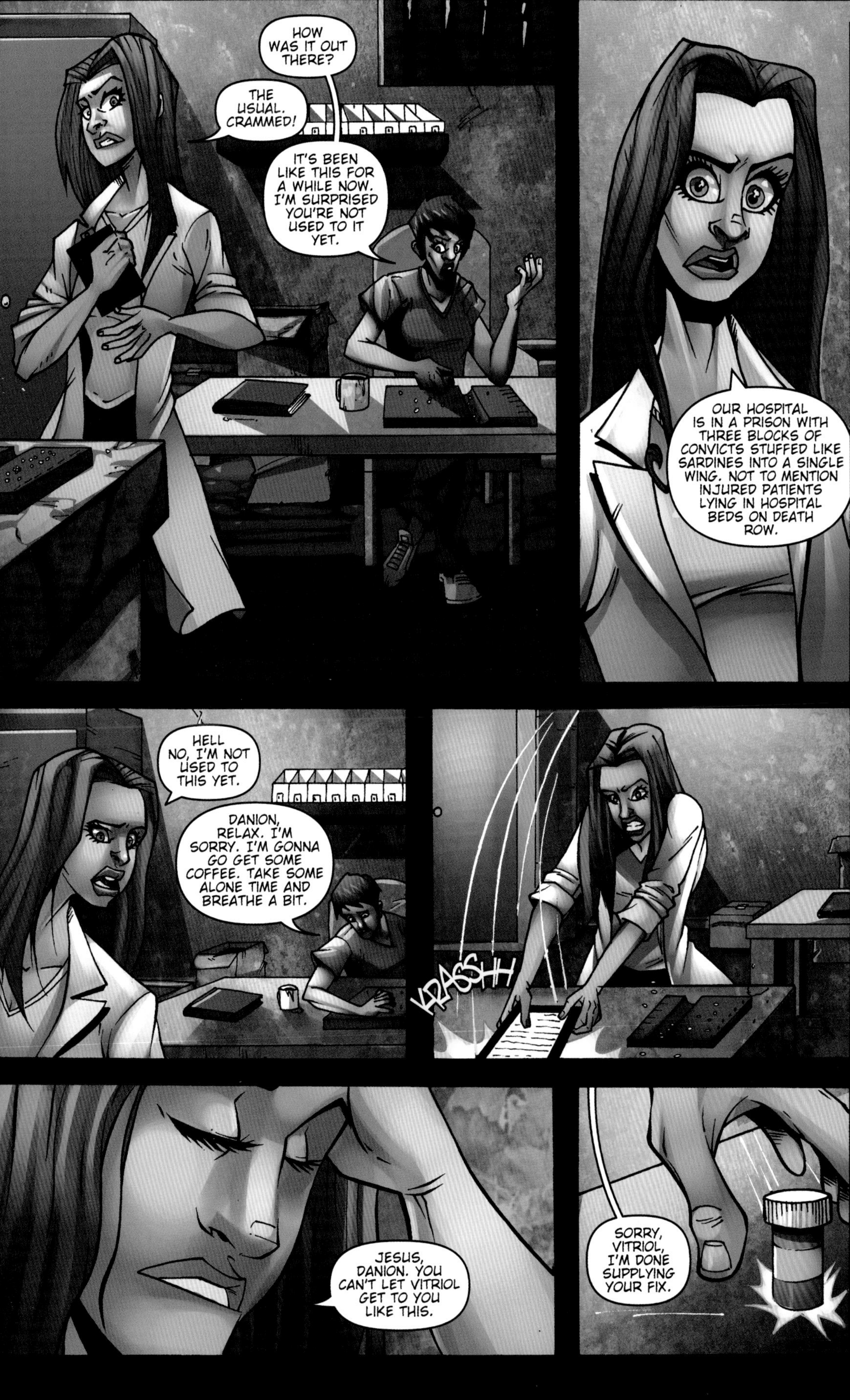
HOW WAS IT OUT THERE?
THE USUAL. CRAMMED!
IT'S BEEN LIKE THIS FOR A WHILE NOW. I'M SURPRISED YOU'RE NOT USED TO IT YET.
OUR HOSPITAL IS IN A PRISON WITH THREE BLOCKS OF CONVICTS STUFFED LIKE SARDINES INTO A SINGLE WING. NOT TO MENTION INJURED PATIENTS LYING IN HOSPITAL BEDS ON DEATH ROW.
HELL NO, I'M NOT USED TO THIS YET.
DANION, RELAX. I'M SORRY. I'M GONNA GO GET SOME COFFEE. TAKE SOME ALONE TIME AND BREATHE A BIT.
KRASSHH
JESUS, DANION. YOU CAN'T LET VITRIOL GET TO YOU LIKE THIS.
SORRY, VITRIOL, I'M DONE SUPPLYING YOUR FIX.

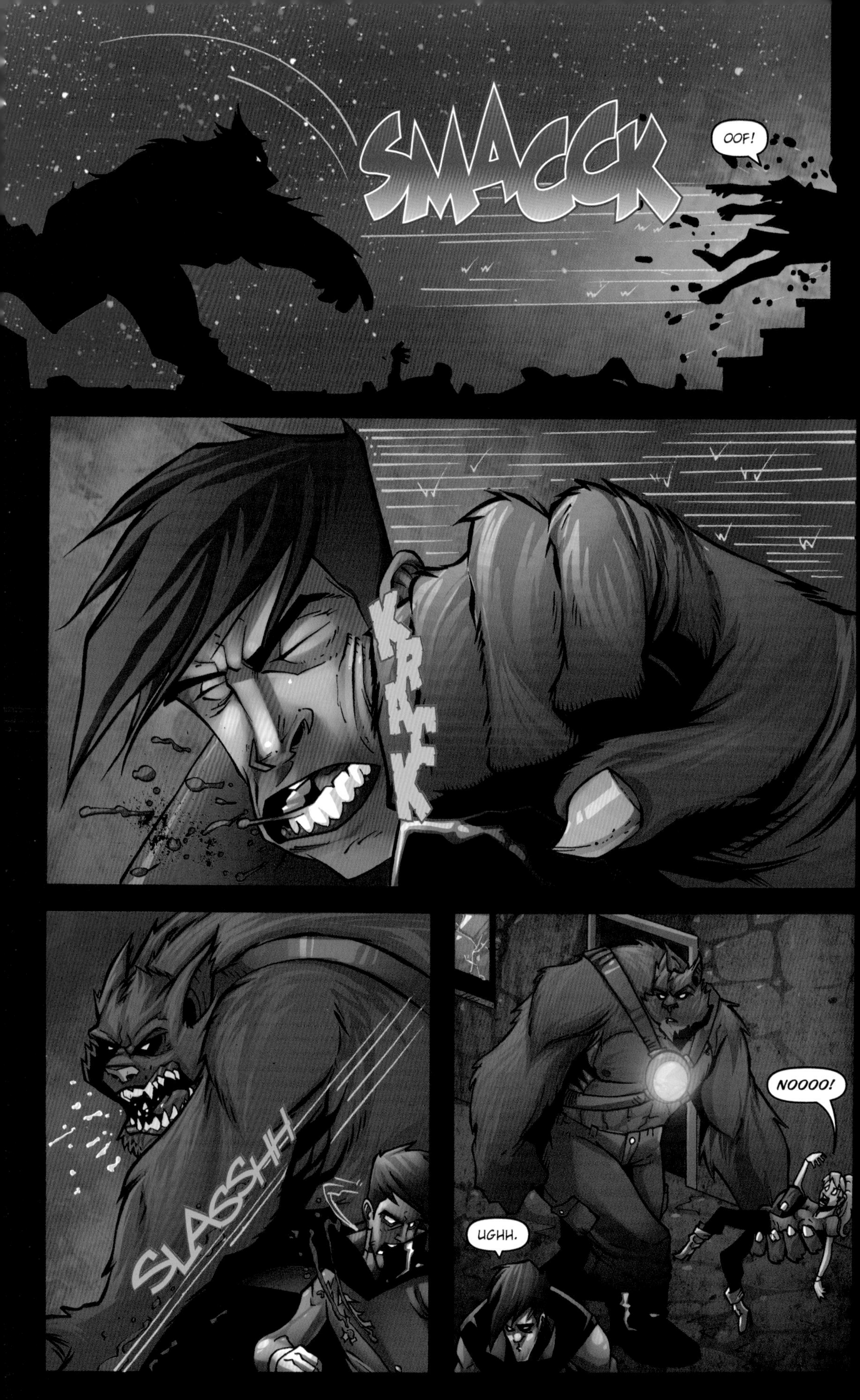
SMACCK
OOF!
KRAK
SLASSHH
NOOOO!
UGHH.

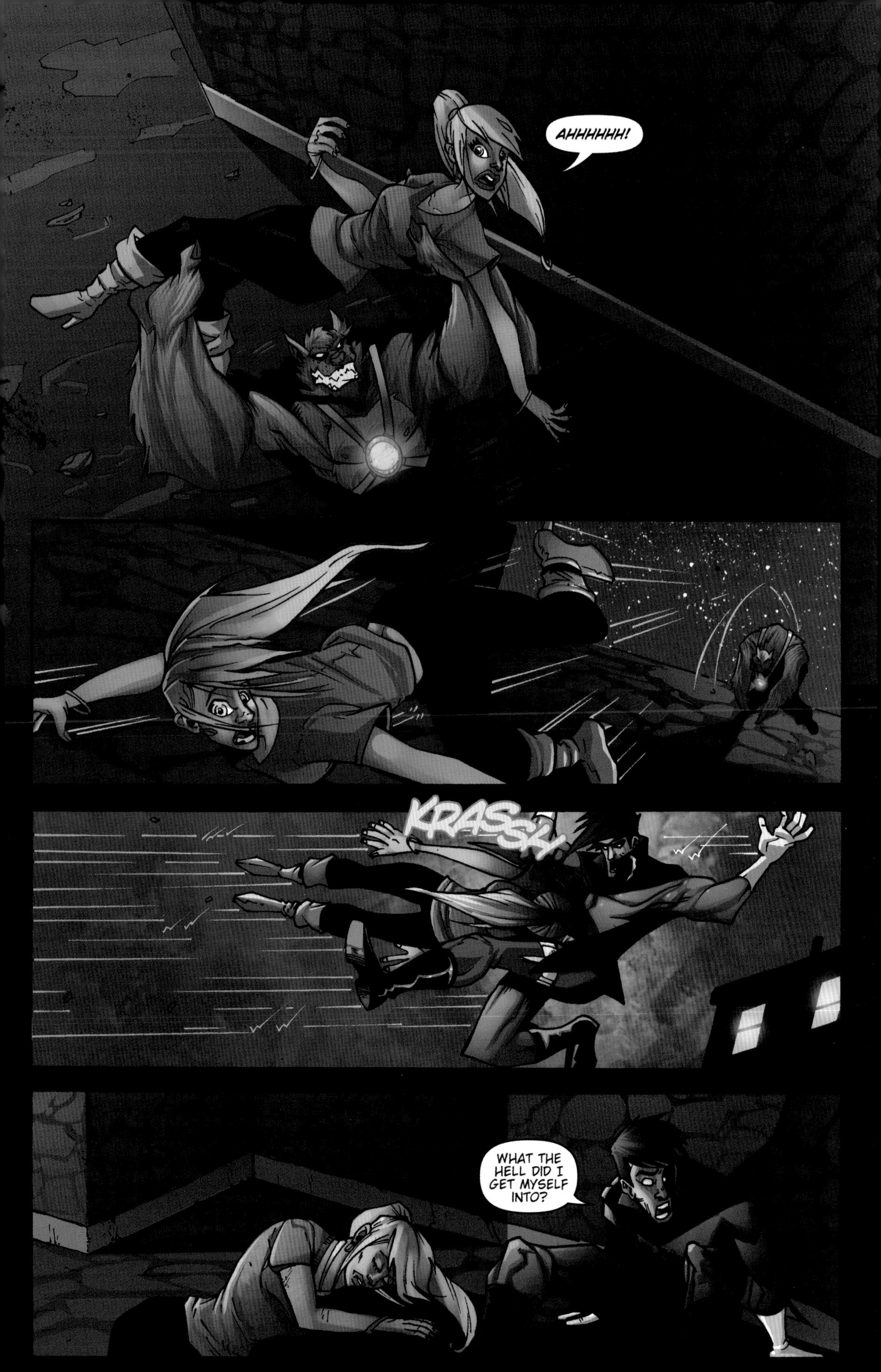
AHHHHHH!
KRASSH
WHAT THE HELL DID I GET MYSELF INTO?

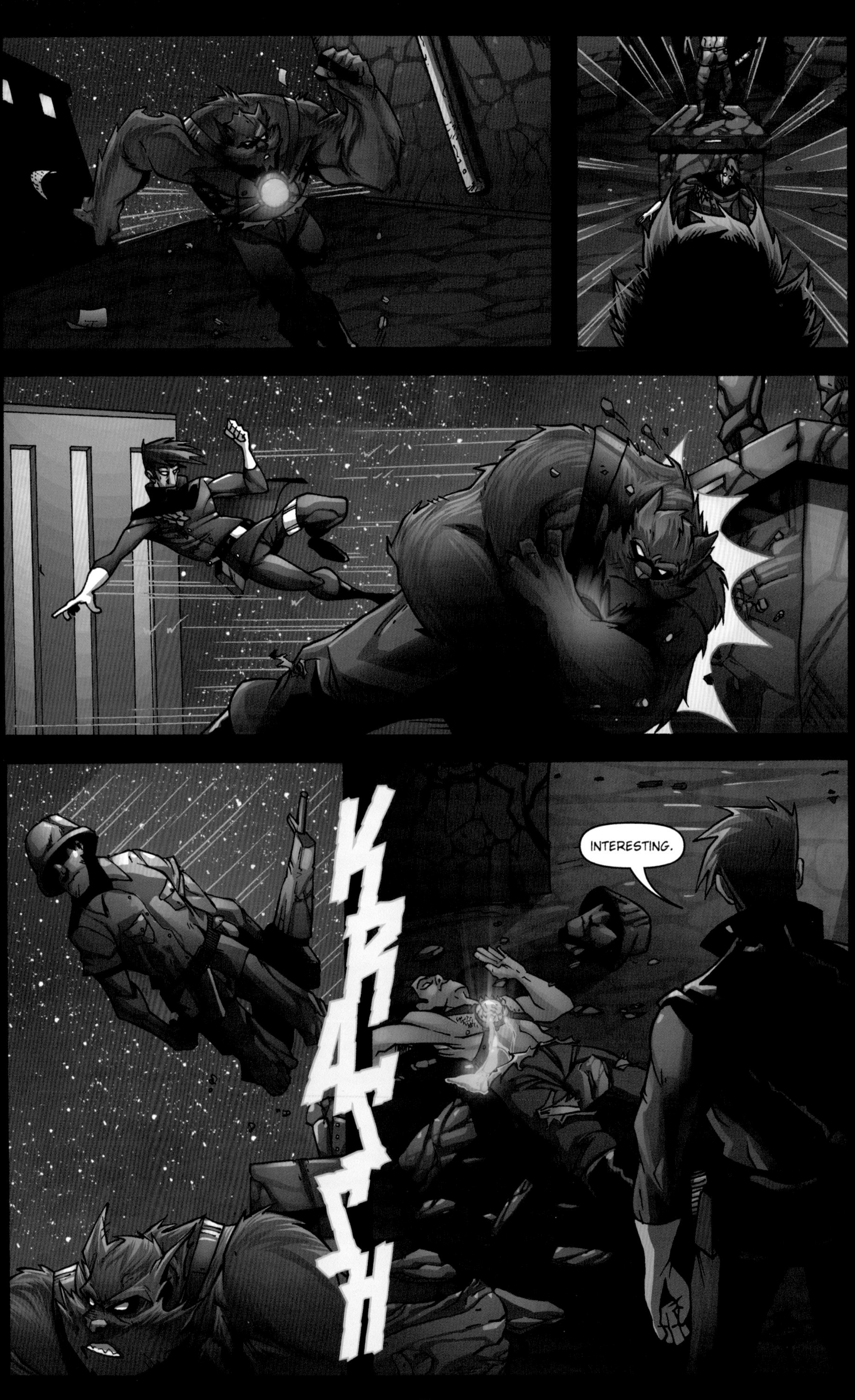
KRASCH
INTERESTING.

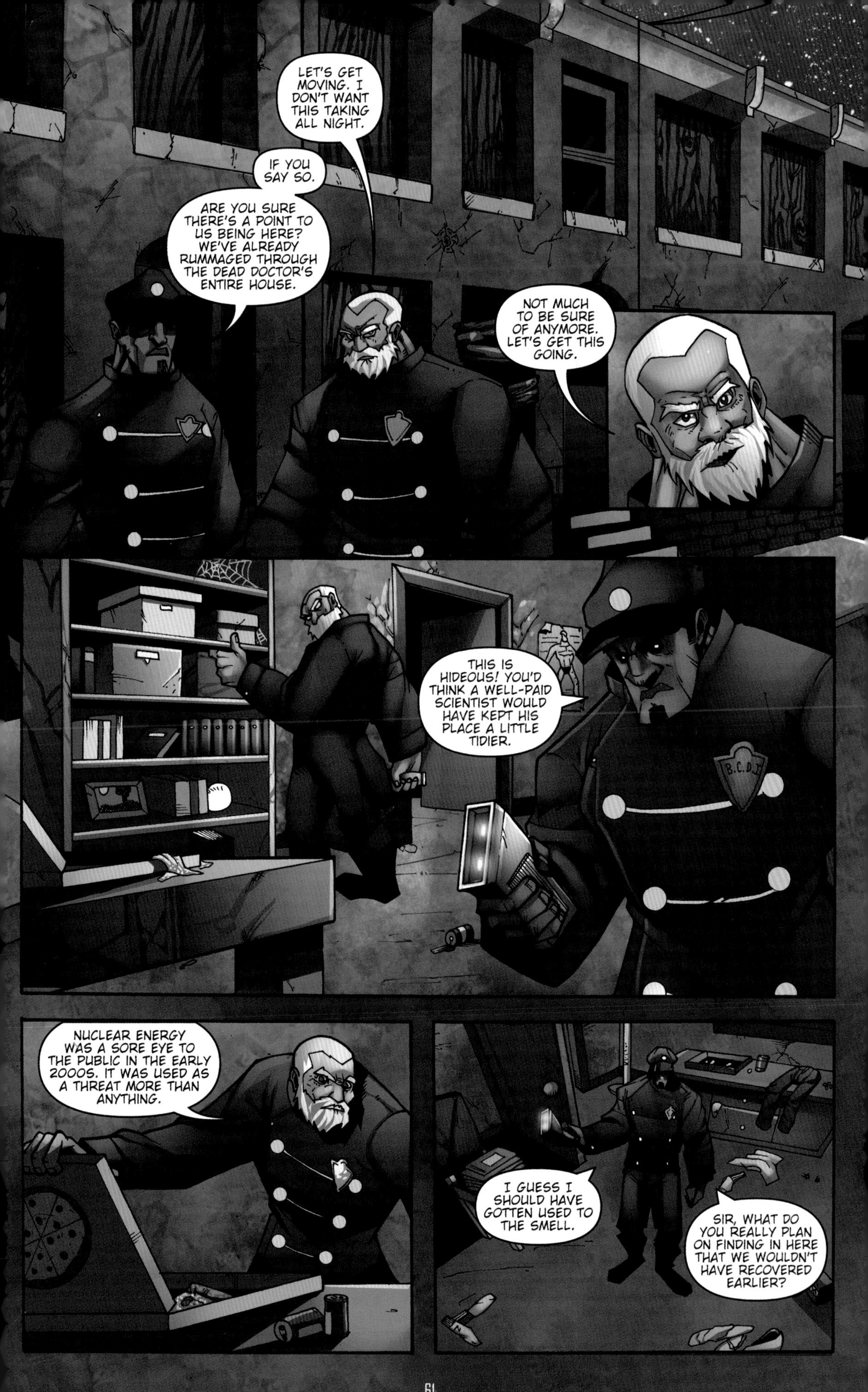

LET'S GET MOVING. I DON'T WANT THIS TAKING ALL NIGHT.
IF YOU SAY SO.
ARE YOU SURE THERE'S A POINT TO US BEING HERE? WE'VE ALREADY RUMMAGED THROUGH THE DEAD DOCTOR'S ENTIRE HOUSE.
NOT MUCH TO BE SURE OF ANYMORE. LET'S GET THIS GOING.
THIS IS HIDEOUS! YOU'D THINK A WELL-PAID SCIENTIST WOULD HAVE KEPT HIS PLACE A LITTLE TIDIER.
B.C.D.
NUCLEAR ENERGY WAS A SORE EYE TO THE PUBLIC IN THE EARLY 2000S. IT WAS USED AS A THREAT MORE THAN ANYTHING.
I GUESS I SHOULD HAVE GOTTEN USED TO THE SMELL.
SIR, WHAT DO YOU REALLY PLAN ON FINDING IN HERE THAT WE WOULDN'T HAVE RECOVERED EARLIER?

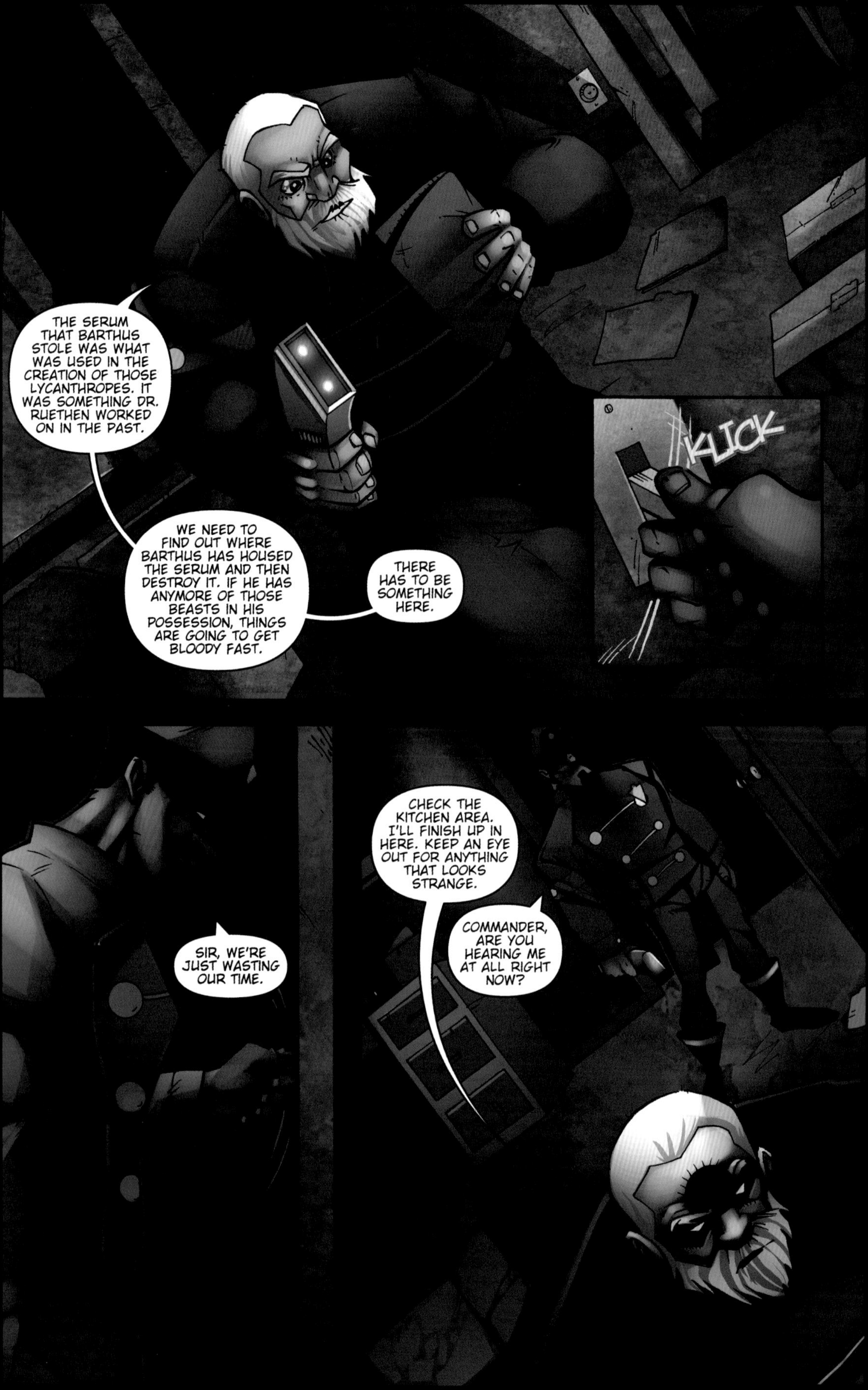
THE SERUM THAT BARTHUS STOLE WAS WHAT WAS USED IN THE CREATION OF THOSE LYCANTHROPES. IT WAS SOMETHING DR. RUETHEN WORKED ON IN THE PAST.
WE NEED TO FIND OUT WHERE BARTHUS HAS HOUSED THE SERUM AND THEN DESTROY IT. IF HE HAS ANYMORE OF THOSE BEASTS IN HIS POSSESSION, THINGS ARE GOING TO GET BLOODY FAST.
THERE HAS TO BE SOMETHING HERE.
KLICK
SIR, WE'RE JUST WASTING OUR TIME.
COMMANDER, ARE YOU HEARING ME AT ALL RIGHT NOW?
CHECK THE KITCHEN AREA. I'LL FINISH UP IN HERE. KEEP AN EYE OUT FOR ANYTHING THAT LOOKS STRANGE.

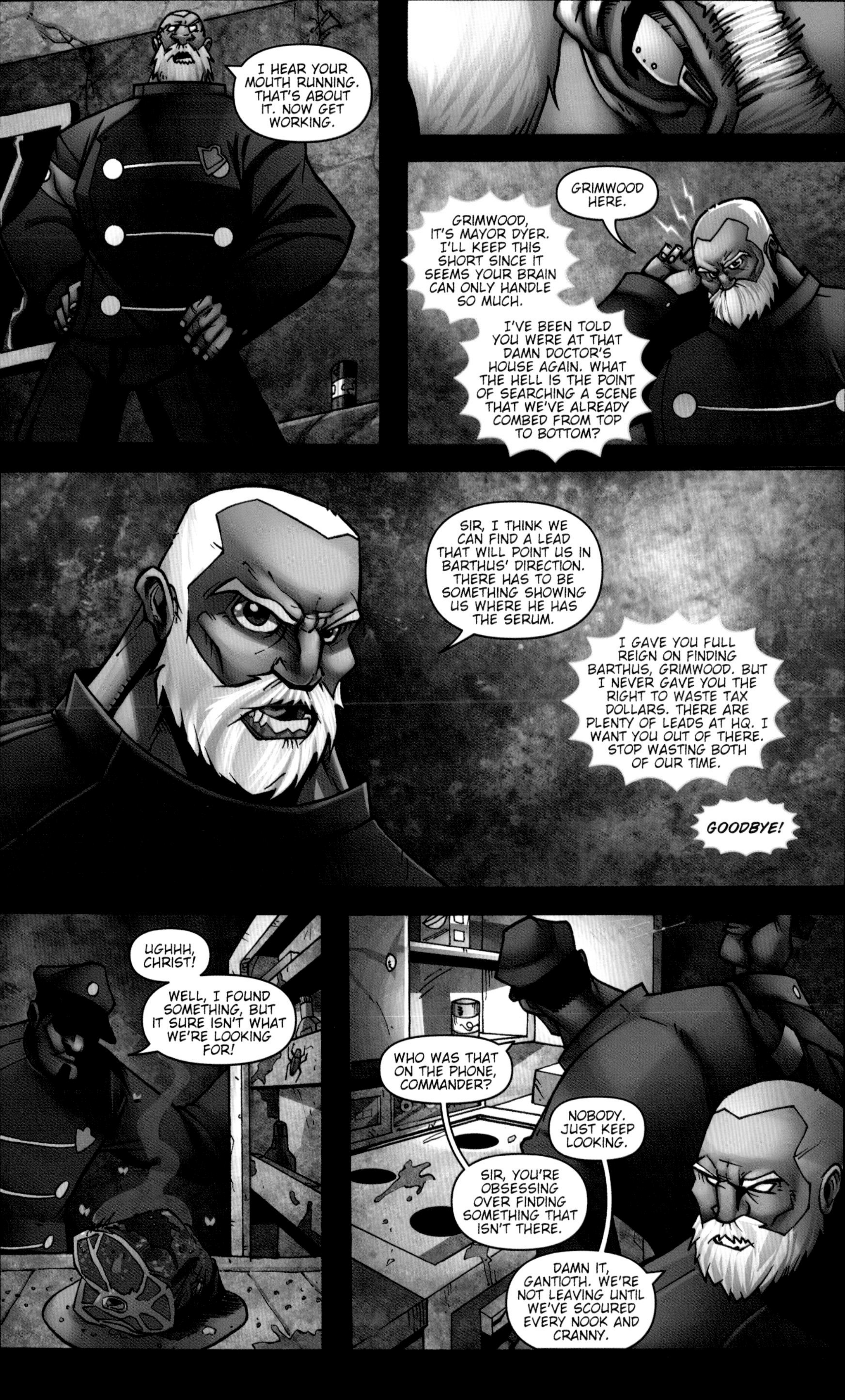
I HEAR YOUR MOUTH RUNNING. THAT'S ABOUT IT. NOW GET WORKING.
GRIMWOOD HERE.
GRIMWOOD, IT'S MAYOR DYER. I'LL KEEP THIS SHORT SINCE IT SEEMS YOUR BRAIN CAN ONLY HANDLE SO MUCH.
I'VE BEEN TOLD YOU WERE AT THAT DAMN DOCTOR'S HOUSE AGAIN. WHAT THE HELL IS THE POINT OF SEARCHING A SCENE THAT WE'VE ALREADY COMBED FROM TOP TO BOTTOM?
SIR, I THINK WE CAN FIND A LEAD THAT WILL POINT US IN BARTHUS' DIRECTION. THERE HAS TO BE SOMETHING SHOWING US WHERE HE HAS THE SERUM.
I GAVE YOU FULL REIGN ON FINDING BARTHUS, GRIMWOOD. BUT I NEVER GAVE YOU THE RIGHT TO WASTE TAX DOLLARS. THERE ARE PLENTY OF LEADS AT HQ. I WANT YOU OUT OF THERE. STOP WASTING BOTH OF OUR TIME.
GOODBYE!
UGHHH, CHRIST!
WELL, I FOUND SOMETHING, BUT IT SURE ISN'T WHAT WE'RE LOOKING FOR!
WHO WAS THAT ON THE PHONE, COMMANDER?
NOBODY. JUST KEEP LOOKING.
SIR, YOU'RE OBSESSING OVER FINDING SOMETHING THAT ISN'T THERE.
DAMN IT, GANTIOTH. WE'RE NOT LEAVING UNTIL WE'VE SCOURED EVERY NOOK AND CRANNY.

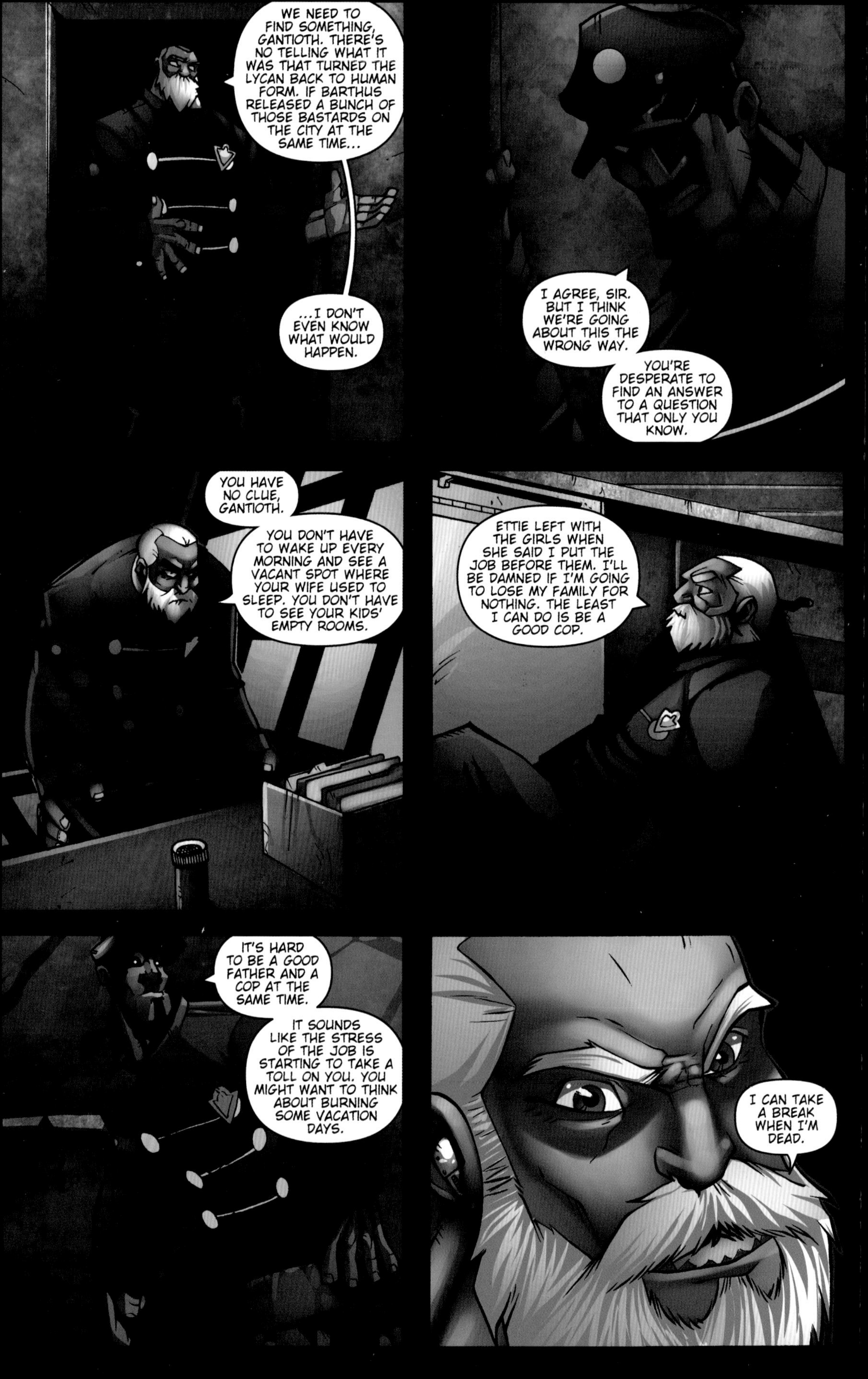
WE NEED TO FIND SOMETHING, GANTIOTH. THERE'S NO TELLING WHAT IT WAS THAT TURNED THE LYCAN BACK TO HUMAN FORM. IF BARTHUS RELEASED A BUNCH OF THOSE BASTARDS ON THE CITY AT THE SAME TIME...
...I DON'T EVEN KNOW WHAT WOULD HAPPEN.
I AGREE, SIR. BUT I THINK WE'RE GOING ABOUT THIS THE WRONG WAY.
YOU'RE DESPERATE TO FIND AN ANSWER TO A QUESTION THAT ONLY YOU KNOW.
YOU HAVE NO CLUE, GANTIOTH.
YOU DON'T HAVE TO WAKE UP EVERY MORNING AND SEE A VACANT SPOT WHERE YOUR WIFE USED TO SLEEP. YOU DON'T HAVE TO SEE YOUR KIDS' EMPTY ROOMS.
ETTIE LEFT WITH THE GIRLS WHEN SHE SAID I PUT THE JOB BEFORE THEM. I'LL BE DAMNED IF I'M GOING TO LOSE MY FAMILY FOR NOTHING. THE LEAST I CAN DO IS BE A GOOD COP.
IT'S HARD TO BE A GOOD FATHER AND A COP AT THE SAME TIME.
IT SOUNDS LIKE THE STRESS OF THE JOB IS STARTING TO TAKE A TOLL ON YOU. YOU MIGHT WANT TO THINK ABOUT BURNING SOME VACATION DAYS.
I CAN TAKE A BREAK WHEN I'M DEAD.

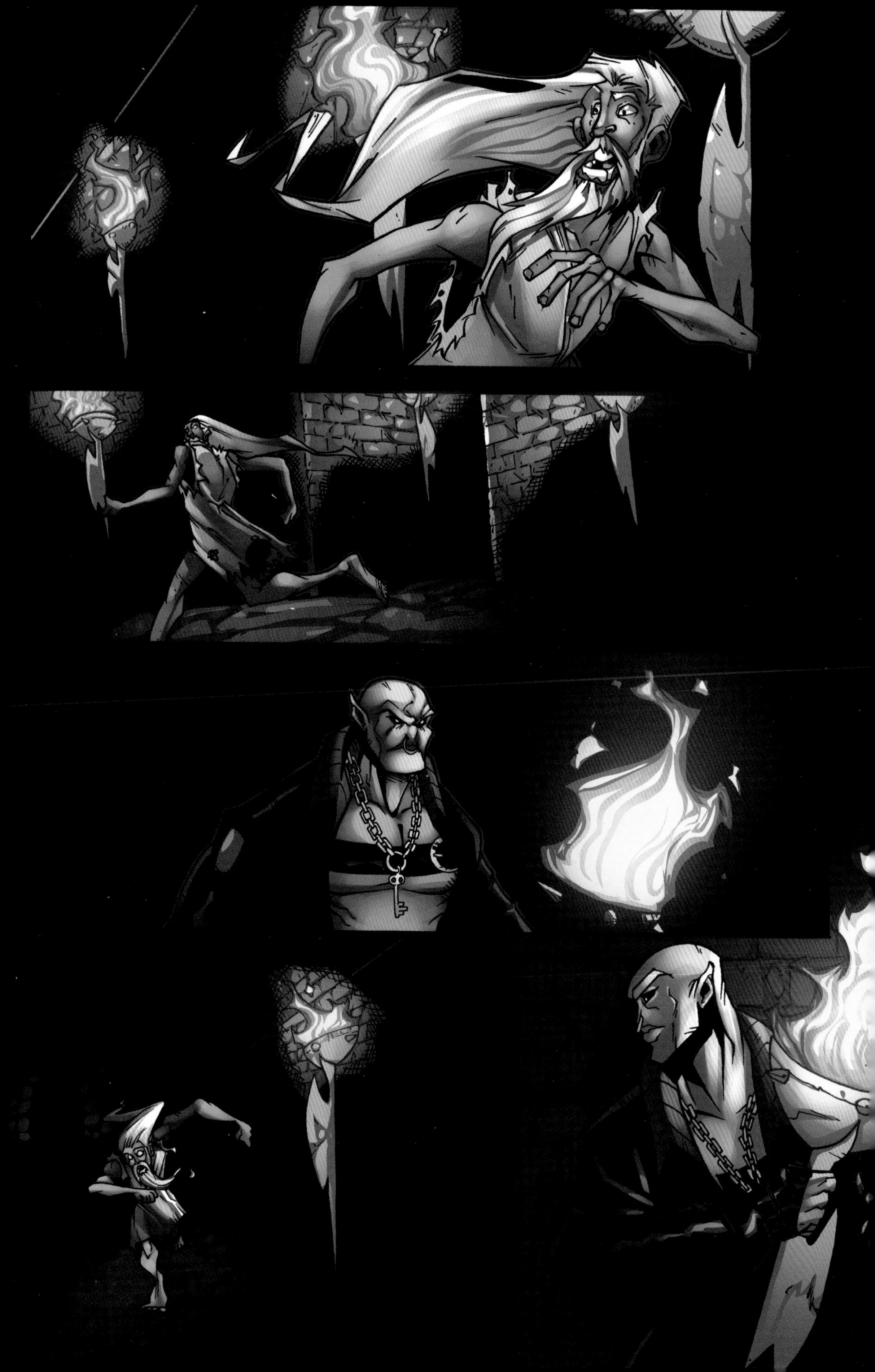

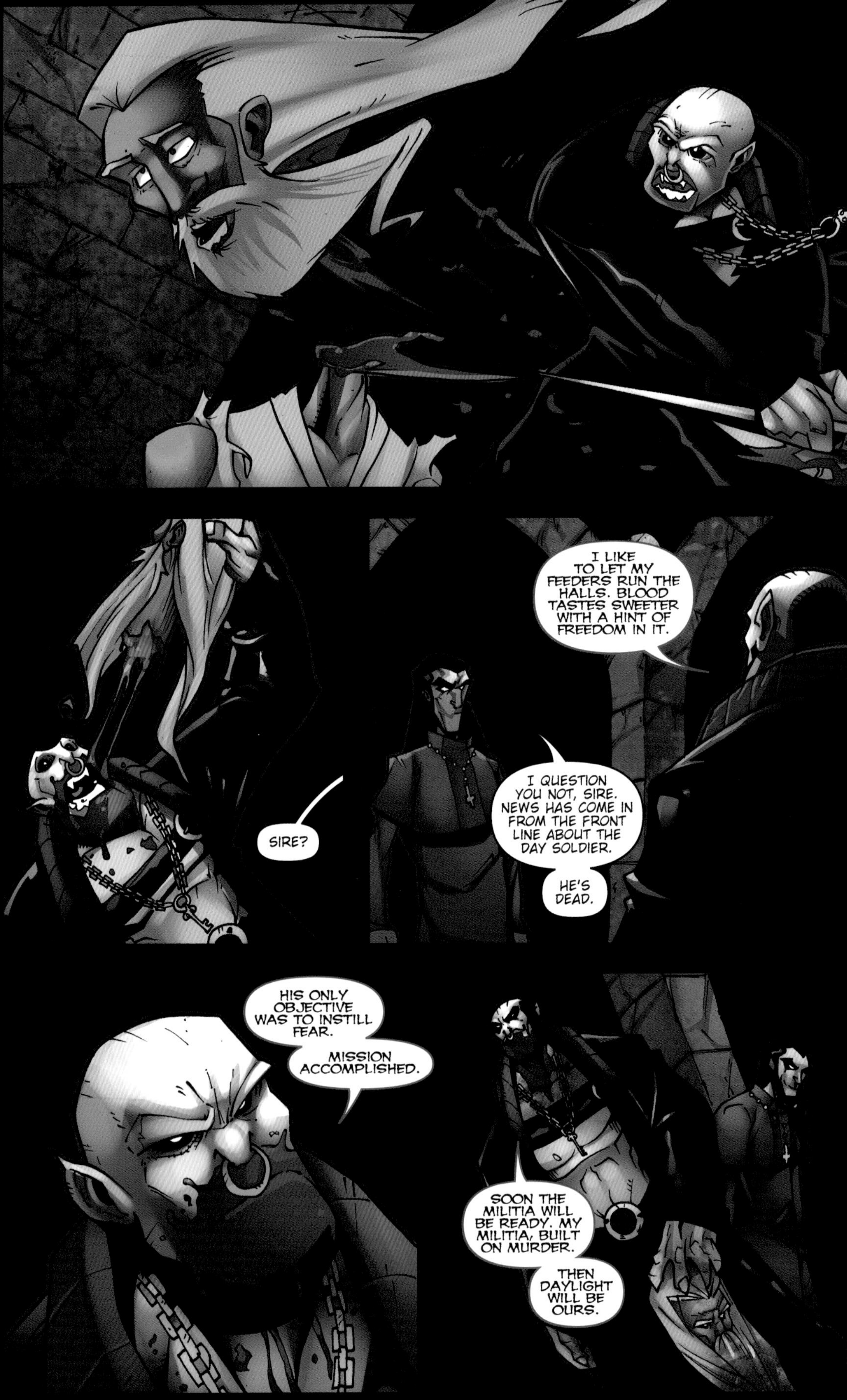
SIRE?
I LIKE TO LET MY FEEDERS RUN THE HALLS. BLOOD TASTES SWEETER WITH A HINT OF FREEDOM IN IT.
I QUESTION YOU NOT, SIRE. NEWS HAS COME IN FROM THE FRONT LINE ABOUT THE DAY SOLDIER.
HE'S DEAD.
HIS ONLY OBJECTIVE WAS TO INSTILL FEAR.
MISSION ACCOMPLISHED.
SOON THE MILITIA WILL BE READY. MY MILITIA, BUILT ON MURDER.
THEN DAYLIGHT WILL BE OURS.

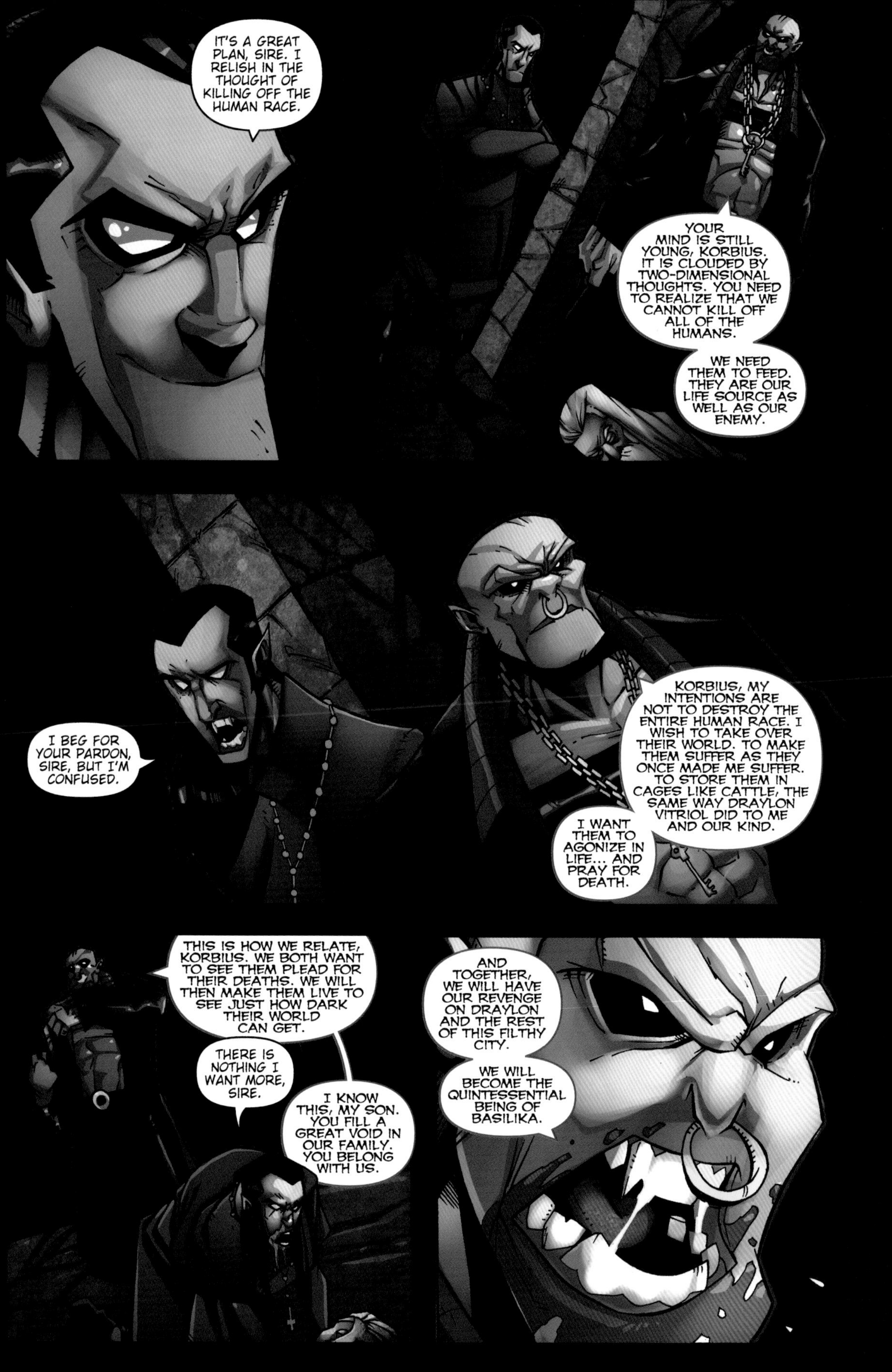
IT'S A GREAT PLAN, SIRE. I RELISH IN THE THOUGHT OF KILLING OFF THE HUMAN RACE.
YOUR MIND IS STILL YOUNG, KORBIUS. IT IS CLOUDED BY TWO-DIMENSIONAL THOUGHTS. YOU NEED TO REALIZE THAT WE CANNOT KILL OFF ALL OF THE HUMANS.
WE NEED THEM TO FEED. THEY ARE OUR LIFE SOURCE AS WELL AS OUR ENEMY.
I BEG FOR YOUR PARDON, SIRE, BUT I'M CONFUSED.
KORBIUS, MY INTENTIONS ARE NOT TO DESTROY THE ENTIRE HUMAN RACE. I WISH TO TAKE OVER THEIR WORLD. TO MAKE THEM SUFFER AS THEY ONCE MADE ME SUFFER. TO STORE THEM IN CAGES LIKE CATTLE, THE SAME WAY DRAYLON VITRIOL DID TO ME AND OUR KIND.
I WANT THEM TO AGONIZE IN LIFE... AND PRAY FOR DEATH.
THIS IS HOW WE RELATE, KORBIUS. WE BOTH WANT TO SEE THEM PLEAD FOR THEIR DEATHS. WE WILL THEN MAKE THEM LIVE TO SEE JUST HOW DARK THEIR WORLD CAN GET.
THERE IS NOTHING I WANT MORE, SIRE.
I KNOW THIS, MY SON. YOU FILL A GREAT VOID IN OUR FAMILY. YOU BELONG WITH US.
AND TOGETHER, WE WILL HAVE OUR REVENGE ON DRAYLON AND THE REST OF THIS FILTHY CITY.
WE WILL BECOME THE QUINTESSENTIAL BEING OF BASILIKA.

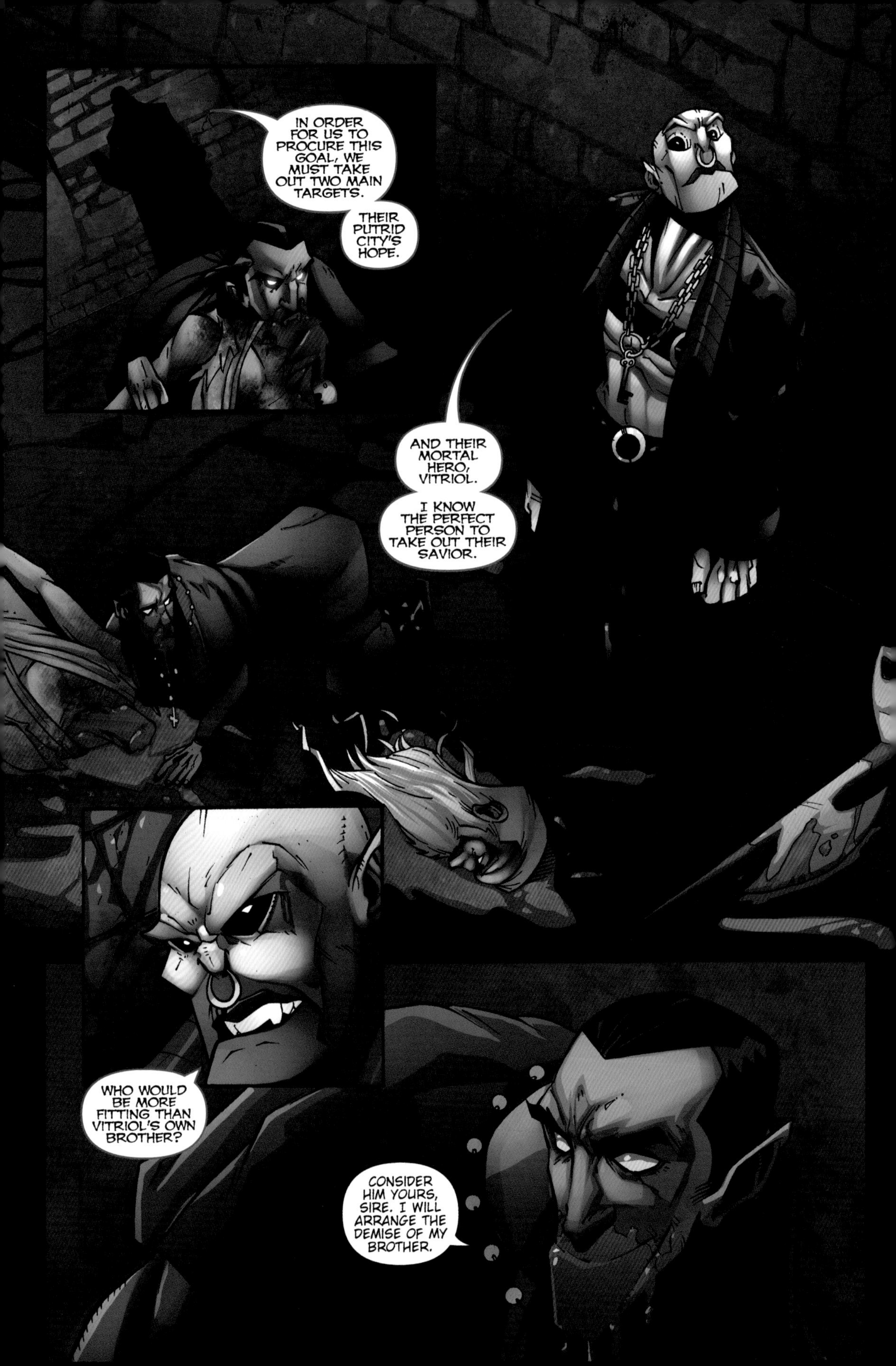
IN ORDER FOR US TO PROCURE THIS GOAL, WE MUST TAKE OUT TWO MAIN TARGETS.
THEIR PUTRID CITY'S HOPE.
AND THEIR MORTAL HERO, VITRIOL.
I KNOW THE PERFECT PERSON TO TAKE OUT THEIR SAVIOR.
WHO WOULD BE MORE FITTING THAN VITRIOL'S OWN BROTHER?
CONSIDER HIM YOURS, SIRE. I WILL ARRANGE THE DEMISE OF MY BROTHER.

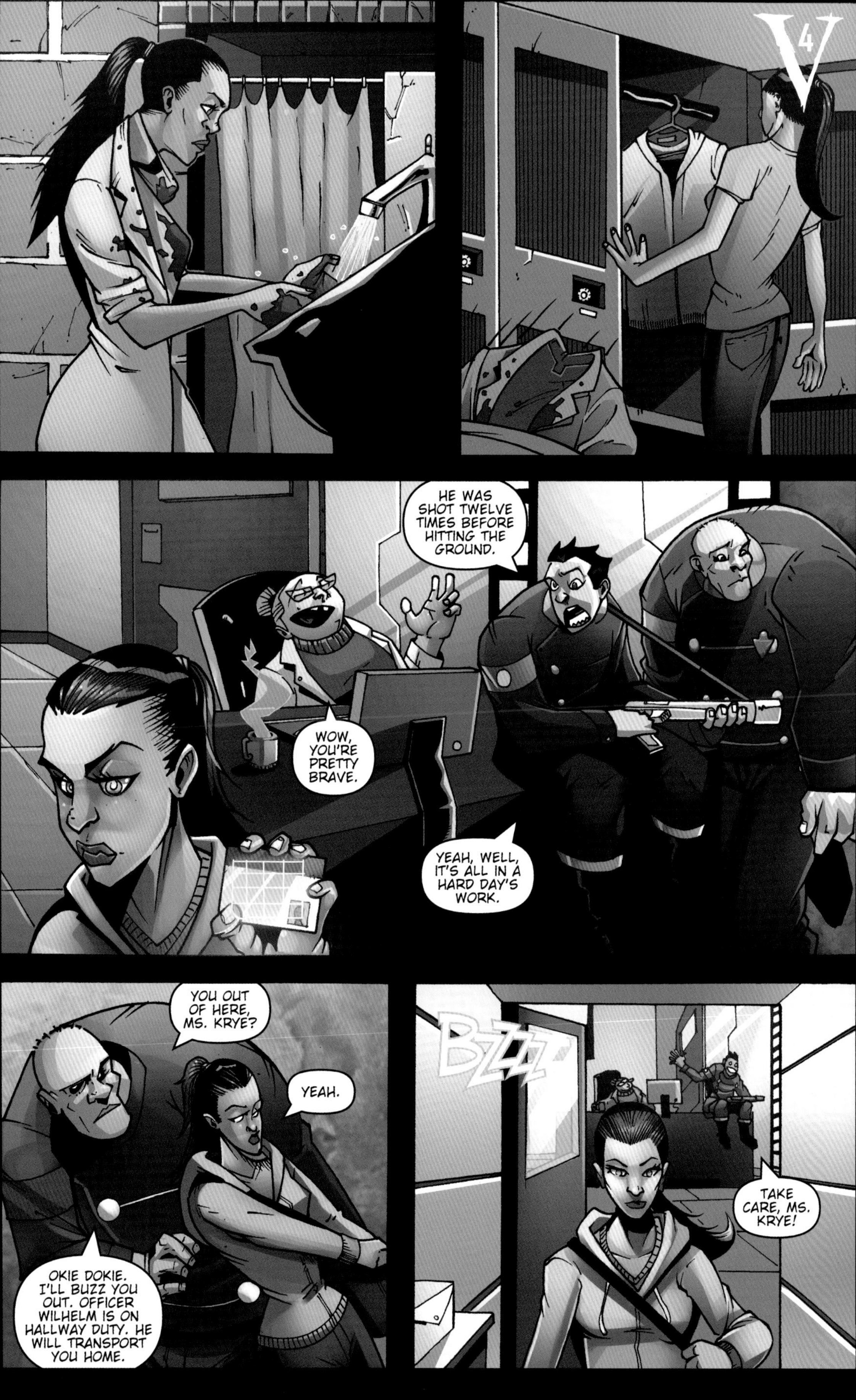
V 4
HE WAS SHOT TWELVE TIMES BEFORE HITTING THE GROUND.
WOW, YOU'RE PRETTY BRAVE.
YEAH, WELL, IT'S ALL IN A HARD DAY'S WORK.
YOU OUT OF HERE, MS. KRYE?
YEAH.
OKIE DOKIE. I'LL BUZZ YOU OUT. OFFICER WILHELM IS ON HALLWAY DUTY. HE WILL TRANSPORT YOU HOME.
BZZZT
TAKE CARE, MS. KRYE!

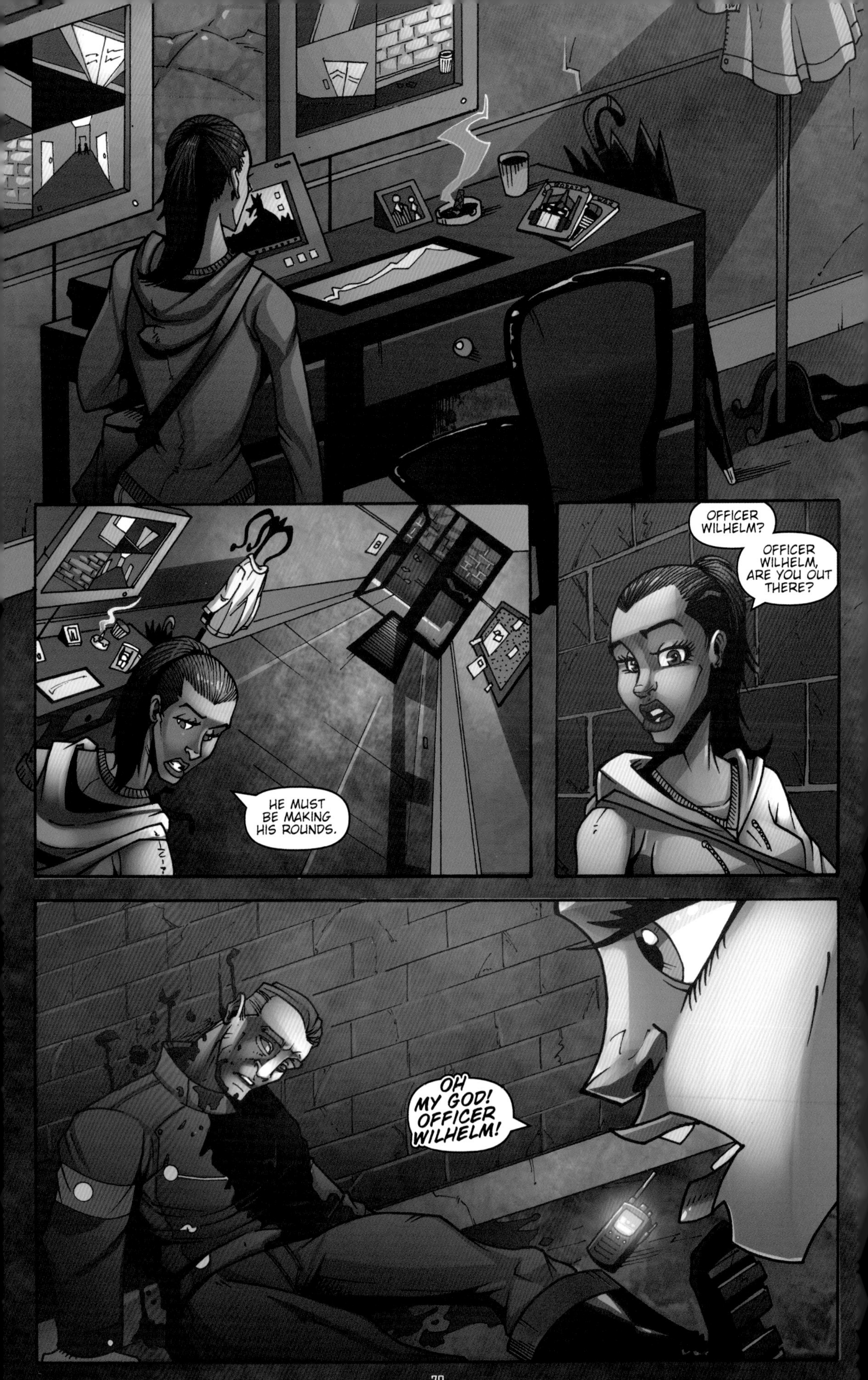
HE MUST BE MAKING HIS ROUNDS.
OFFICER WILHELM?
OFFICER WILHELM, ARE YOU OUT THERE?
OH MY GOD! OFFICER WILHELM!

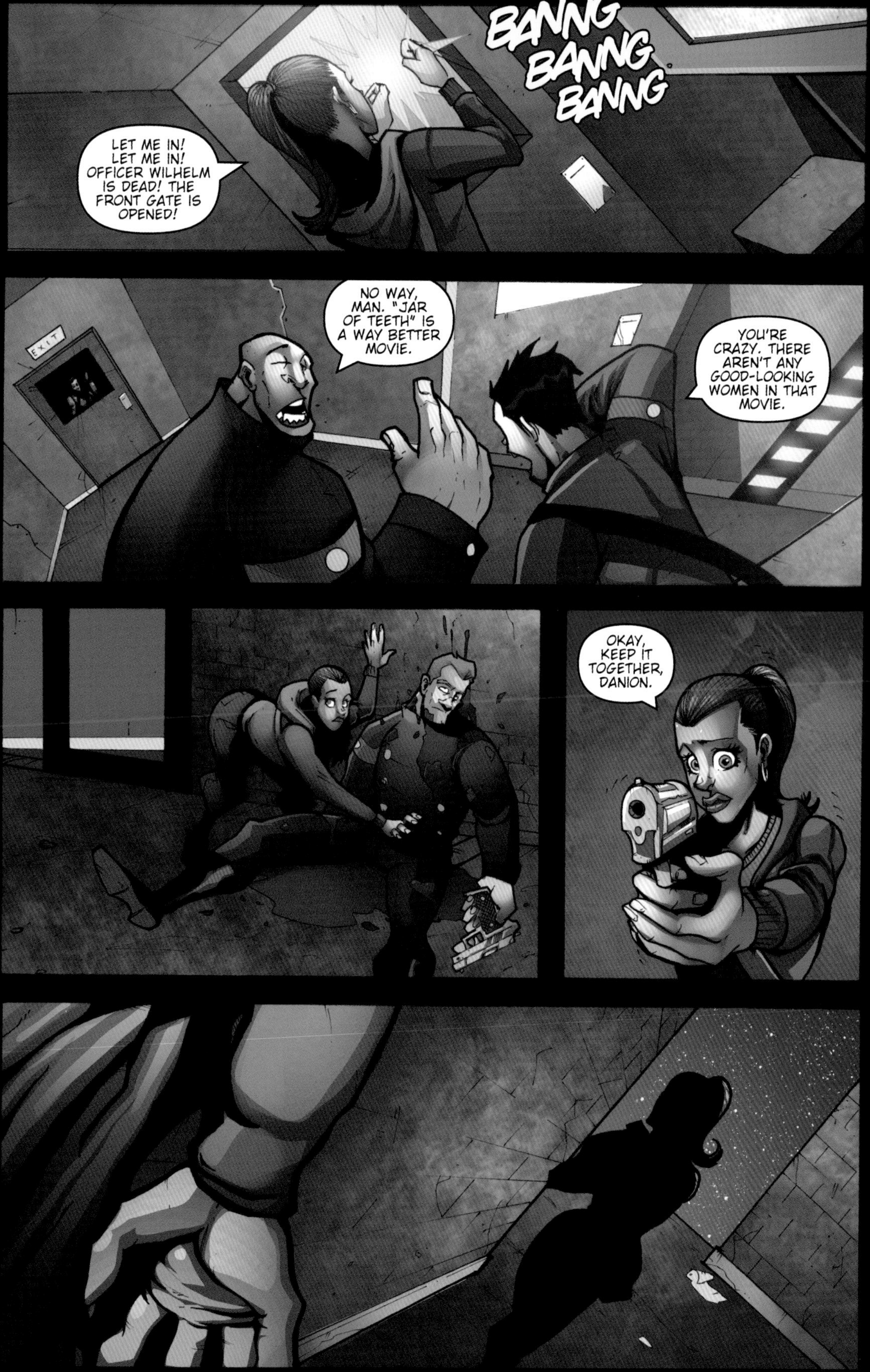
BANNG BANNG BANNG
LET ME IN! LET ME IN! OFFICER WILHELM IS DEAD! THE FRONT GATE IS OPENED!
NO WAY, MAN. "JAR OF TEETH" IS A WAY BETTER MOVIE.
EXIT
YOU'RE CRAZY. THERE AREN'T ANY GOOD-LOOKING WOMEN IN THAT MOVIE.
OKAY, KEEP IT TOGETHER, DANION.

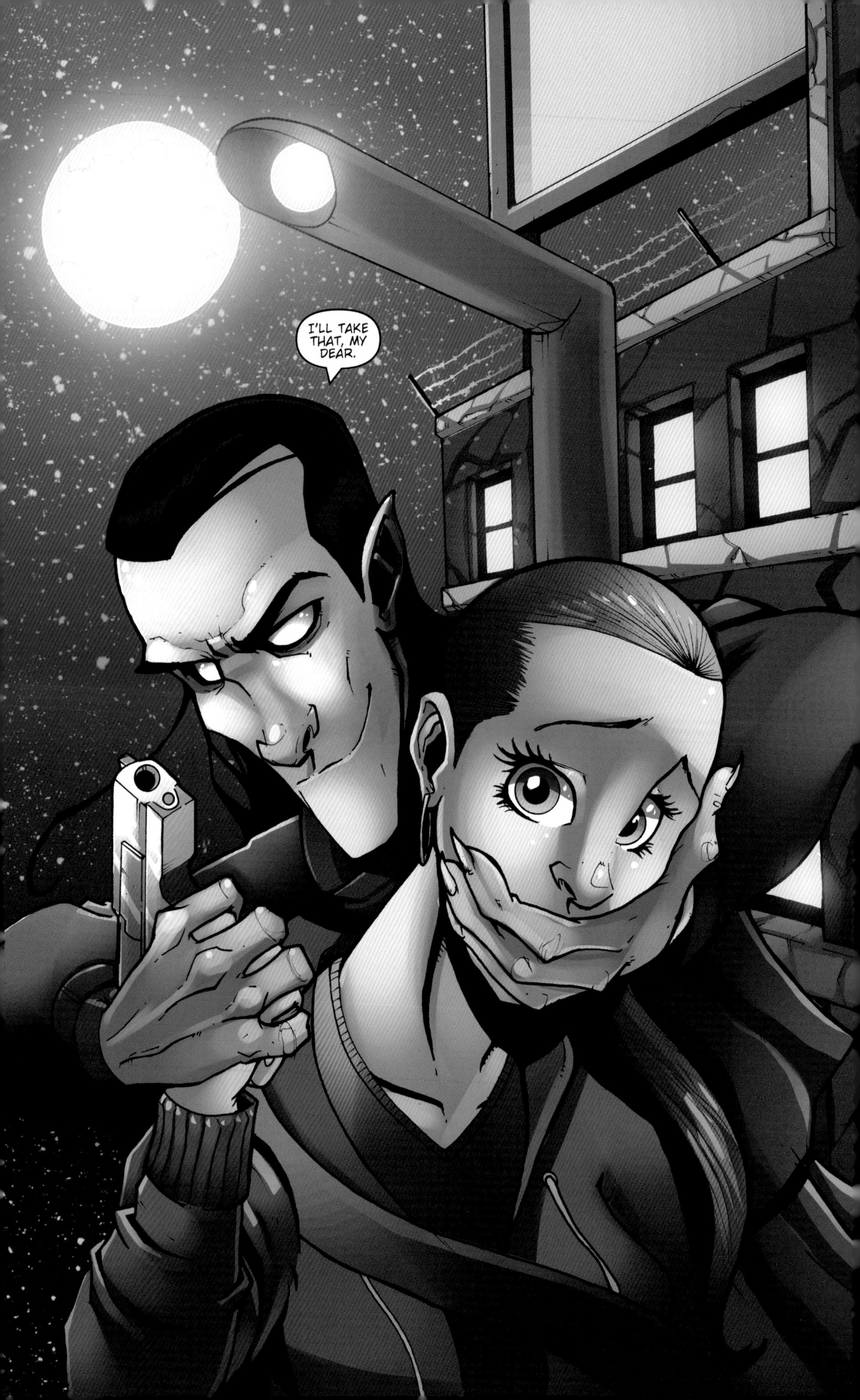
I'LL TAKE THAT, MY DEAR.

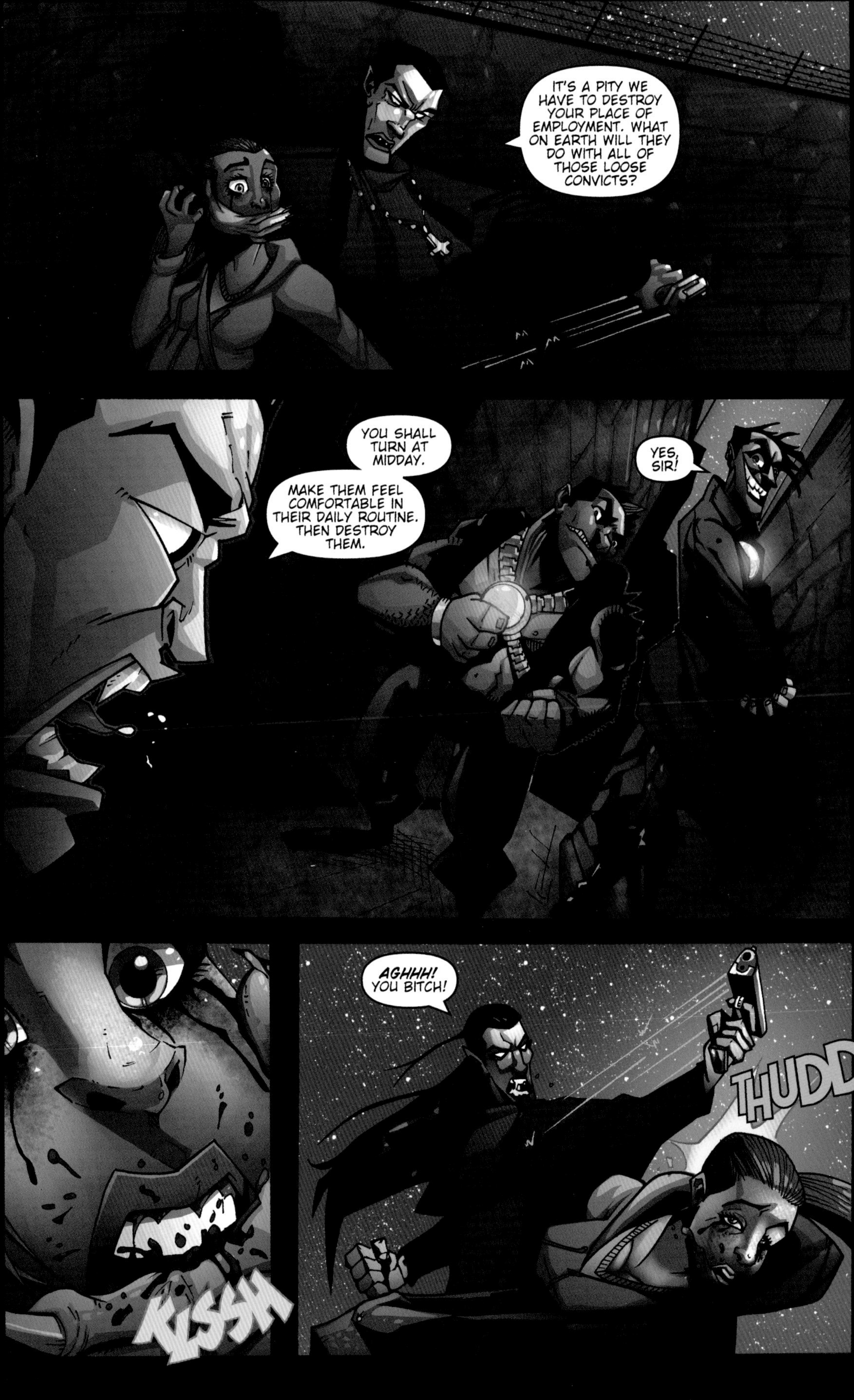
IT'S A PITY WE HAVE TO DESTROY YOUR PLACE OF EMPLOYMENT. WHAT ON EARTH WILL THEY DO WITH ALL OF THOSE LOOSE CONVICTS?
YOU SHALL TURN AT MIDDAY.
MAKE THEM FEEL COMFORTABLE IN THEIR DAILY ROUTINE. THEN DESTROY THEM.
YES, SIR!
KSSH
AGHHH! YOU BITCH!
THUDD

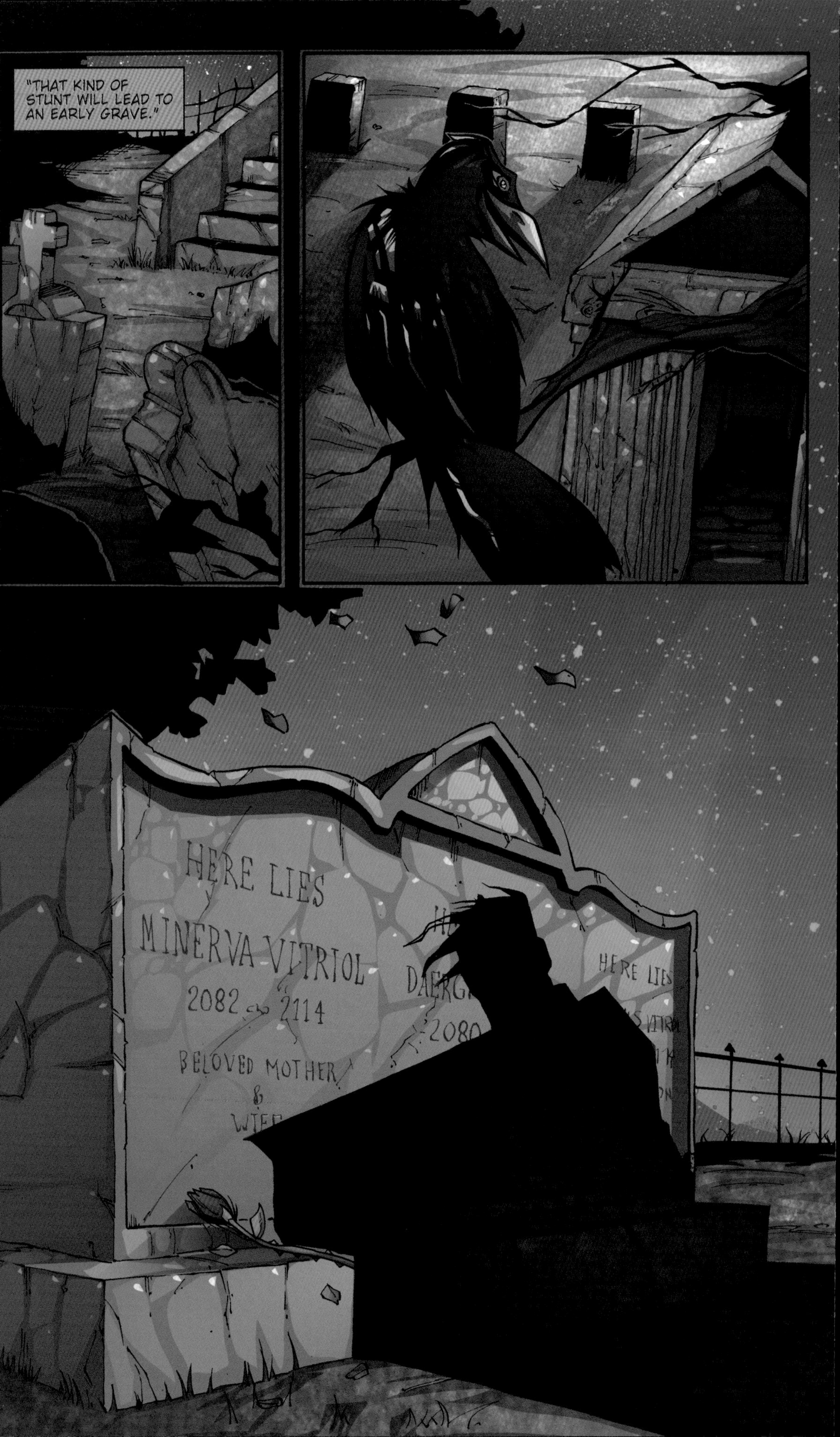
"THAT KIND OF STUNT WILL LEAD TO AN EARLY GRAVE."
HERE LIES
MINERVA VITRIOL
2082 ~ 2114
BELOVED MOTHER
&
HERE LIES

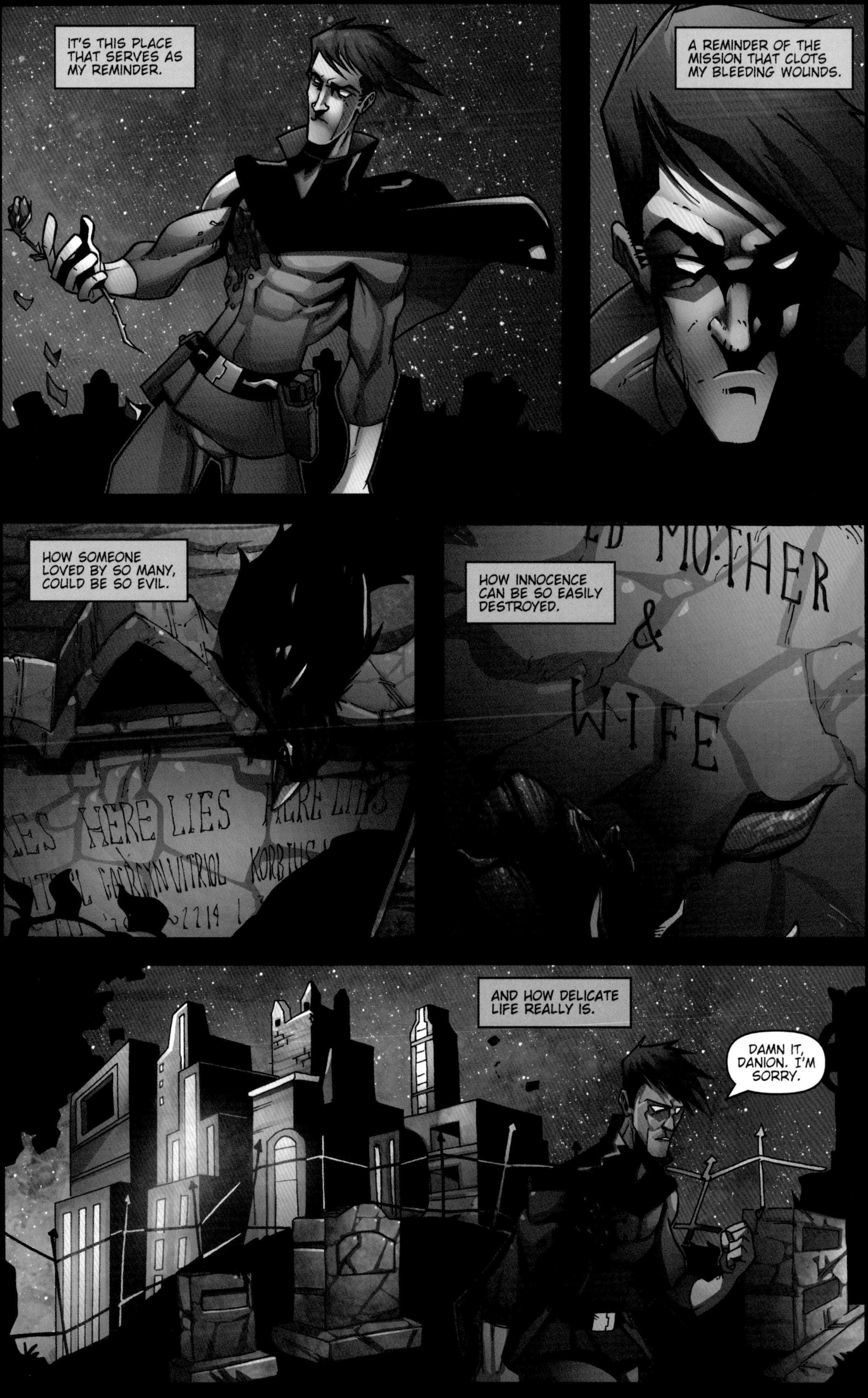
IT'S THIS PLACE THAT SERVES AS MY REMINDER.
A REMINDER OF THE MISSION THAT CLOTS MY BLEEDING WOUNDS.
HOW SOMEONE LOVED BY SO MANY, COULD BE SO EVIL.
HERE LIES
HOW INNOCENCE CAN BE SO EASILY DESTROYED.
MOTHER
&
WIFE
AND HOW DELICATE LIFE REALLY IS.
DAMN IT, DANION. I'M SORRY.

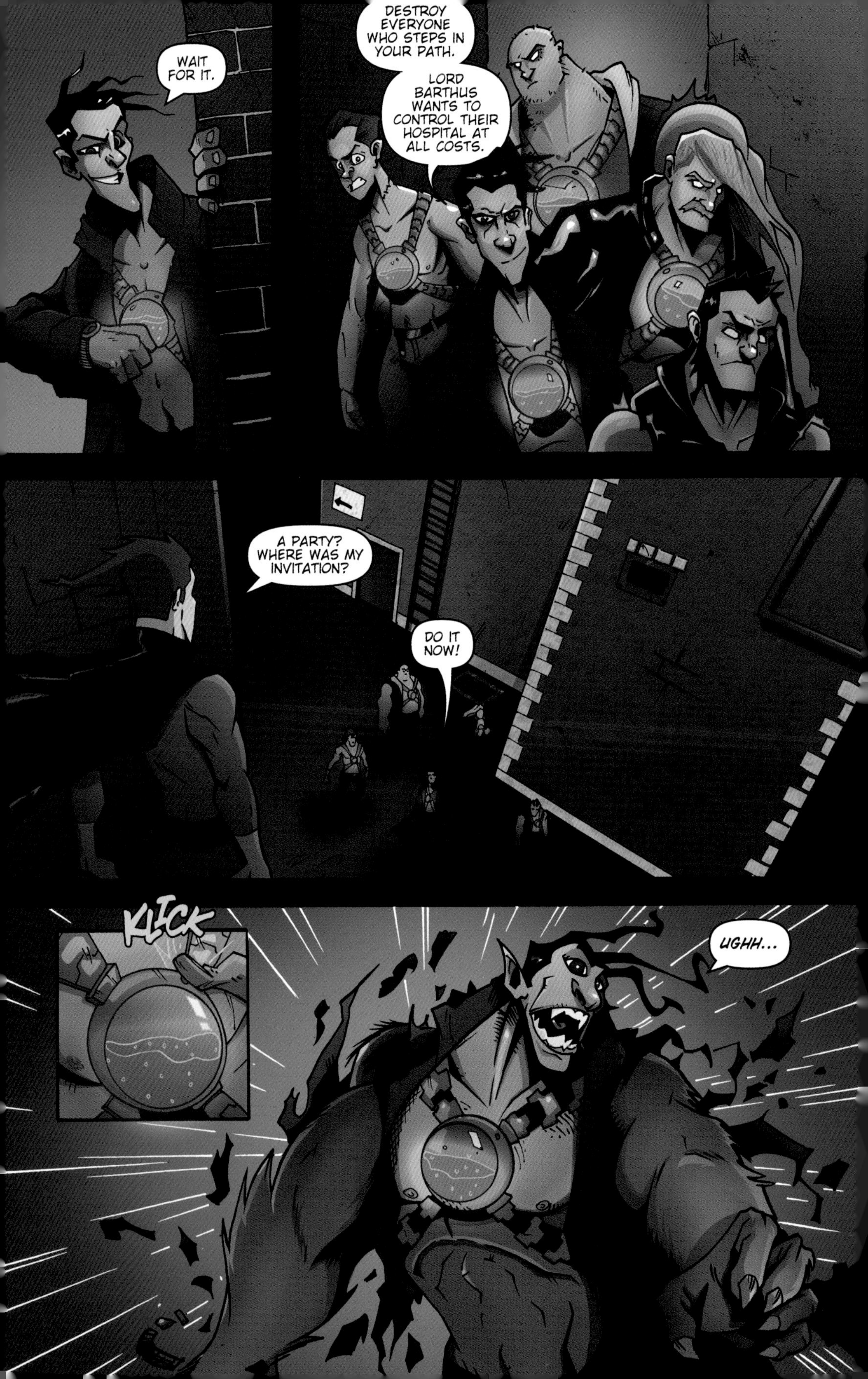
WAIT FOR IT.
DESTROY EVERYONE WHO STEPS IN YOUR PATH.
LORD BARTHUS WANTS TO CONTROL THEIR HOSPITAL AT ALL COSTS.
A PARTY? WHERE WAS MY INVITATION?
DO IT NOW!
KLICK
UGHH...

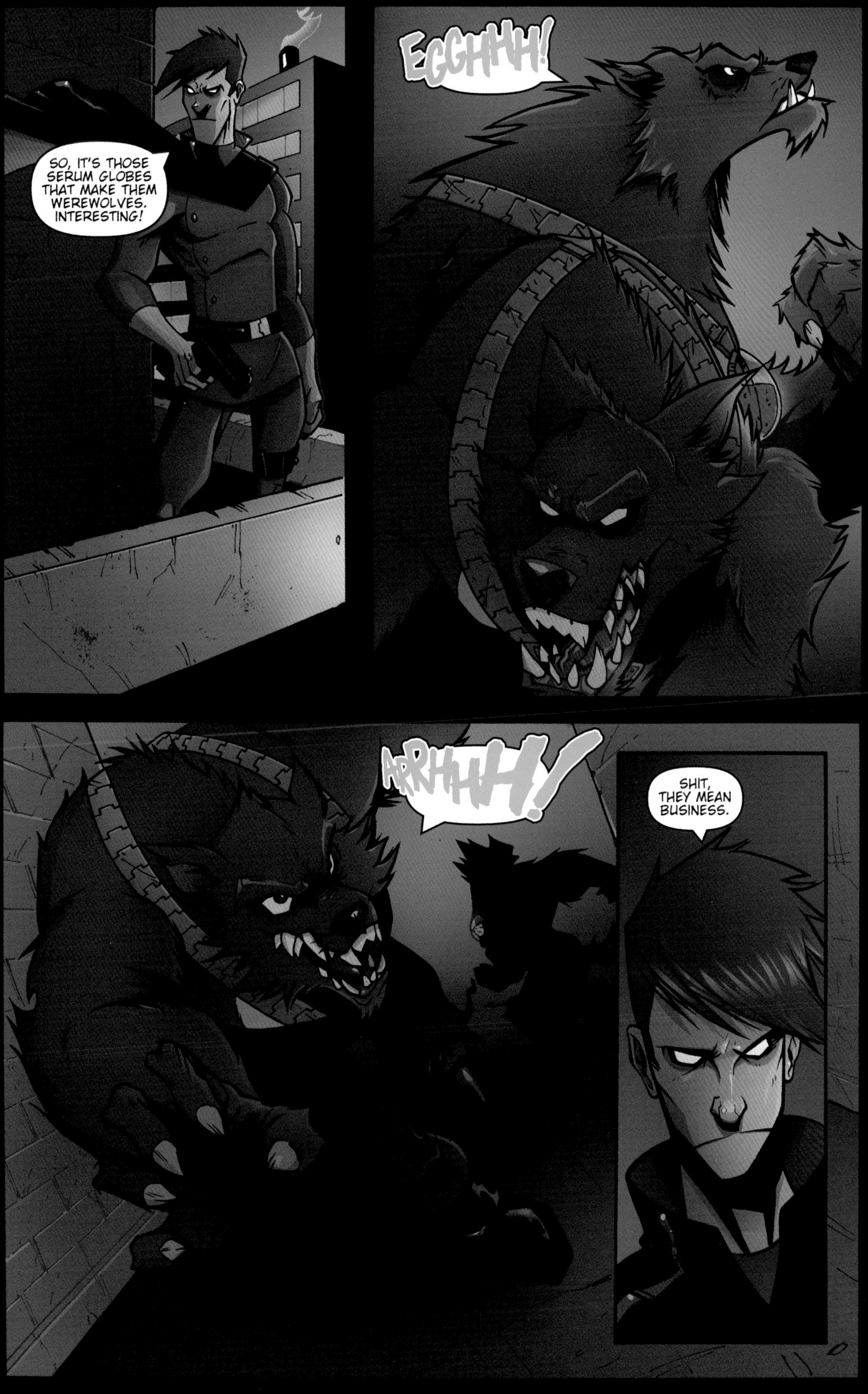
SO, IT'S THOSE SERUM GLOBES THAT MAKE THEM WEREWOLVES. INTERESTING!
EGGHHH!
ARRHHHH!
SHIT, THEY MEAN BUSINESS.

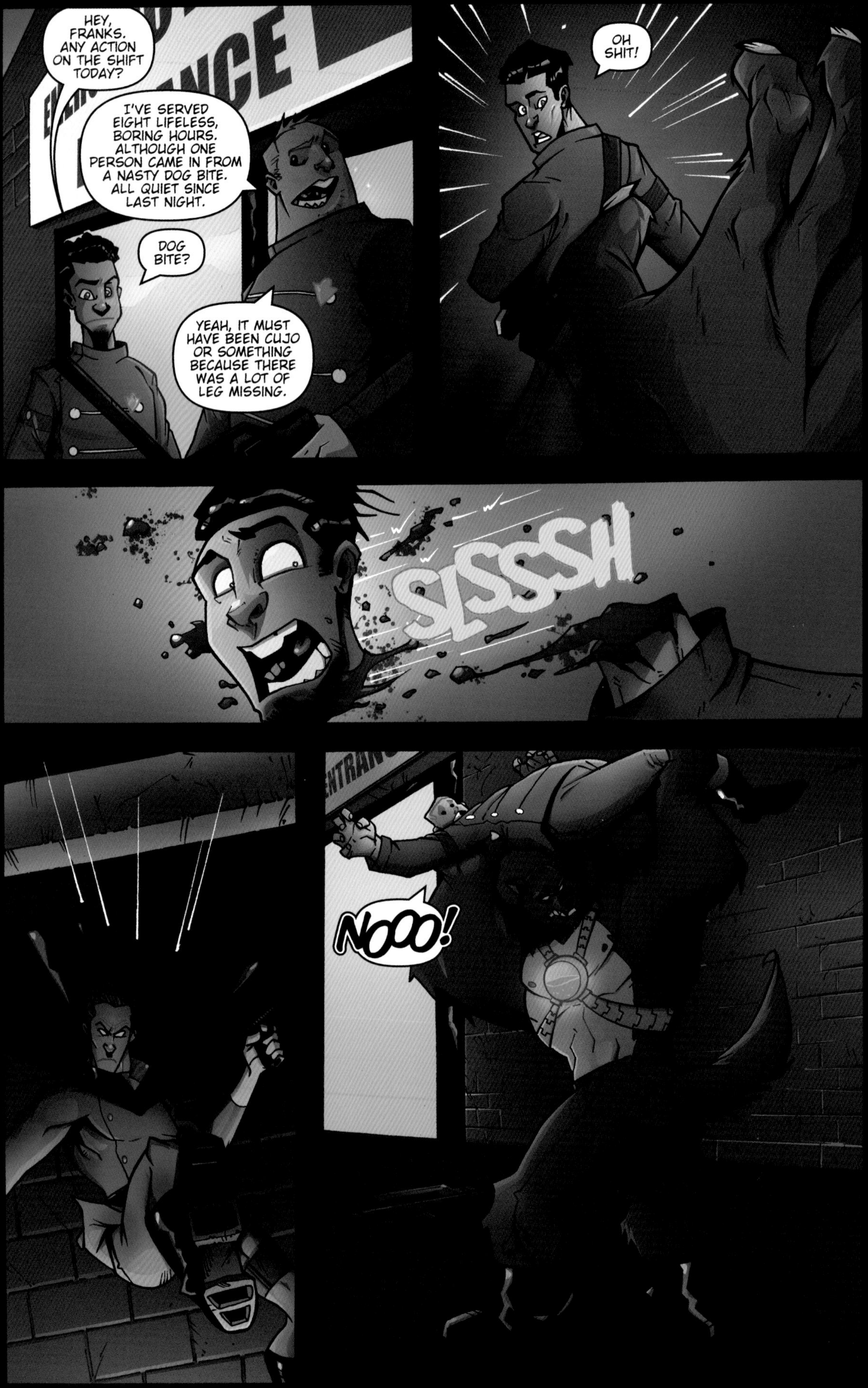
HEY, FRANKS. ANY ACTION ON THE SHIFT TODAY?
I'VE SERVED EIGHT LIFELESS, BORING HOURS. ALTHOUGH ONE PERSON CAME IN FROM A NASTY DOG BITE. ALL QUIET SINCE LAST NIGHT.
DOG BITE?
YEAH, IT MUST HAVE BEEN CUJO OR SOMETHING BECAUSE THERE WAS A LOT OF LEG MISSING.
OH SHIT!
SLSSSH
NOOO!

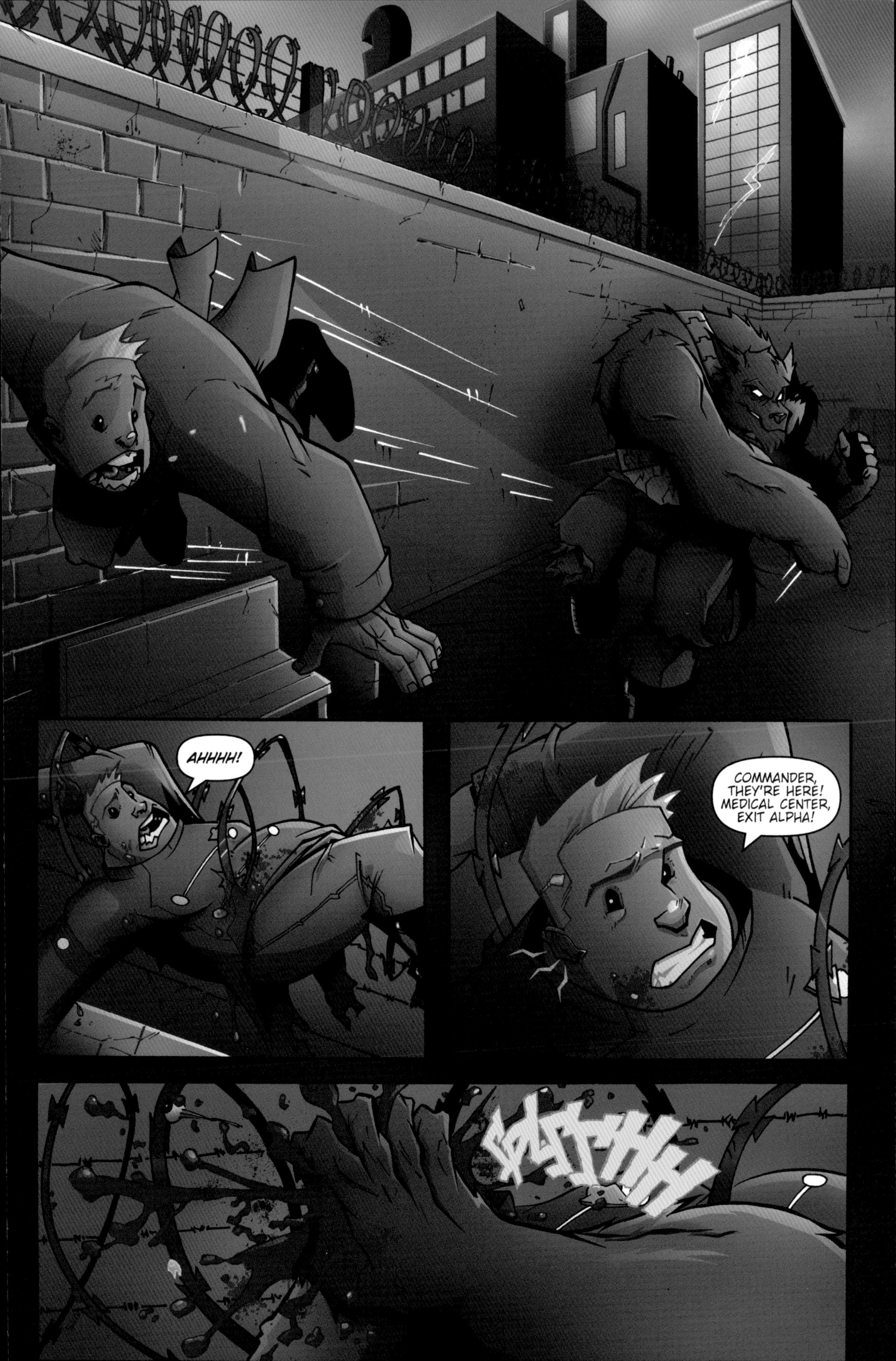
AHHHH!
COMMANDER, THEY'RE HERE! MEDICAL CENTER, EXIT ALPHA!

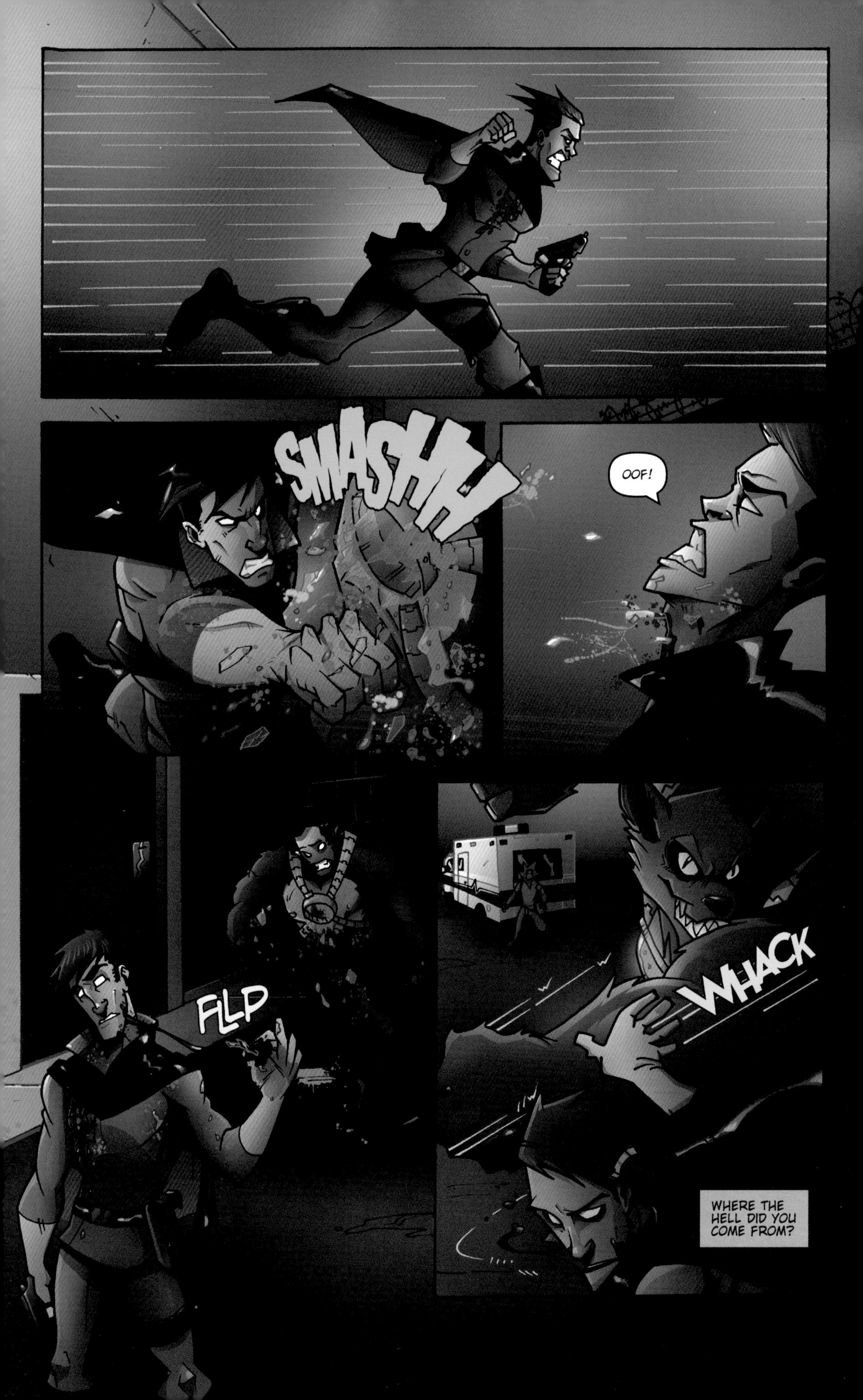
SMASHH
OOF!
FLLP
WHACK
WHERE THE HELL DID YOU COME FROM?

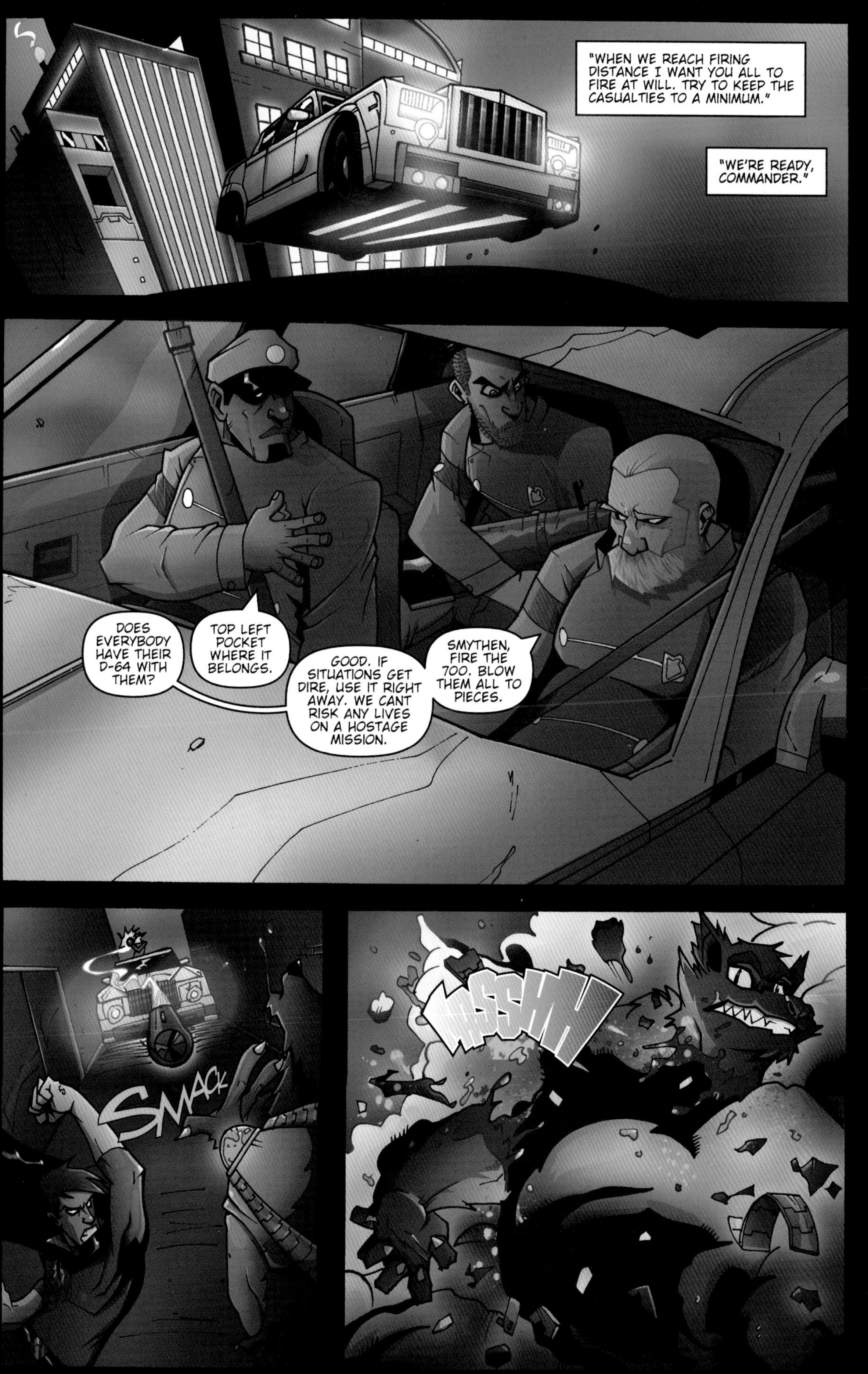
"WHEN WE REACH FIRING DISTANCE I WANT YOU ALL TO FIRE AT WILL. TRY TO KEEP THE CASUALTIES TO A MINIMUM."
"WE'RE READY, COMMANDER."
DOES EVERYBODY HAVE THEIR D-64 WITH THEM?
TOP LEFT POCKET WHERE IT BELONGS.
GOOD. IF SITUATIONS GET DIRE, USE IT RIGHT AWAY. WE CANT RISK ANY LIVES ON A HOSTAGE MISSION.
SMYTHEN, FIRE THE 700. BLOW THEM ALL TO PIECES.
SMACK

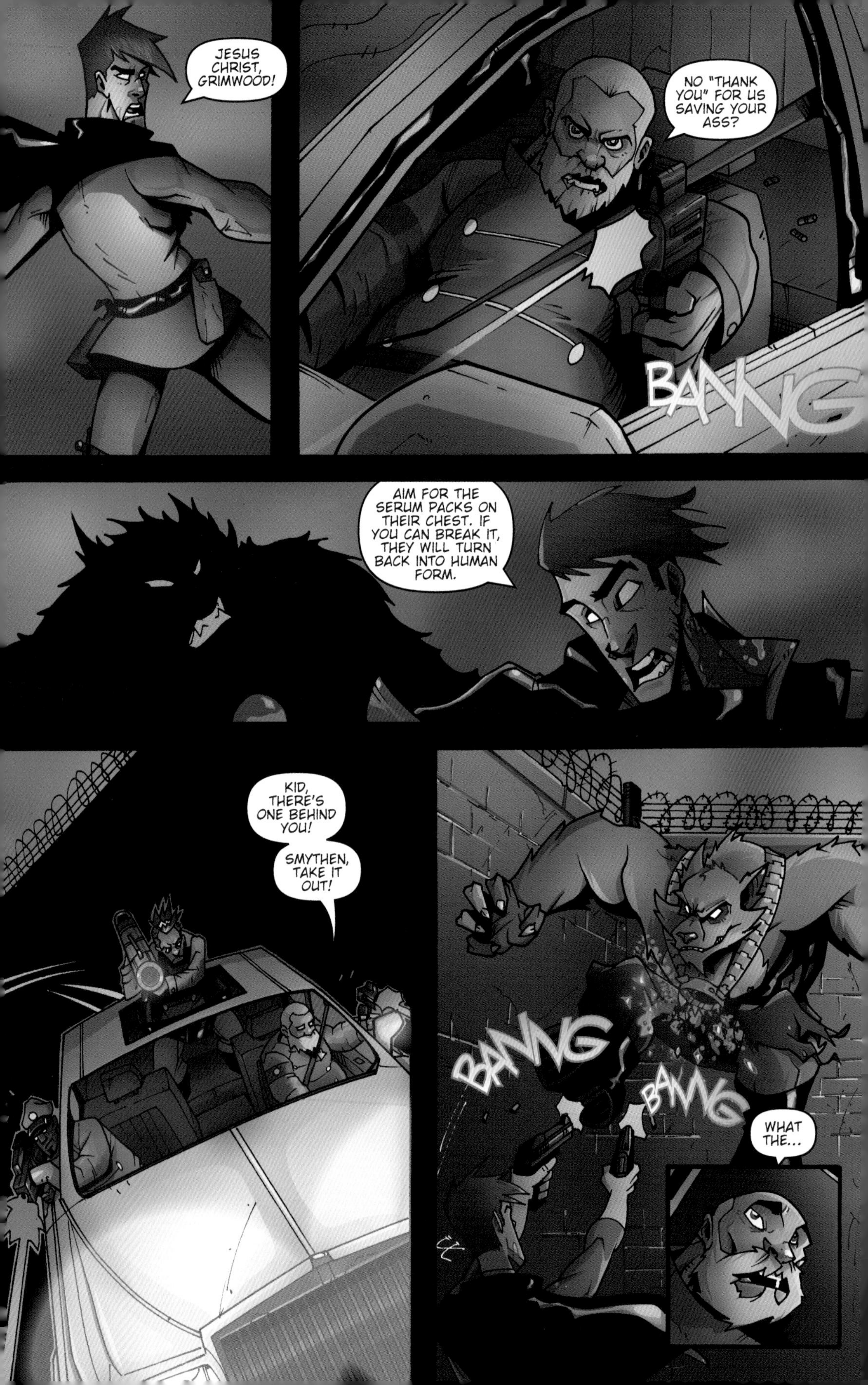
JESUS CHRIST, GRIMWOOD!
NO "THANK YOU" FOR US SAVING YOUR ASS?
BANNG
AIM FOR THE SERUM PACKS ON THEIR CHEST. IF YOU CAN BREAK IT, THEY WILL TURN BACK INTO HUMAN FORM.
KID, THERE'S ONE BEHIND YOU!
SMYTHEN, TAKE IT OUT!
BANNG
BANNG
WHAT THE...

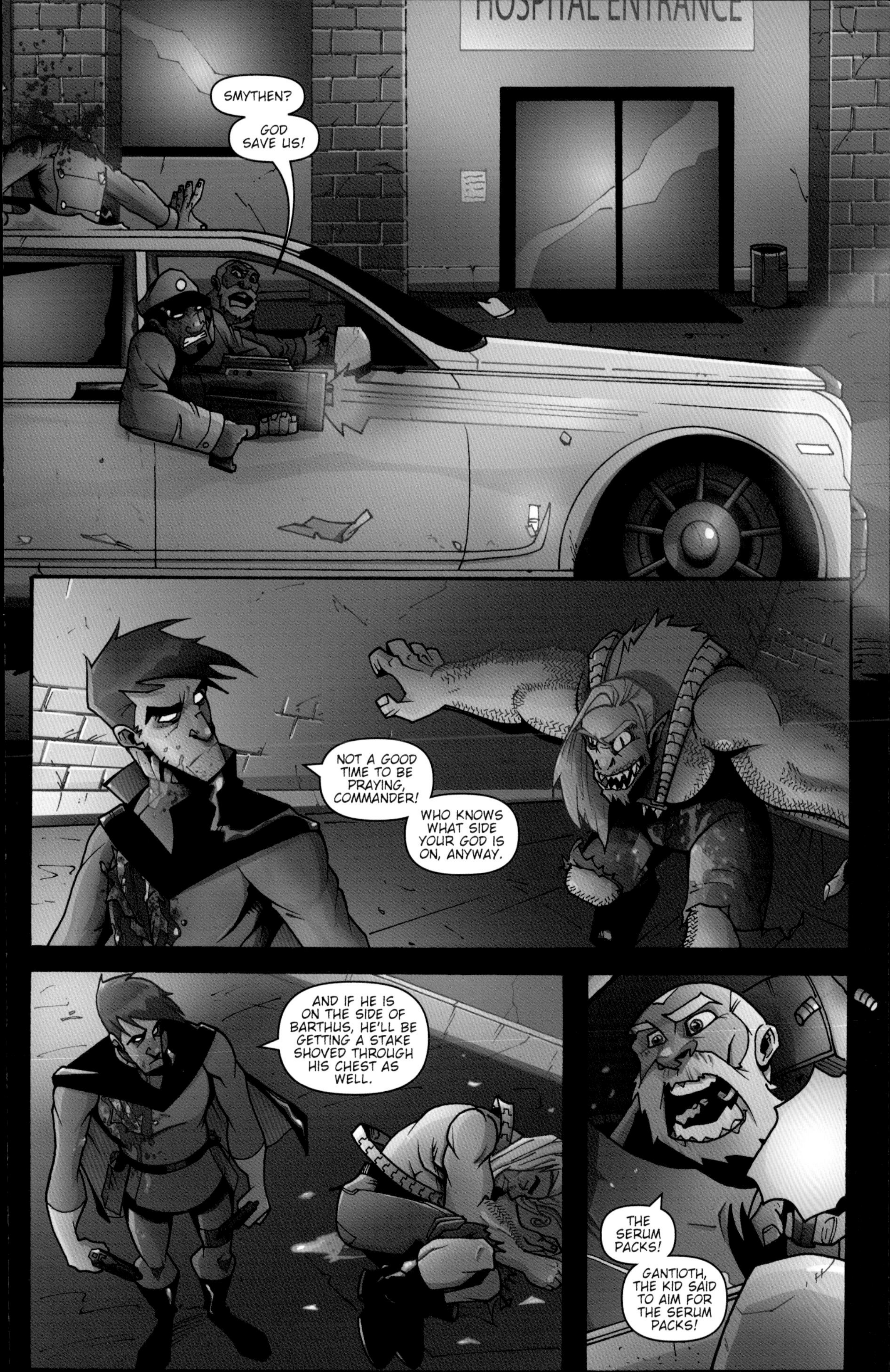
HOSPITAL ENTRANCE
SMYTHEN?
GOD SAVE US!
NOT A GOOD TIME TO BE PRAYING, COMMANDER!
WHO KNOWS WHAT SIDE YOUR GOD IS ON, ANYWAY.
AND IF HE IS ON THE SIDE OF BARTHUS, HE'LL BE GETTING A STAKE SHOVED THROUGH HIS CHEST AS WELL.
THE SERUM PACKS!
GANTIOTH, THE KID SAID TO AIM FOR THE SERUM PACKS!

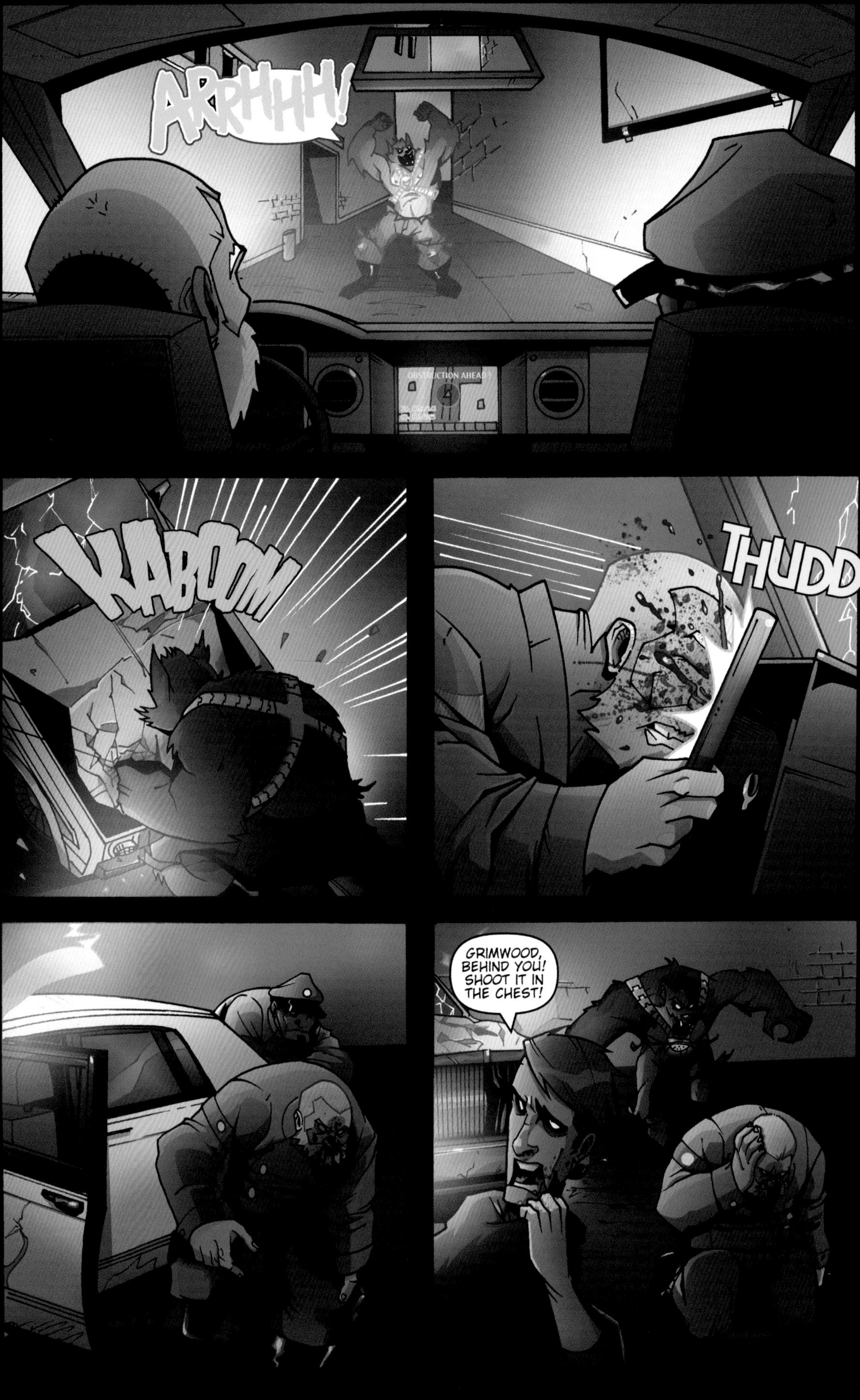
ARRHHH!
OBSTRUCTION AHEAD !
KABOOM
THUDD
GRIMWOOD, BEHIND YOU! SHOOT IT IN THE CHEST!

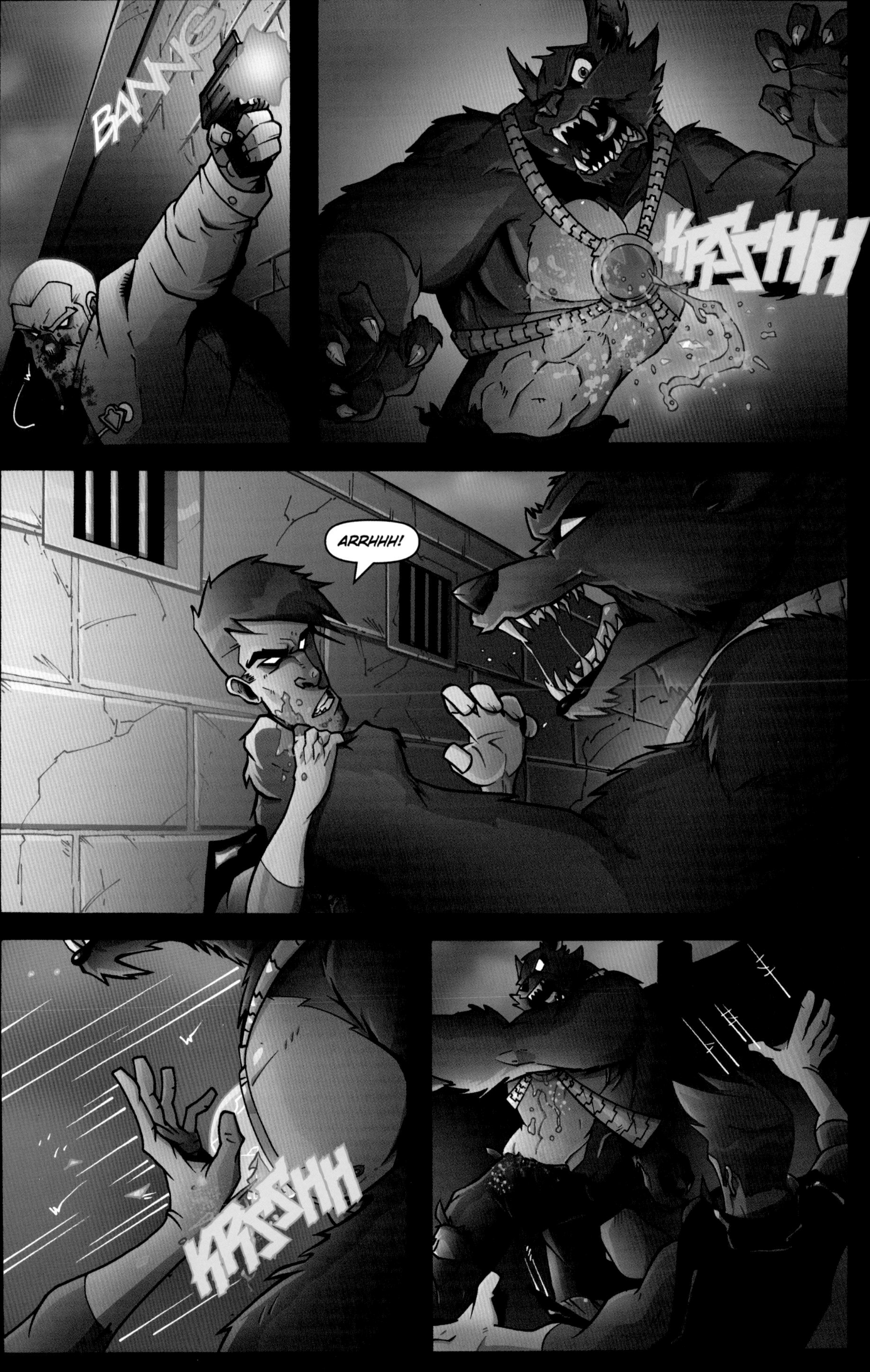
BANG
KRSHH
ARRHHH!
KRSHH

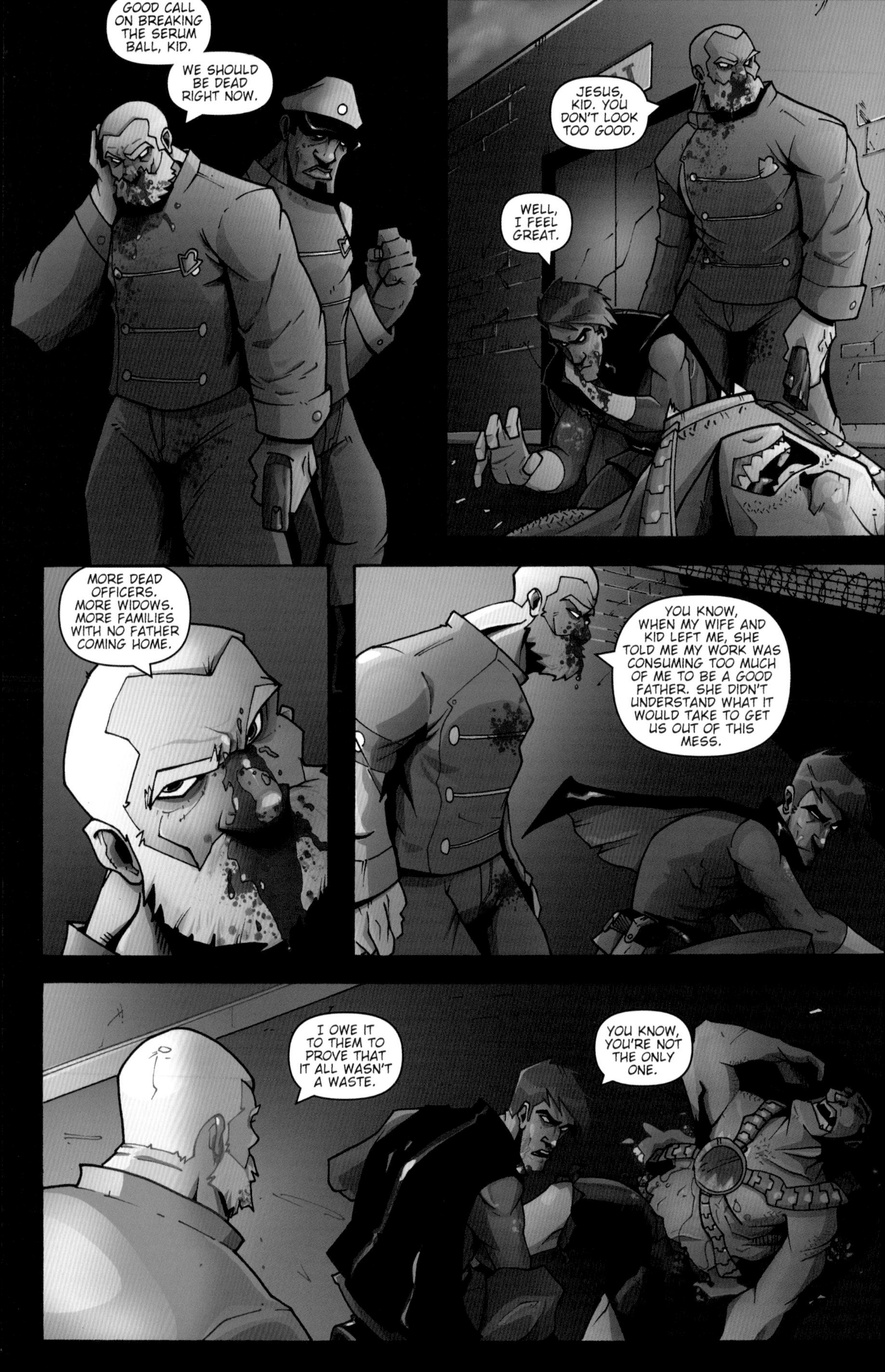
GOOD CALL ON BREAKING THE SERUM BALL, KID.
WE SHOULD BE DEAD RIGHT NOW.
JESUS, KID. YOU DON'T LOOK TOO GOOD.
WELL, I FEEL GREAT.
MORE DEAD OFFICERS. MORE WIDOWS. MORE FAMILIES WITH NO FATHER COMING HOME.
YOU KNOW, WHEN MY WIFE AND KID LEFT ME, SHE TOLD ME MY WORK WAS CONSUMING TOO MUCH OF ME TO BE A GOOD FATHER. SHE DIDN'T UNDERSTAND WHAT IT WOULD TAKE TO GET US OUT OF THIS MESS.
I OWE IT TO THEM TO PROVE THAT IT ALL WASN'T A WASTE.
YOU KNOW, YOU'RE NOT THE ONLY ONE.

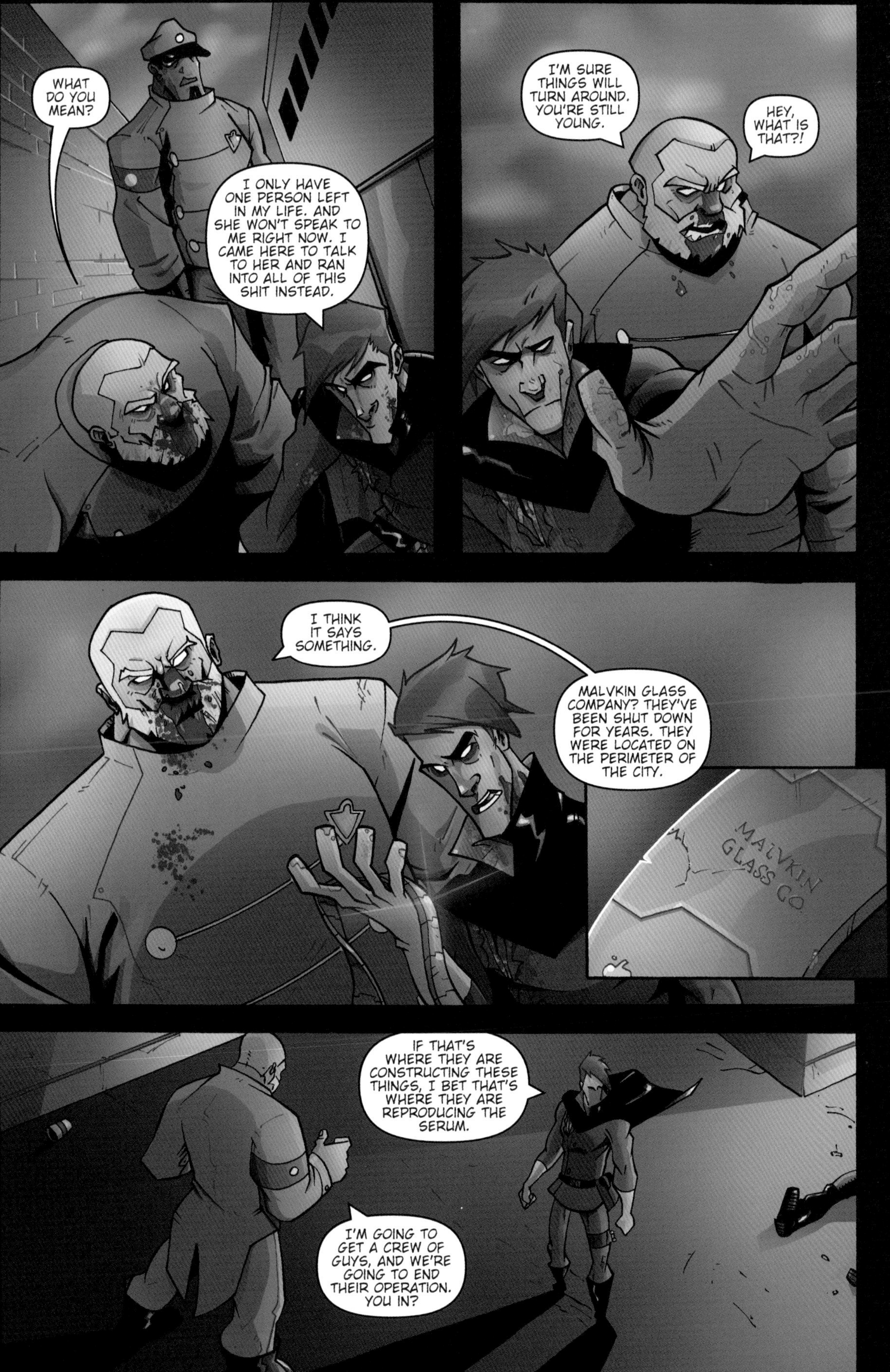
WHAT DO YOU MEAN?
I ONLY HAVE ONE PERSON LEFT IN MY LIFE. AND SHE WON'T SPEAK TO ME RIGHT NOW. I CAME HERE TO TALK TO HER AND RAN INTO ALL OF THIS SHIT INSTEAD.
I'M SURE THINGS WILL TURN AROUND. YOU'RE STILL YOUNG.
HEY, WHAT IS THAT?!
I THINK IT SAYS SOMETHING.
MALVKIN GLASS COMPANY? THEY'VE BEEN SHUT DOWN FOR YEARS. THEY WERE LOCATED ON THE PERIMETER OF THE CITY.
MALVKIN GLASS CO.
IF THAT'S WHERE THEY ARE CONSTRUCTING THESE THINGS, I BET THAT'S WHERE THEY ARE REPRODUCING THE SERUM.
I'M GOING TO GET A CREW OF GUYS, AND WE'RE GOING TO END THEIR OPERATION. YOU IN?

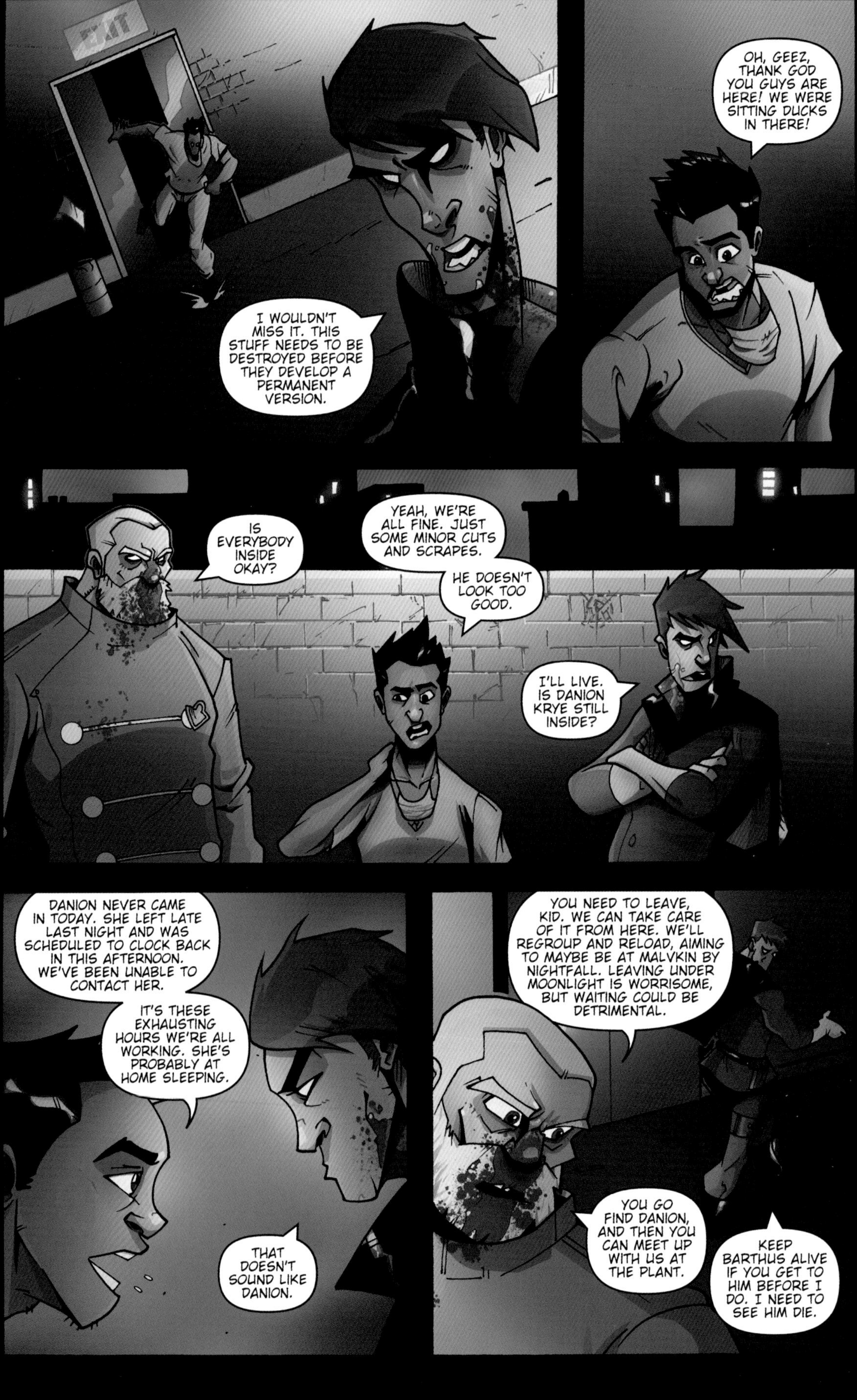
EXIT
I WOULDN'T MISS IT. THIS STUFF NEEDS TO BE DESTROYED BEFORE THEY DEVELOP A PERMANENT VERSION.
OH, GEEZ, THANK GOD YOU GUYS ARE HERE! WE WERE SITTING DUCKS IN THERE!
IS EVERYBODY INSIDE OKAY?
YEAH, WE'RE ALL FINE. JUST SOME MINOR CUTS AND SCRAPES.
HE DOESN'T LOOK TOO GOOD.
I'LL LIVE. IS DANION KRYE STILL INSIDE?
DANION NEVER CAME IN TODAY. SHE LEFT LATE LAST NIGHT AND WAS SCHEDULED TO CLOCK BACK IN THIS AFTERNOON. WE'VE BEEN UNABLE TO CONTACT HER.
IT'S THESE EXHAUSTING HOURS WE'RE ALL WORKING. SHE'S PROBABLY AT HOME SLEEPING.
THAT DOESN'T SOUND LIKE DANION.
YOU NEED TO LEAVE, KID. WE CAN TAKE CARE OF IT FROM HERE. WE'LL REGROUP AND RELOAD, AIMING TO MAYBE BE AT MALVKIN BY NIGHTFALL. LEAVING UNDER MOONLIGHT IS WORRISOME, BUT WAITING COULD BE DETRIMENTAL.
YOU GO FIND DANION, AND THEN YOU CAN MEET UP WITH US AT THE PLANT.
KEEP BARTHUS ALIVE IF YOU GET TO HIM BEFORE I DO. I NEED TO SEE HIM DIE.

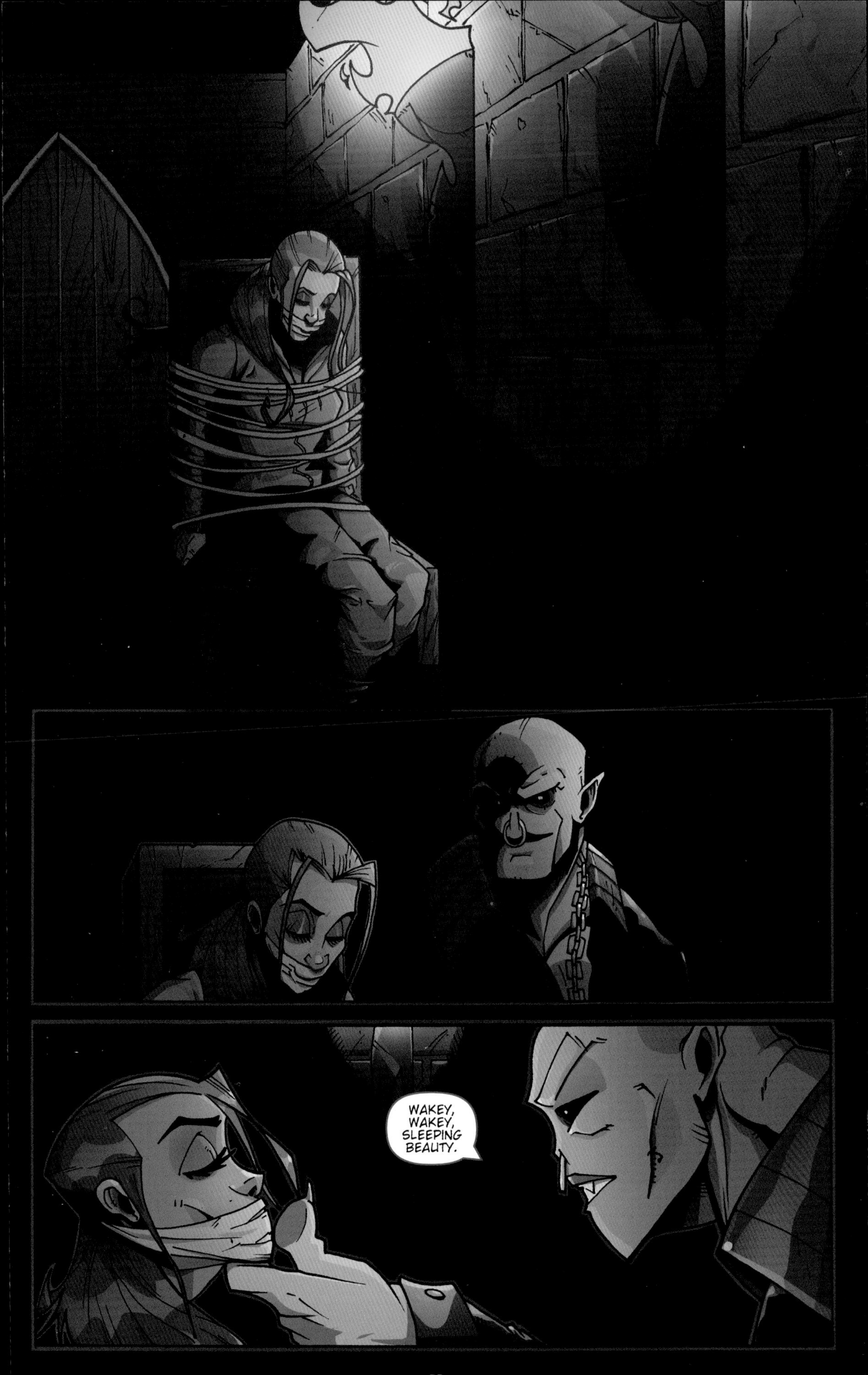
WAKEY, WAKEY, SLEEPING BEAUTY.

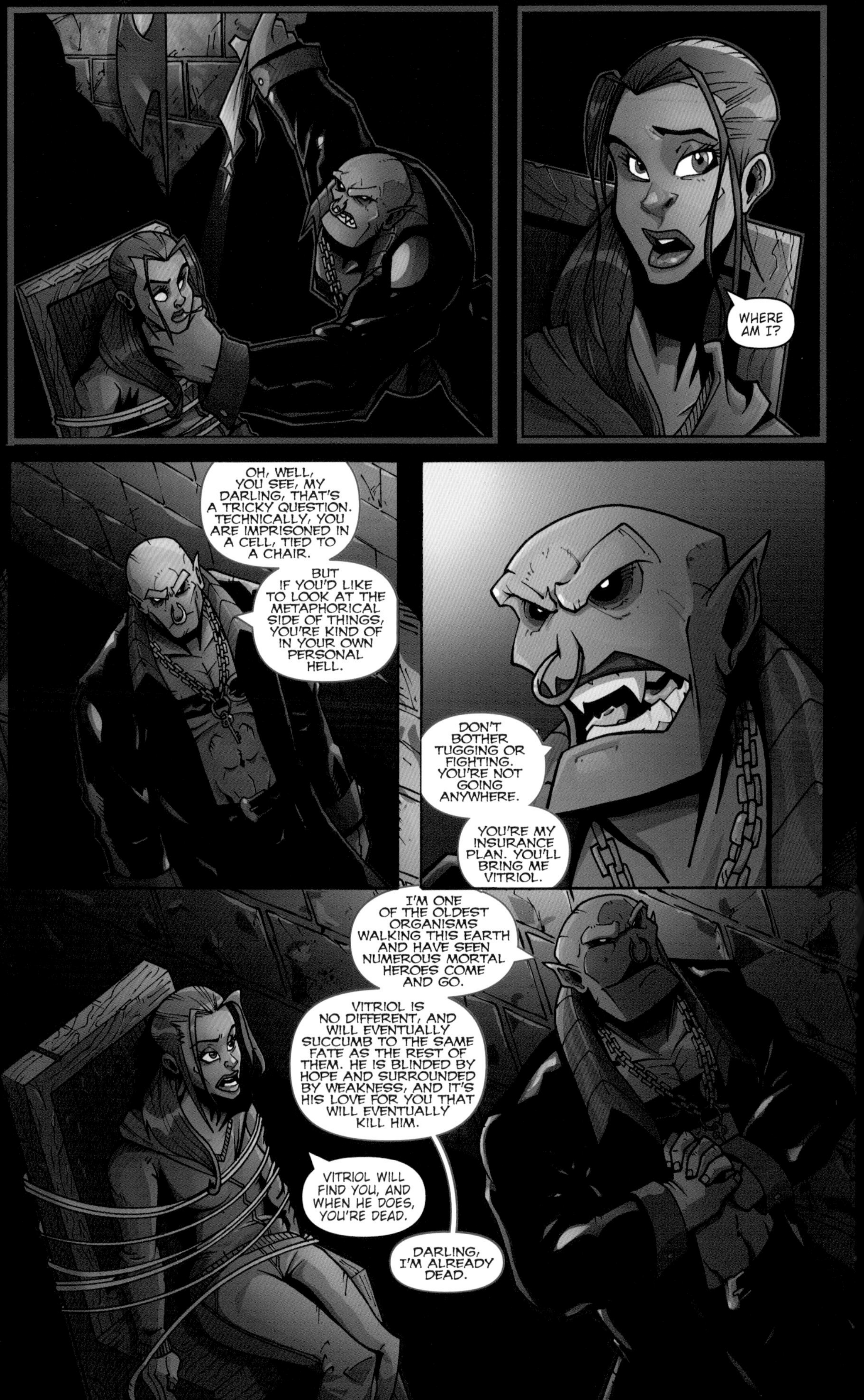
WHERE AM I?
OH, WELL, YOU SEE, MY DARLING, THAT'S A TRICKY QUESTION. TECHNICALLY, YOU ARE IMPRISONED IN A CELL, TIED TO A CHAIR.
BUT IF YOU'D LIKE TO LOOK AT THE METAPHORICAL SIDE OF THINGS, YOU'RE KIND OF IN YOUR OWN PERSONAL HELL.
DON'T BOTHER TUGGING OR FIGHTING. YOU'RE NOT GOING ANYWHERE.
YOU'RE MY INSURANCE PLAN. YOU'LL BRING ME VITRIOL.
I'M ONE OF THE OLDEST ORGANISMS WALKING THIS EARTH AND HAVE SEEN NUMEROUS MORTAL HEROES COME AND GO.
VITRIOL IS NO DIFFERENT, AND WILL EVENTUALLY SUCCUMB TO THE SAME FATE AS THE REST OF THEM. HE IS BLINDED BY HOPE AND SURROUNDED BY WEAKNESS, AND IT'S HIS LOVE FOR YOU THAT WILL EVENTUALLY KILL HIM.
VITRIOL WILL FIND YOU, AND WHEN HE DOES, YOU'RE DEAD.
DARLING, I'M ALREADY DEAD.

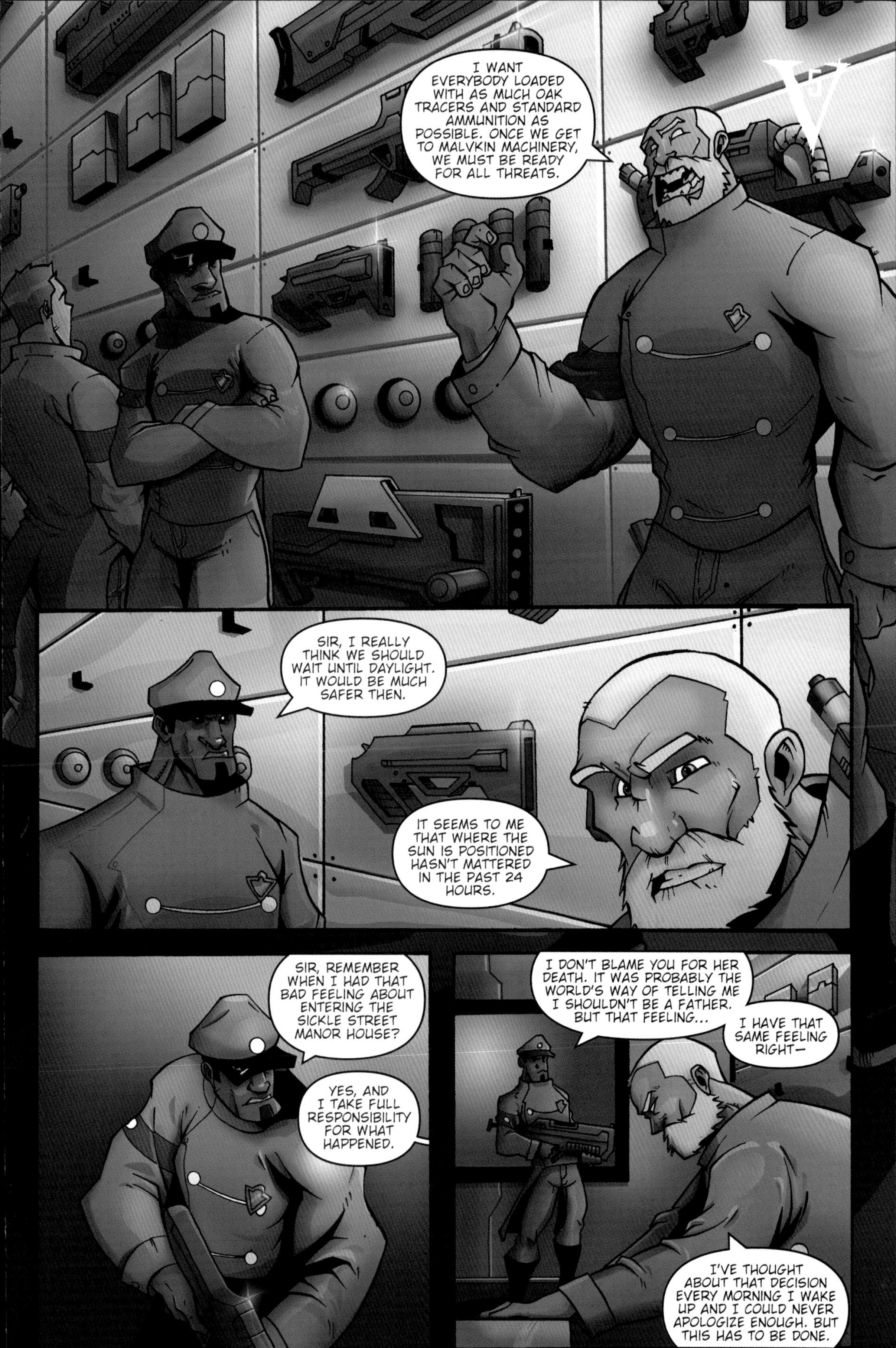
I WANT EVERYBODY LOADED WITH AS MUCH OAK TRACERS AND STANDARD AMMUNITION AS POSSIBLE. ONCE WE GET TO MALVKIN MACHINERY, WE MUST BE READY FOR ALL THREATS.
SIR, I REALLY THINK WE SHOULD WAIT UNTIL DAYLIGHT. IT WOULD BE MUCH SAFER THEN.
IT SEEMS TO ME THAT WHERE THE SUN IS POSITIONED HASN'T MATTERED IN THE PAST 24 HOURS.
SIR, REMEMBER WHEN I HAD THAT BAD FEELING ABOUT ENTERING THE SICKLE STREET MANOR HOUSE?
YES, AND I TAKE FULL RESPONSIBILITY FOR WHAT HAPPENED.
I DON'T BLAME YOU FOR HER DEATH. IT WAS PROBABLY THE WORLD'S WAY OF TELLING ME I SHOULDN'T BE A FATHER. BUT THAT FEELING...
I HAVE THAT SAME FEELING RIGHT—
I'VE THOUGHT ABOUT THAT DECISION EVERY MORNING I WAKE UP AND I COULD NEVER APOLOGIZE ENOUGH. BUT THIS HAS TO BE DONE.

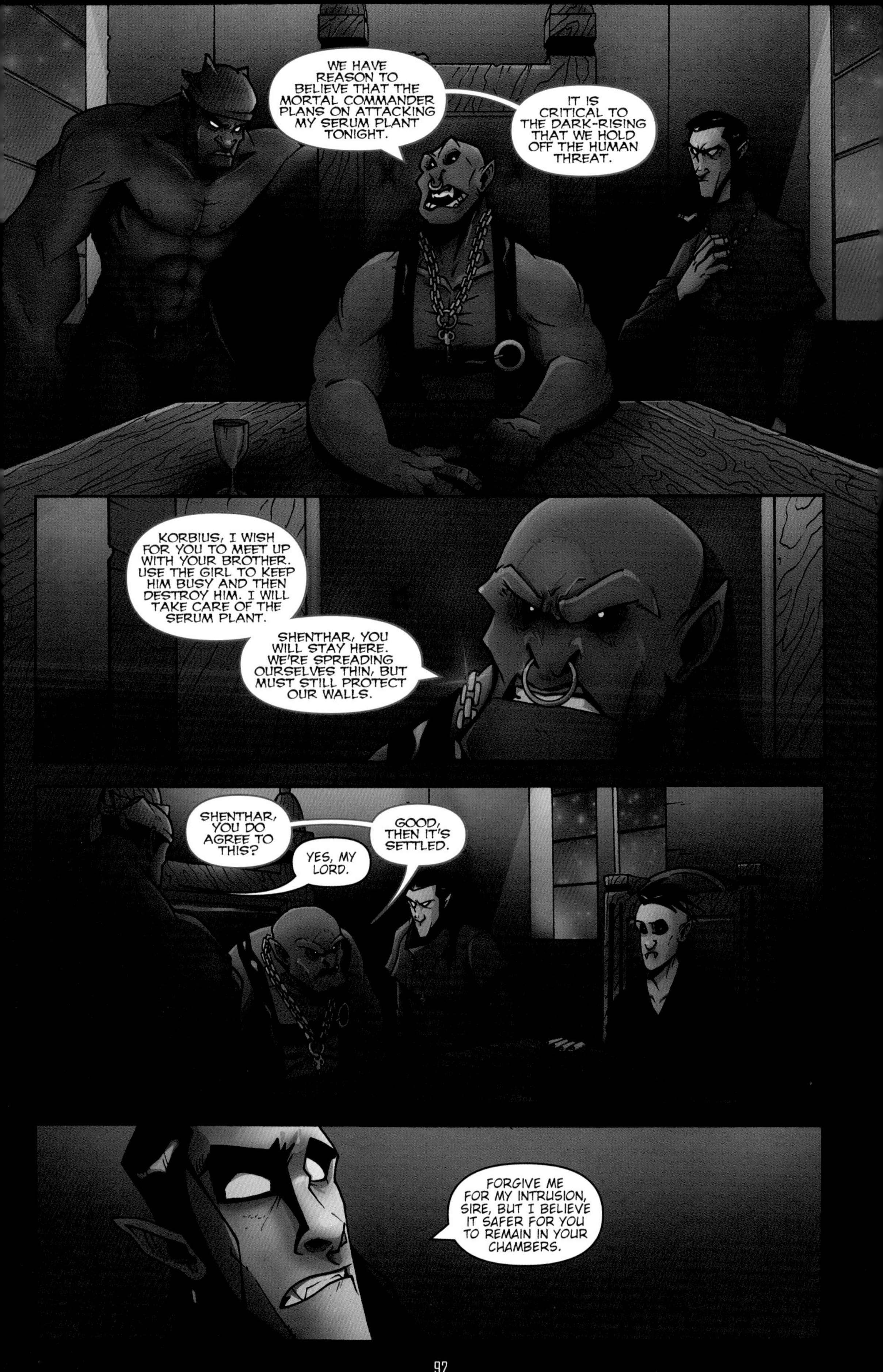
WE HAVE REASON TO BELIEVE THAT THE MORTAL COMMANDER PLANS ON ATTACKING MY SERUM PLANT TONIGHT.
IT IS CRITICAL TO THE DARK-RISING THAT WE HOLD OFF THE HUMAN THREAT.
KORBIUS, I WISH FOR YOU TO MEET UP WITH YOUR BROTHER. USE THE GIRL TO KEEP HIM BUSY AND THEN DESTROY HIM. I WILL TAKE CARE OF THE SERUM PLANT.
SHENTHAR, YOU WILL STAY HERE. WE'RE SPREADING OURSELVES THIN, BUT MUST STILL PROTECT OUR WALLS.
SHENTHAR, YOU DO AGREE TO THIS?
YES, MY LORD.
GOOD, THEN IT'S SETTLED.
FORGIVE ME FOR MY INTRUSION, SIRE, BUT I BELIEVE IT SAFER FOR YOU TO REMAIN IN YOUR CHAMBERS.

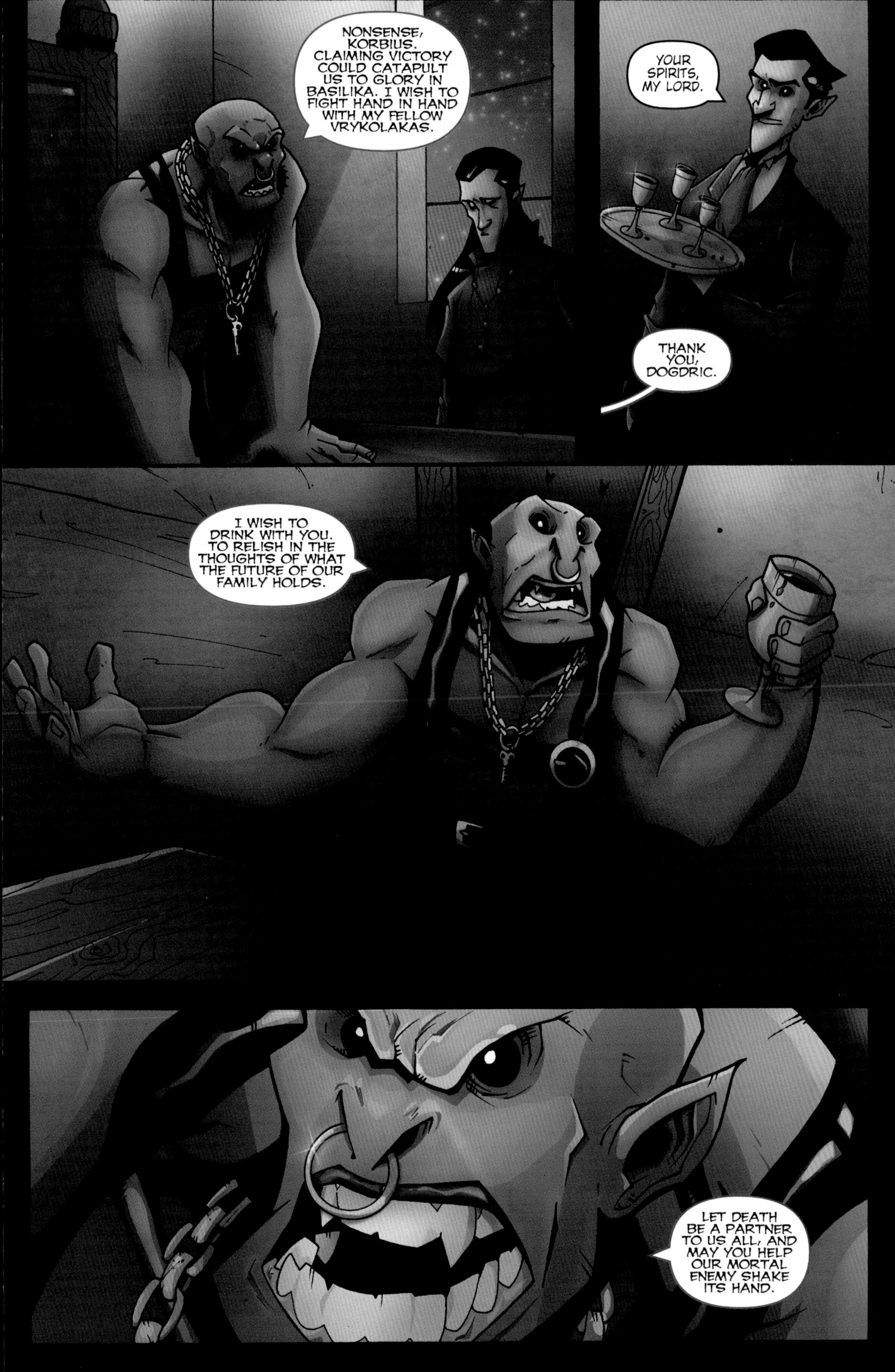
NONSENSE, KORBIUS. CLAIMING VICTORY COULD CATAPULT US TO GLORY IN BASILIKA. I WISH TO FIGHT HAND IN HAND WITH MY FELLOW VRYKOLAKAS.
YOUR SPIRITS, MY LORD.
THANK YOU, DOGDRIC.
I WISH TO DRINK WITH YOU. TO RELISH IN THE THOUGHTS OF WHAT THE FUTURE OF OUR FAMILY HOLDS.
LET DEATH BE A PARTNER TO US ALL, AND MAY YOU HELP OUR MORTAL ENEMY SHAKE ITS HAND.

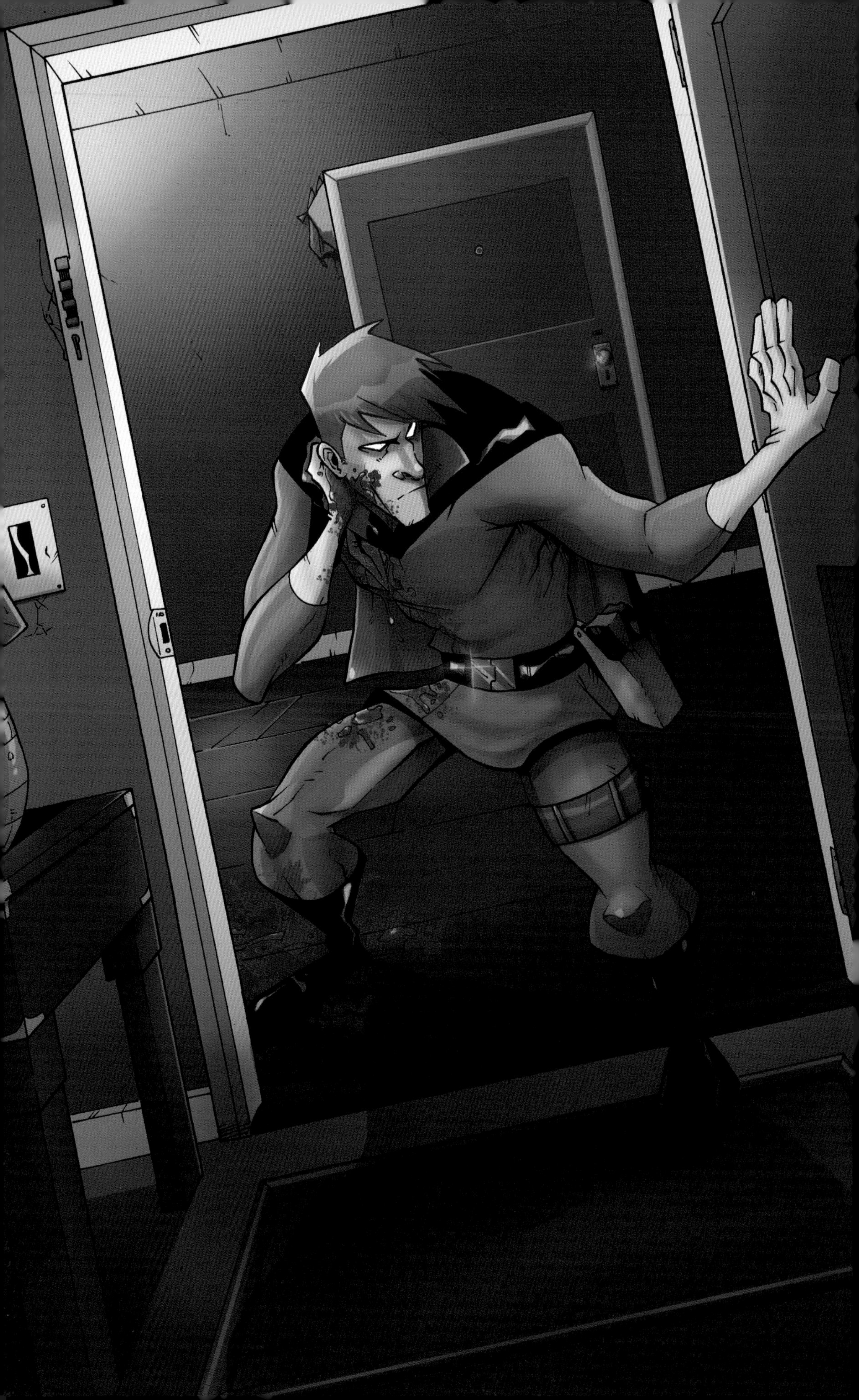

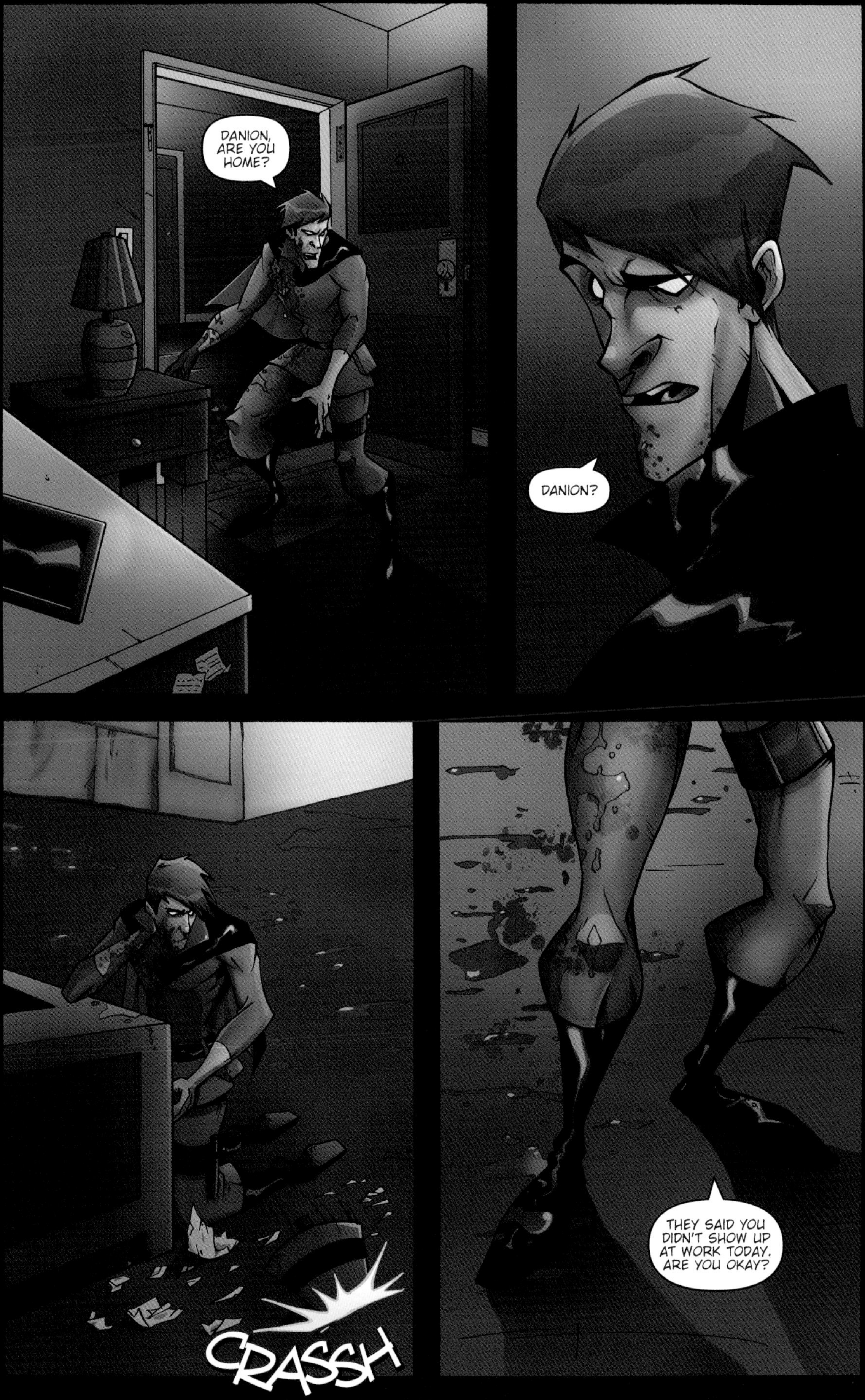
DANION, ARE YOU HOME?
DANION?
CRASSH
THEY SAID YOU DIDN'T SHOW UP AT WORK TODAY. ARE YOU OKAY?

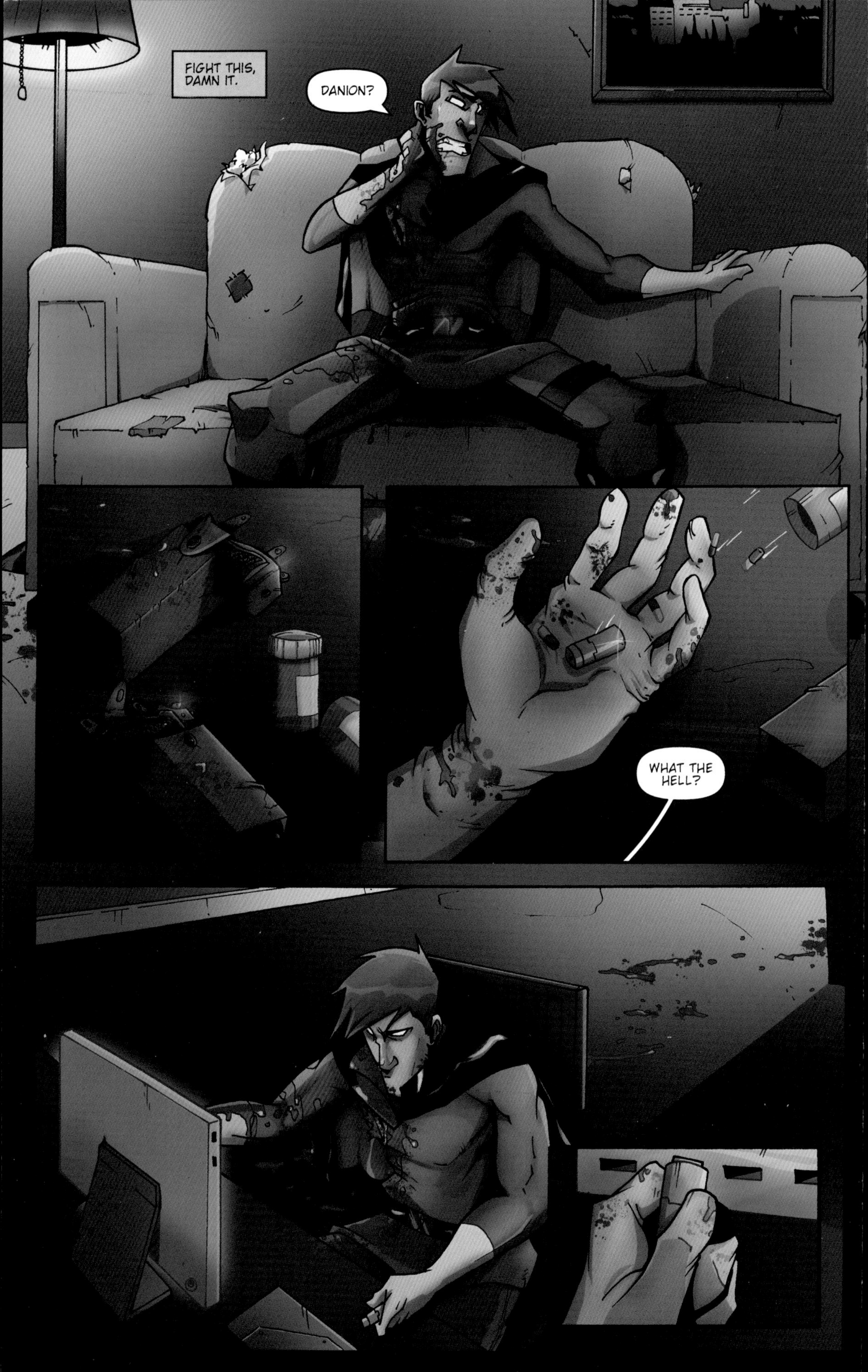
FIGHT THIS, DAMN IT.
DANION?
WHAT THE HELL?

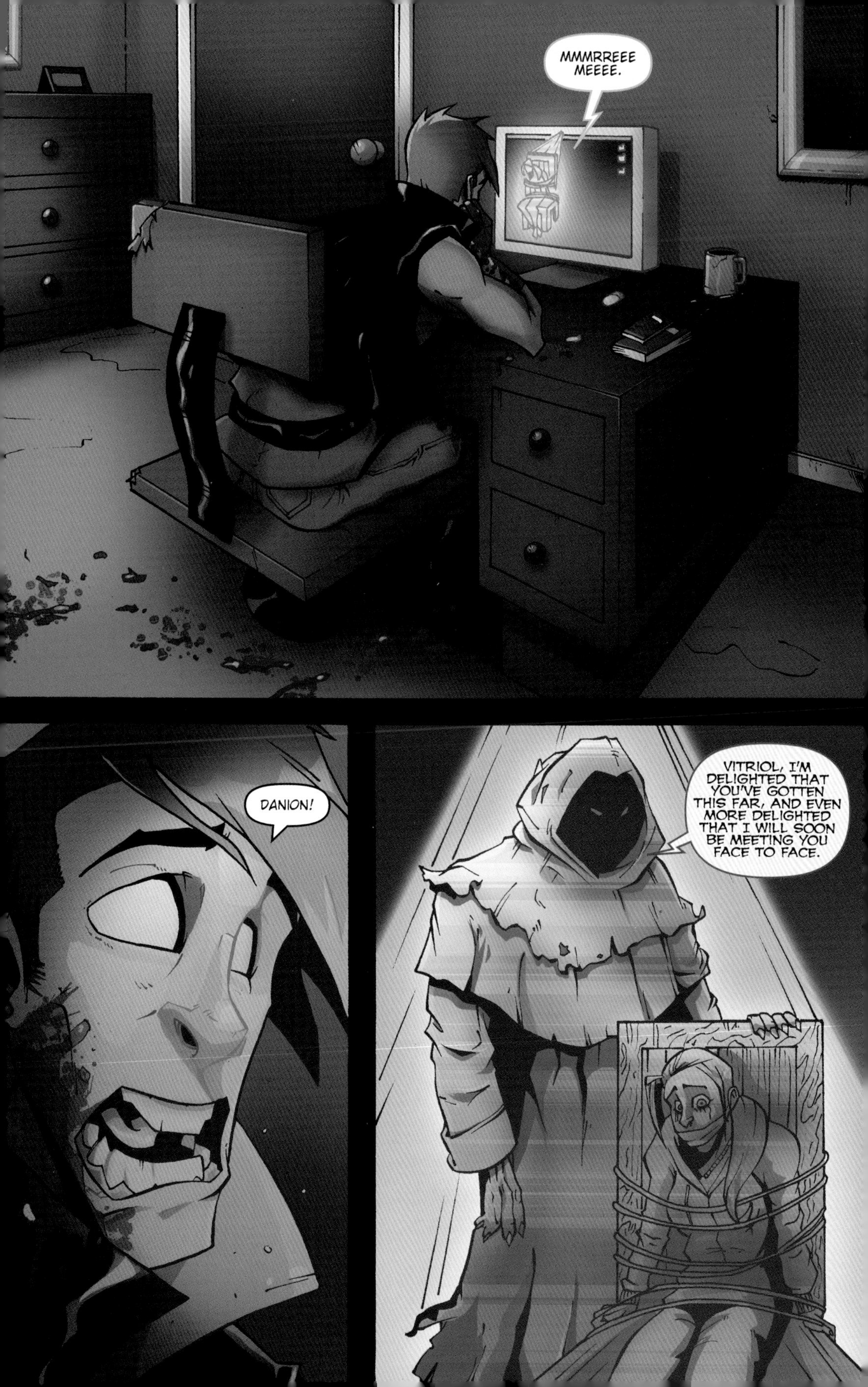
MMMRREEE MEEEE.
DANION!
VITRIOL, I'M DELIGHTED THAT YOU'VE GOTTEN THIS FAR, AND EVEN MORE DELIGHTED THAT I WILL SOON BE MEETING YOU FACE TO FACE.

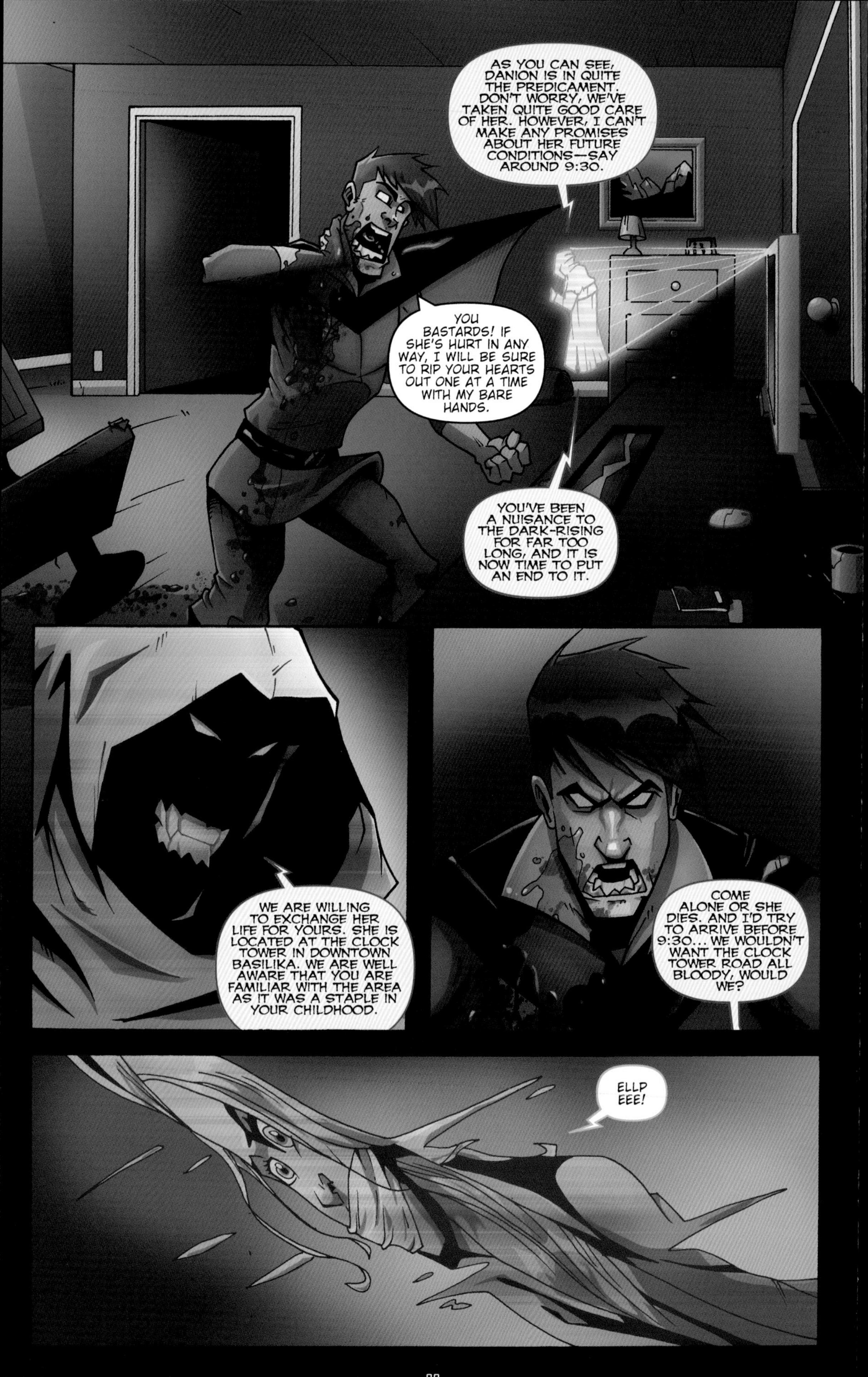
AS YOU CAN SEE, DANION IS IN QUITE THE PREDICAMENT. DON'T WORRY, WE'VE TAKEN QUITE GOOD CARE OF HER. HOWEVER, I CAN'T MAKE ANY PROMISES ABOUT HER FUTURE CONDITIONS—SAY AROUND 9:30.
YOU BASTARDS! IF SHE'S HURT IN ANY WAY, I WILL BE SURE TO RIP YOUR HEARTS OUT ONE AT A TIME WITH MY BARE HANDS.
YOU'VE BEEN A NUISANCE TO THE DARK-RISING FOR FAR TOO LONG, AND IT IS NOW TIME TO PUT AN END TO IT.
WE ARE WILLING TO EXCHANGE HER LIFE FOR YOURS. SHE IS LOCATED AT THE CLOCK TOWER IN DOWNTOWN BASILIKA. WE ARE WELL AWARE THAT YOU ARE FAMILIAR WITH THE AREA AS IT WAS A STAPLE IN YOUR CHILDHOOD.
COME ALONE OR SHE DIES. AND I'D TRY TO ARRIVE BEFORE 9:30... WE WOULDN'T WANT THE CLOCK TOWER ROAD ALL BLOODY, WOULD WE?
ELLP EEE!

GODDAMN IT, DANION. SURE COULD USE YOUR SEWING SKILLS RIGHT NOW.

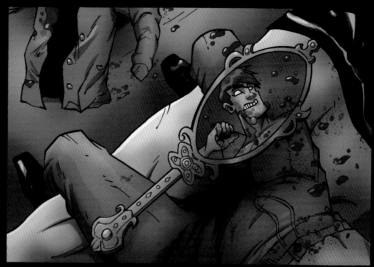

IN THE DAYS LONG AGO, THEY USED GASOLINE INSTEAD OF ELECTRICAL GEL. HARD TO BELIEVE, I KNOW.

TECHNOLOGY WAS BOOMING, AND THEN WE WERE HIT WITH THE RECESSION OF THE MID-2000s.

WE LOST MANY YEARS OF TECHNOLOGICAL BREAKTHROUGHS. THIS IS WHY YOU ONLY SEE THE D.I. AND THE WEALTHY WITH HOVER CARS. REFURBISHED CLASSICS WILL DO FOR US REGULAR FOLK.

THIS STUFF HERE IS A SOLAR NANOCRYSTAL SOLUTION COMPRISED OF THE SEMICONDUCTOR CADMIUM SELENIDE.

IT CAPTURES THE SUN'S RAYS SO WHEN YOU'RE RIDING YOUR BIKE YOUR HANDS WON'T GET COLD.

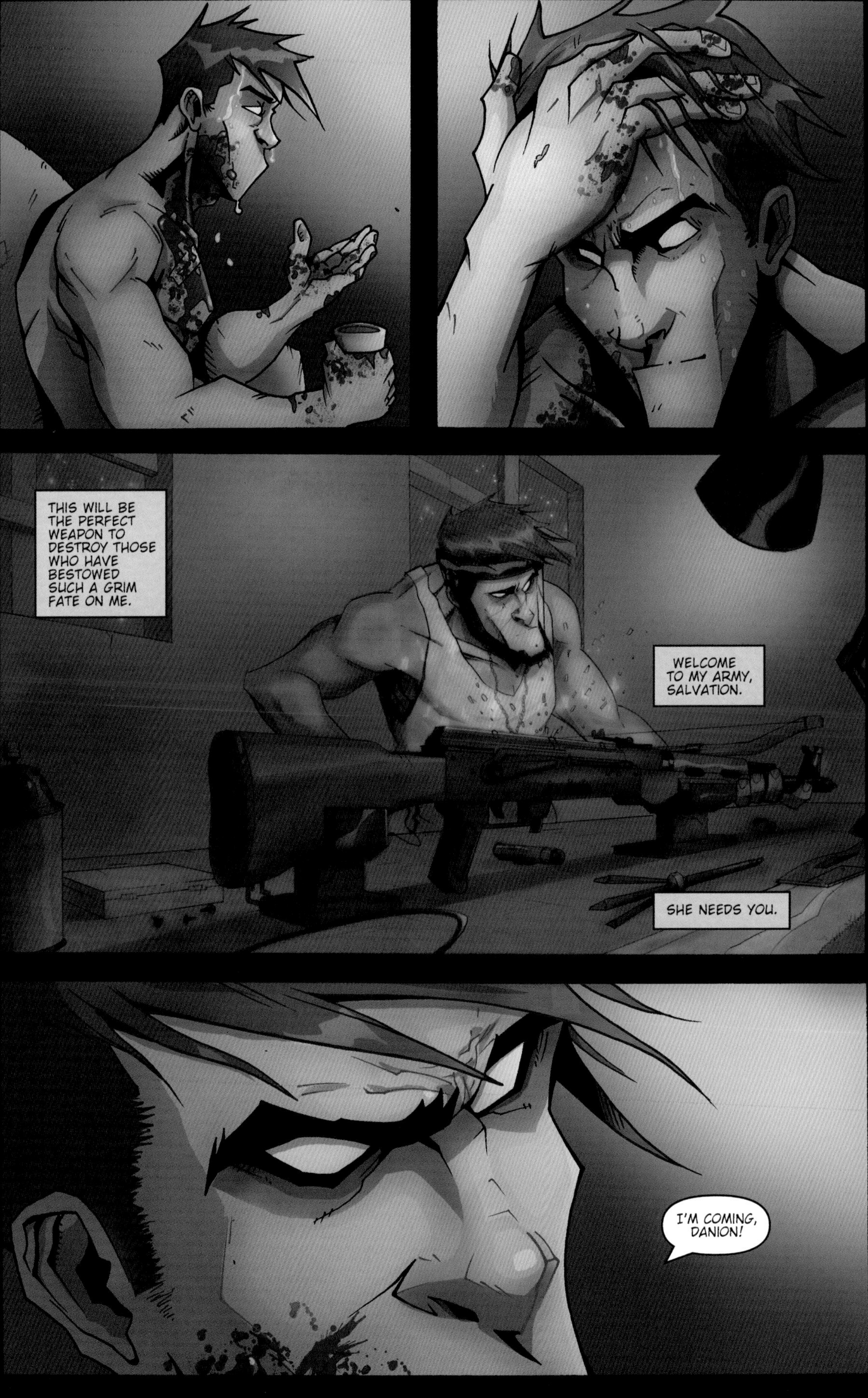
THIS WILL BE THE PERFECT WEAPON TO DESTROY THOSE WHO HAVE BESTOWED SUCH A GRIM FATE ON ME.
WELCOME TO MY ARMY, SALVATION.
SHE NEEDS YOU.
I'M COMING, DANION!

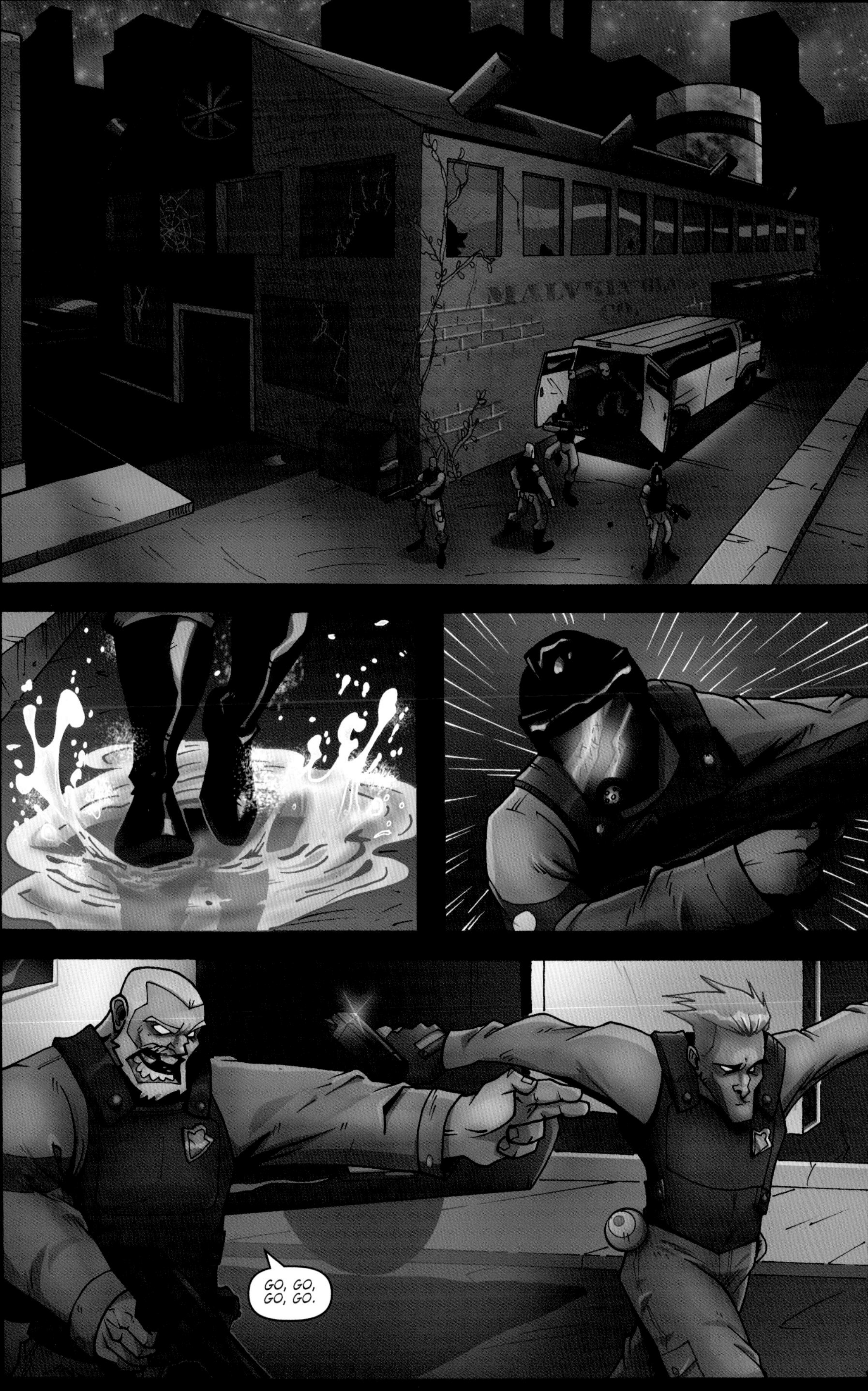
GO, GO,
GO, GO.

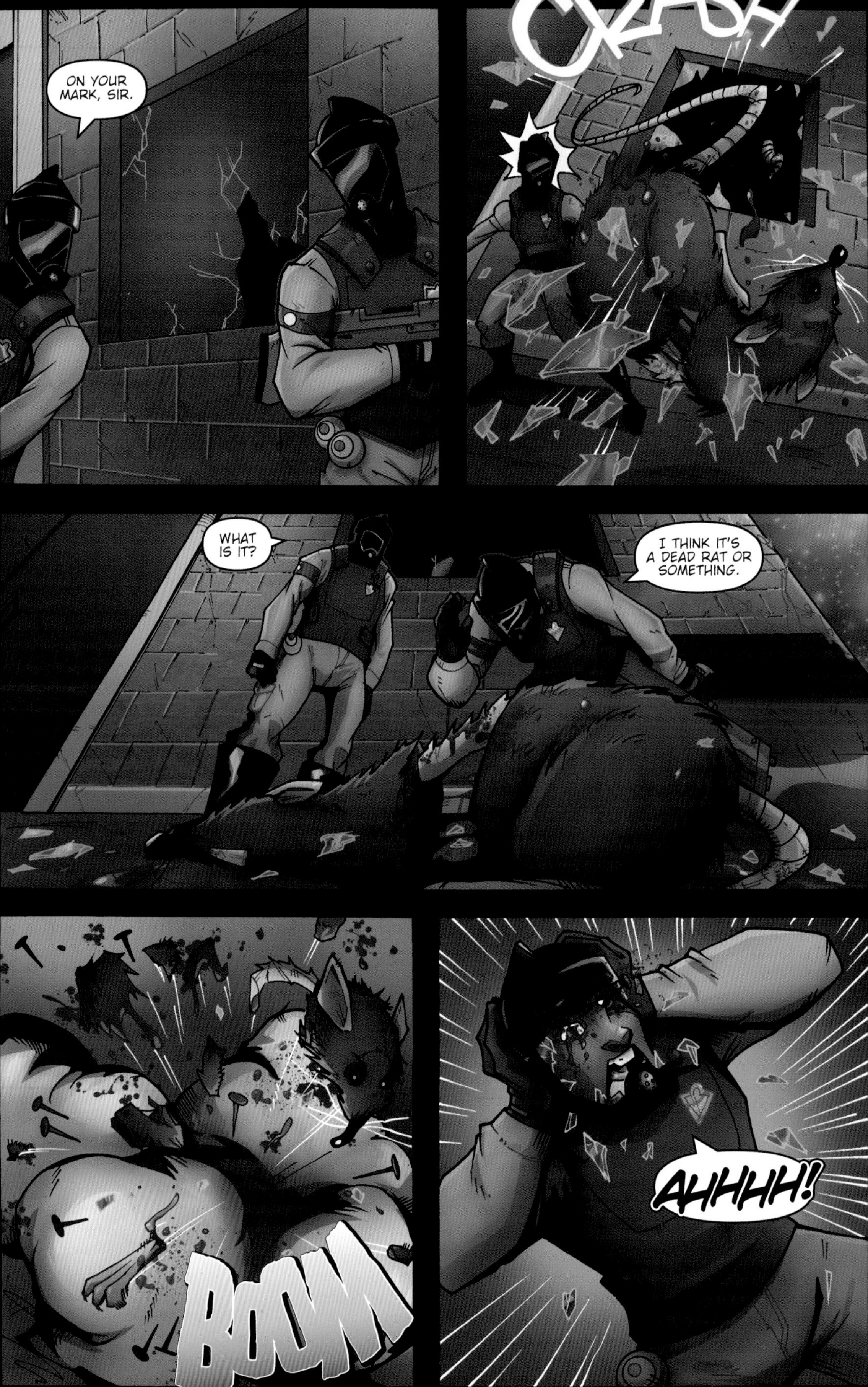
ON YOUR MARK, SIR.
CRASH
WHAT IS IT?
I THINK IT'S A DEAD RAT OR SOMETHING.
BOOM
AHHHH!

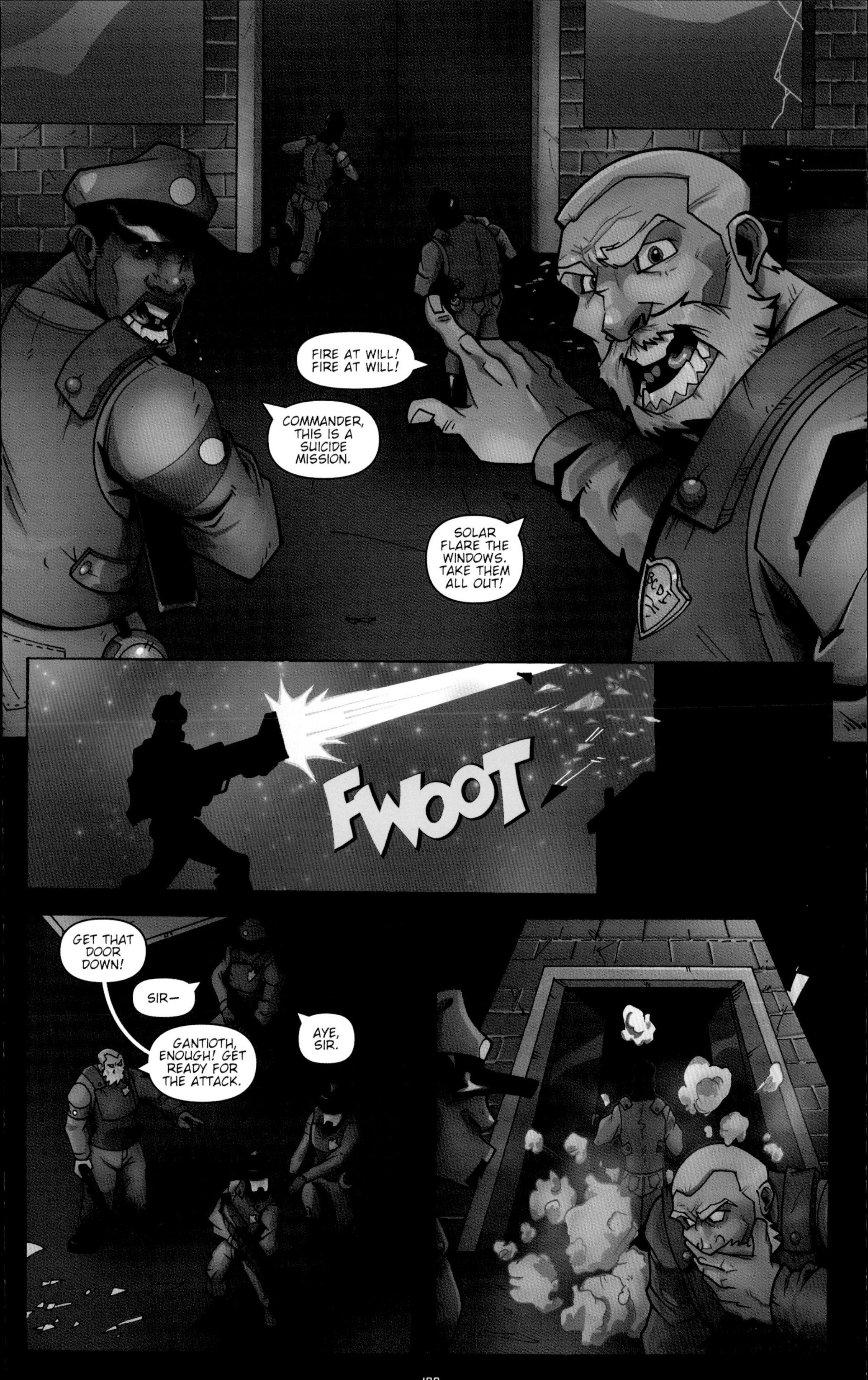
FIRE AT WILL! FIRE AT WILL!
COMMANDER, THIS IS A SUICIDE MISSION.
SOLAR FLARE THE WINDOWS. TAKE THEM ALL OUT!
FWOOT
GET THAT DOOR DOWN!
SIR—
GANTIOTH, ENOUGH! GET READY FOR THE ATTACK.
AYE, SIR.

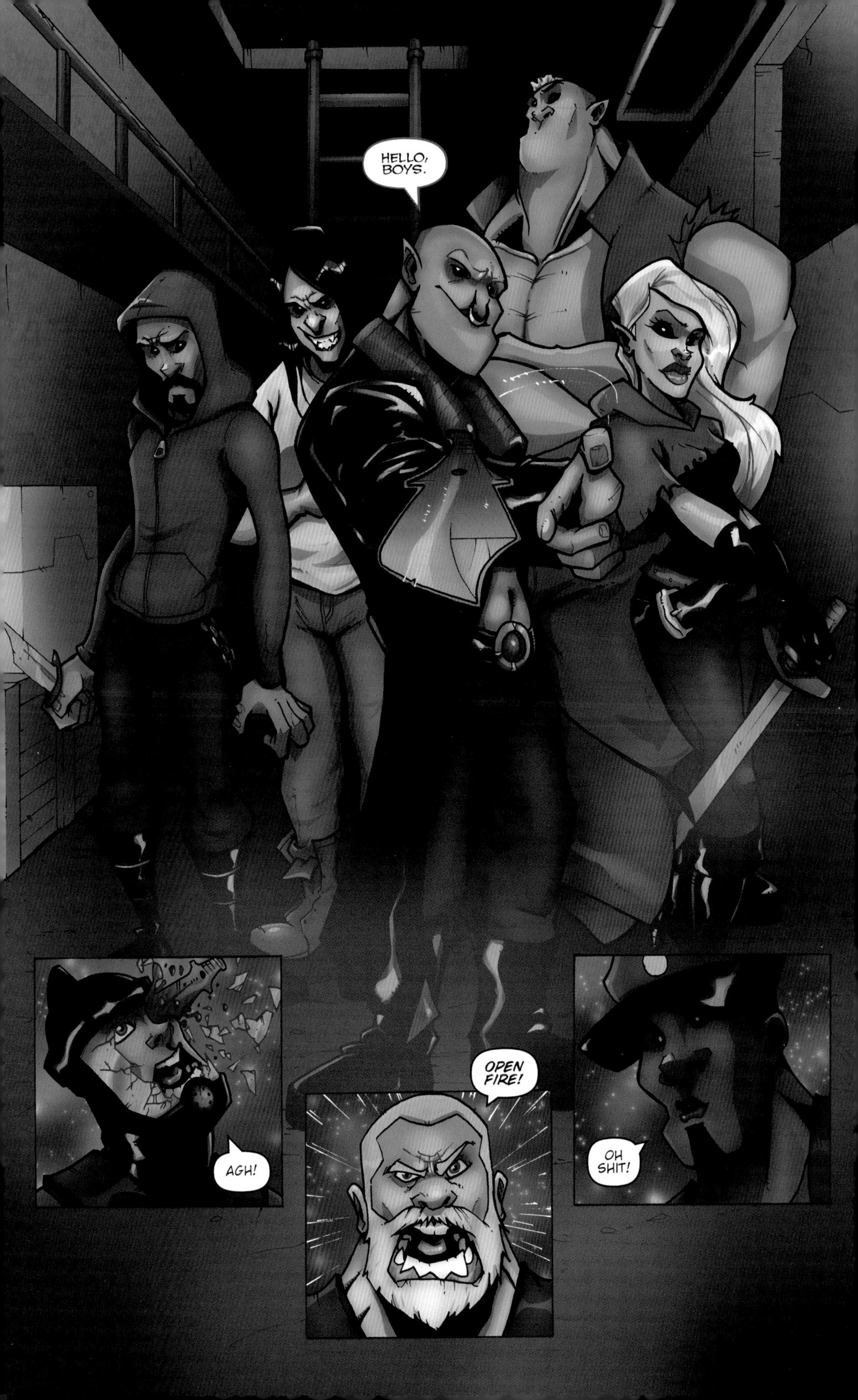
HELLO, BOYS.
AGH!
OPEN FIRE!
OH SHIT!

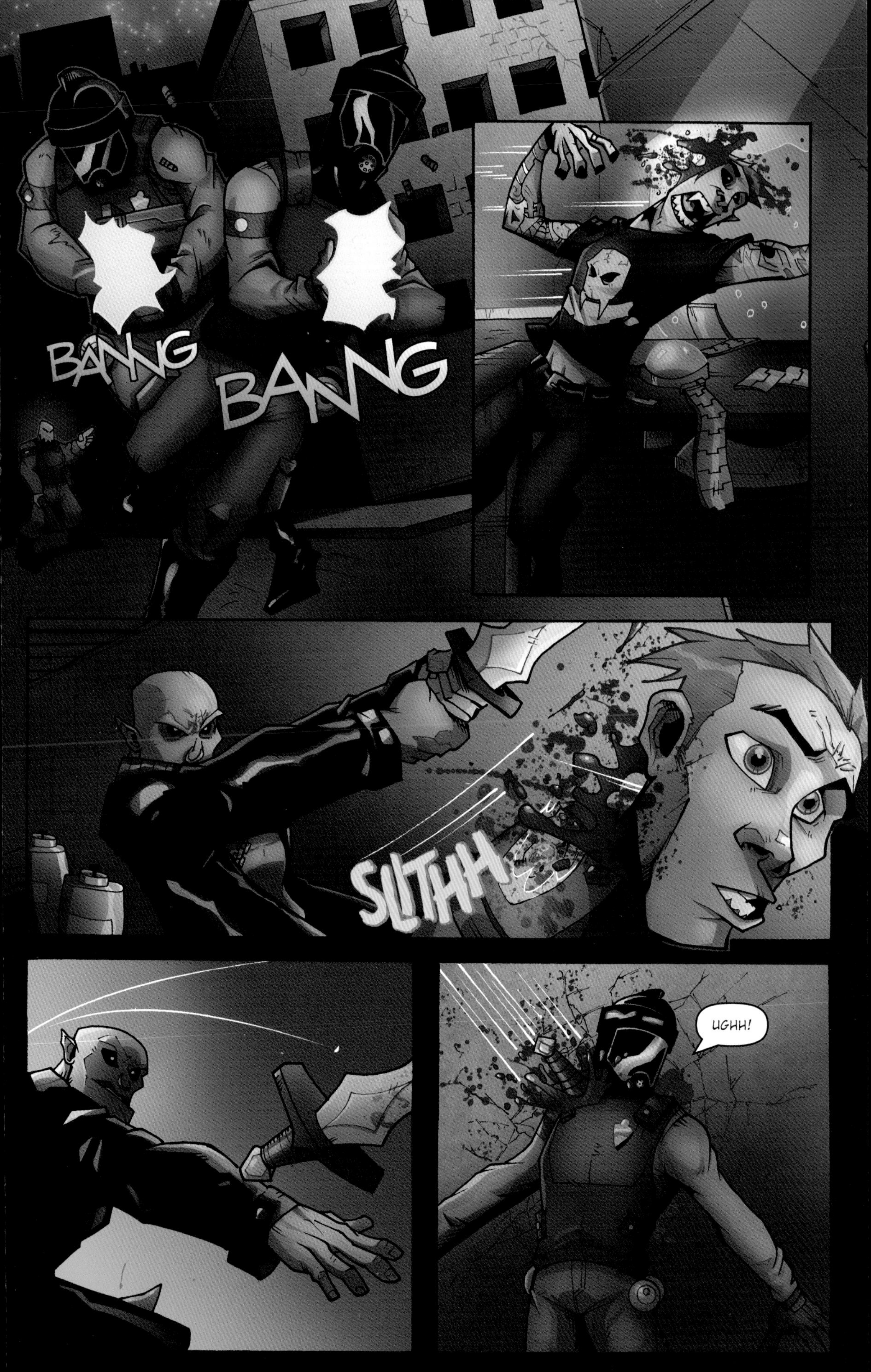
BANNG
BANNG
SLITHH
UGHH!

SEE YOU IN HELL!

TAKE CARE OF YOURSELF, OFFICER ZYLAND. I DON'T WANT TO HAVE TO KILL ANY OF MY BOYS IF THEY TURN.

WELL DONE, COMMANDER. LET'S SEE IF YOUR LUCK CONTINUES.

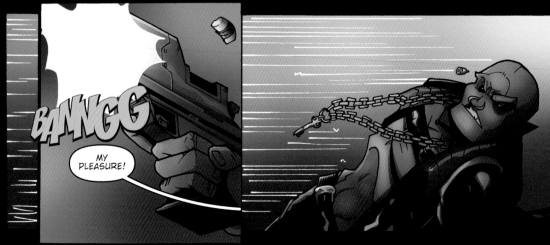

BANNGG

MY PLEASURE!

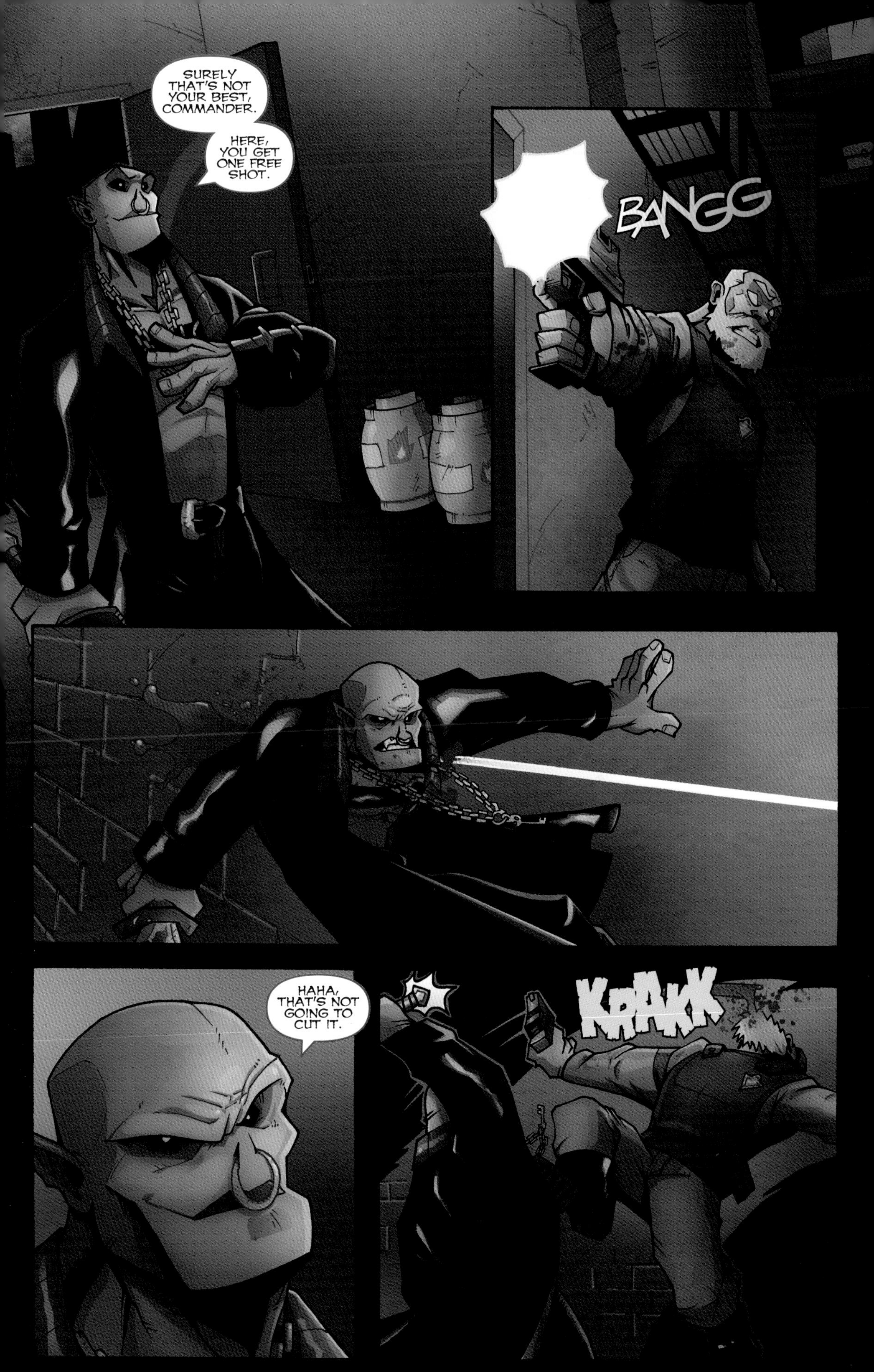
SURELY THAT'S NOT YOUR BEST, COMMANDER.
HERE, YOU GET ONE FREE SHOT.
BANGG
HAHA, THAT'S NOT GOING TO CUT IT.
KRAKK

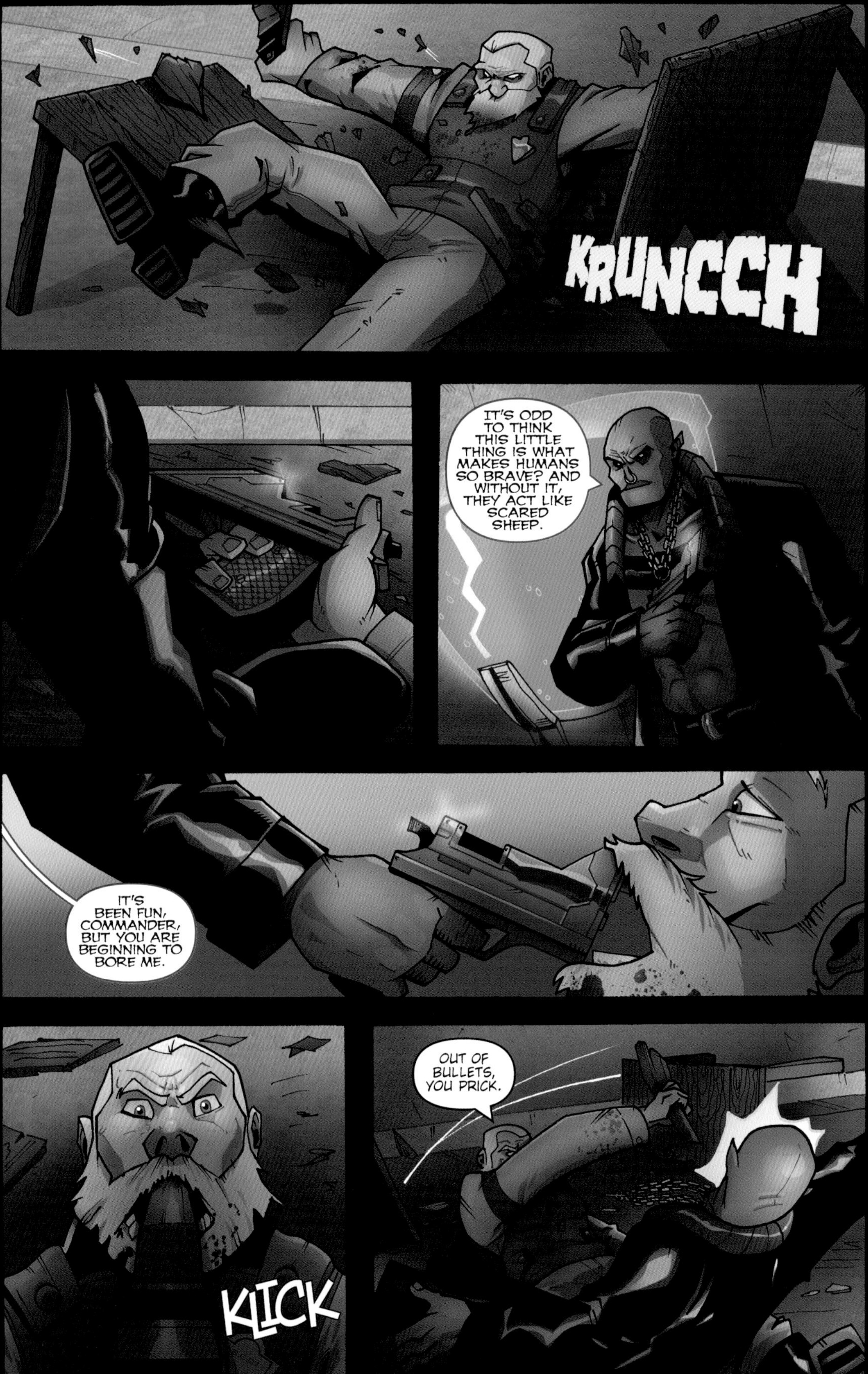
KRUNCCH
IT'S ODD TO THINK THIS LITTLE THING IS WHAT MAKES HUMANS SO BRAVE? AND WITHOUT IT, THEY ACT LIKE SCARED SHEEP.
IT'S BEEN FUN, COMMANDER, BUT YOU ARE BEGINNING TO BORE ME.
KLICK
OUT OF BULLETS, YOU PRICK.

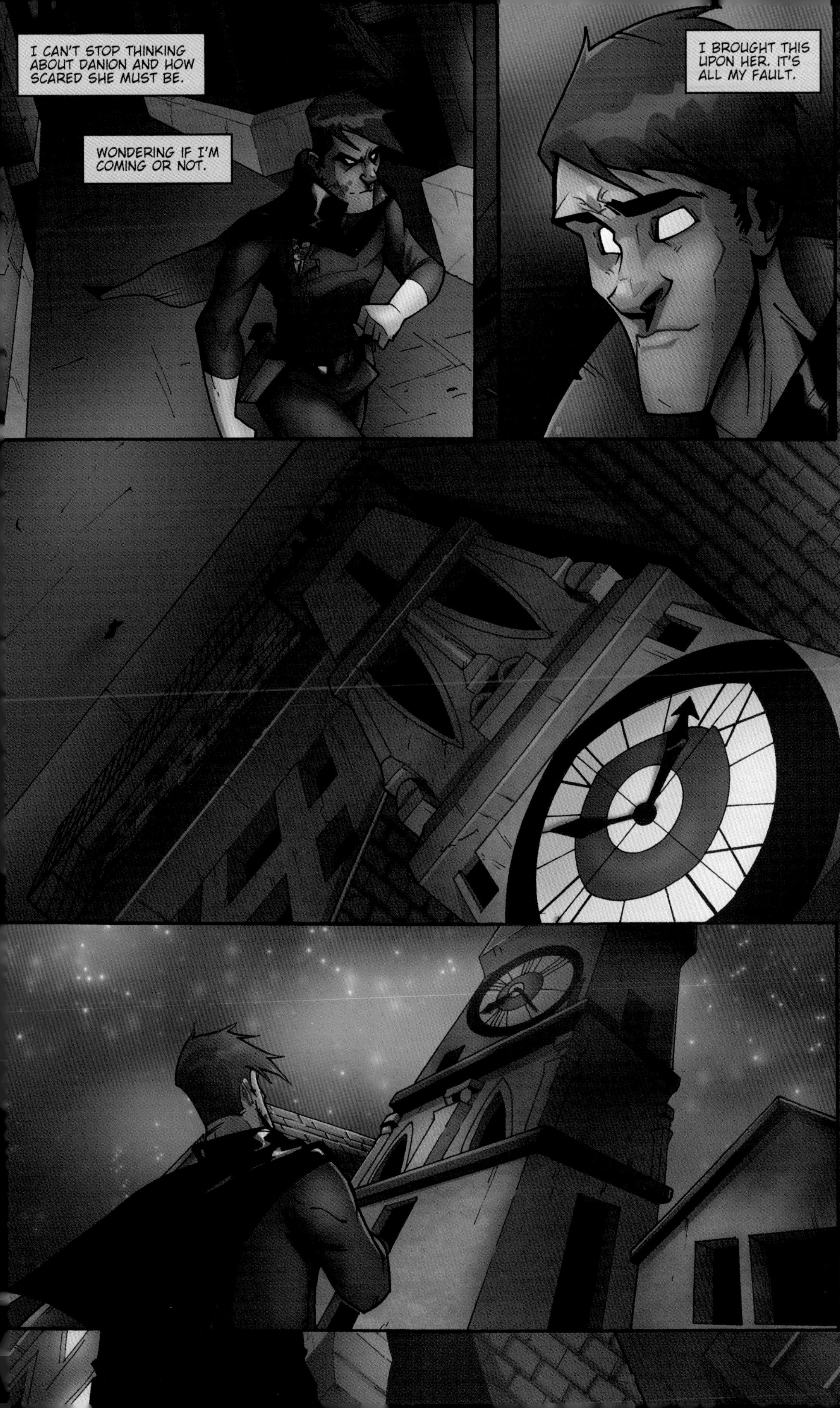
I CAN'T STOP THINKING ABOUT DANION AND HOW SCARED SHE MUST BE.
WONDERING IF I'M COMING OR NOT.
I BROUGHT THIS UPON HER. IT'S ALL MY FAULT.

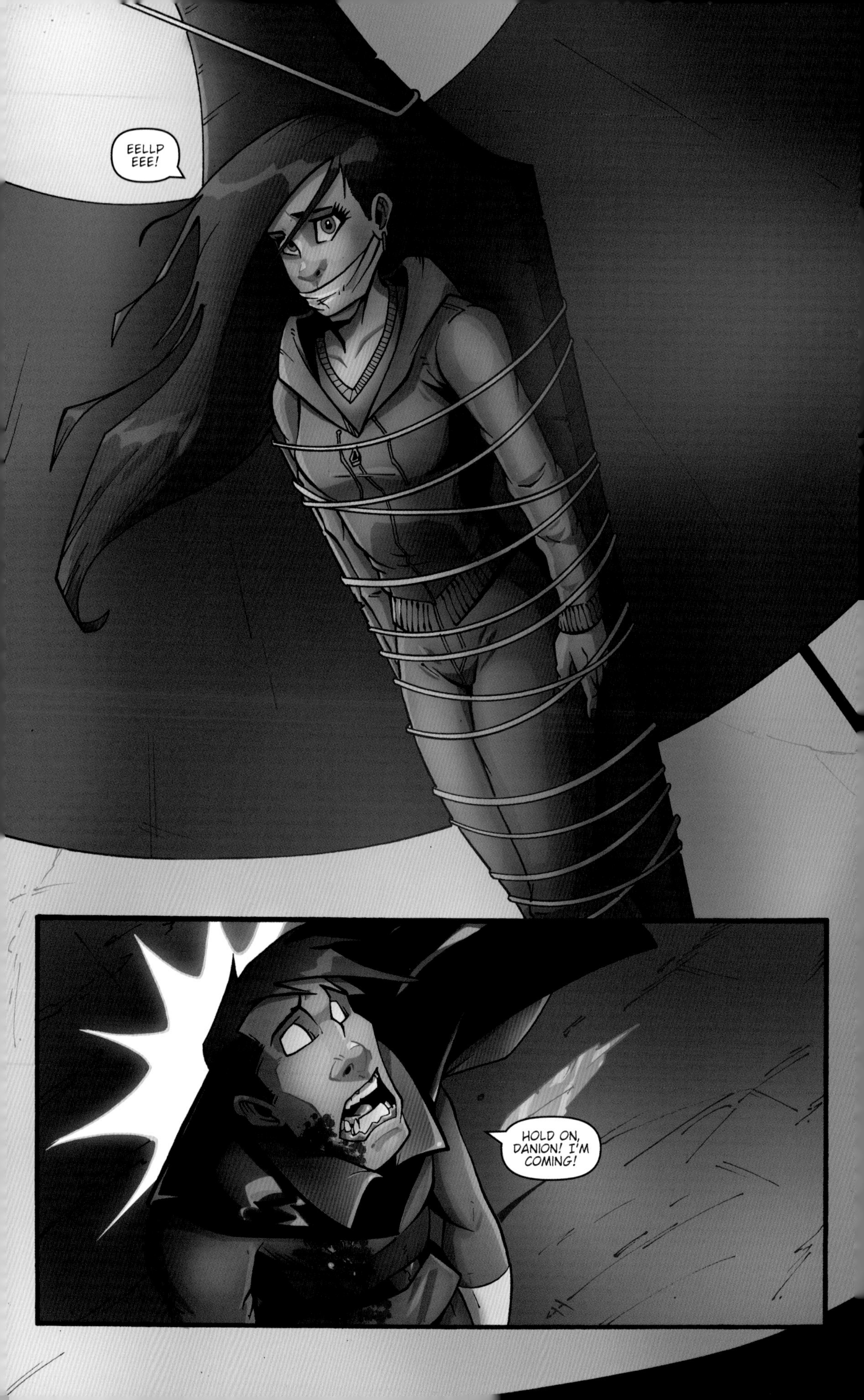
EELLP EEE!
HOLD ON, DANION! I'M COMING!

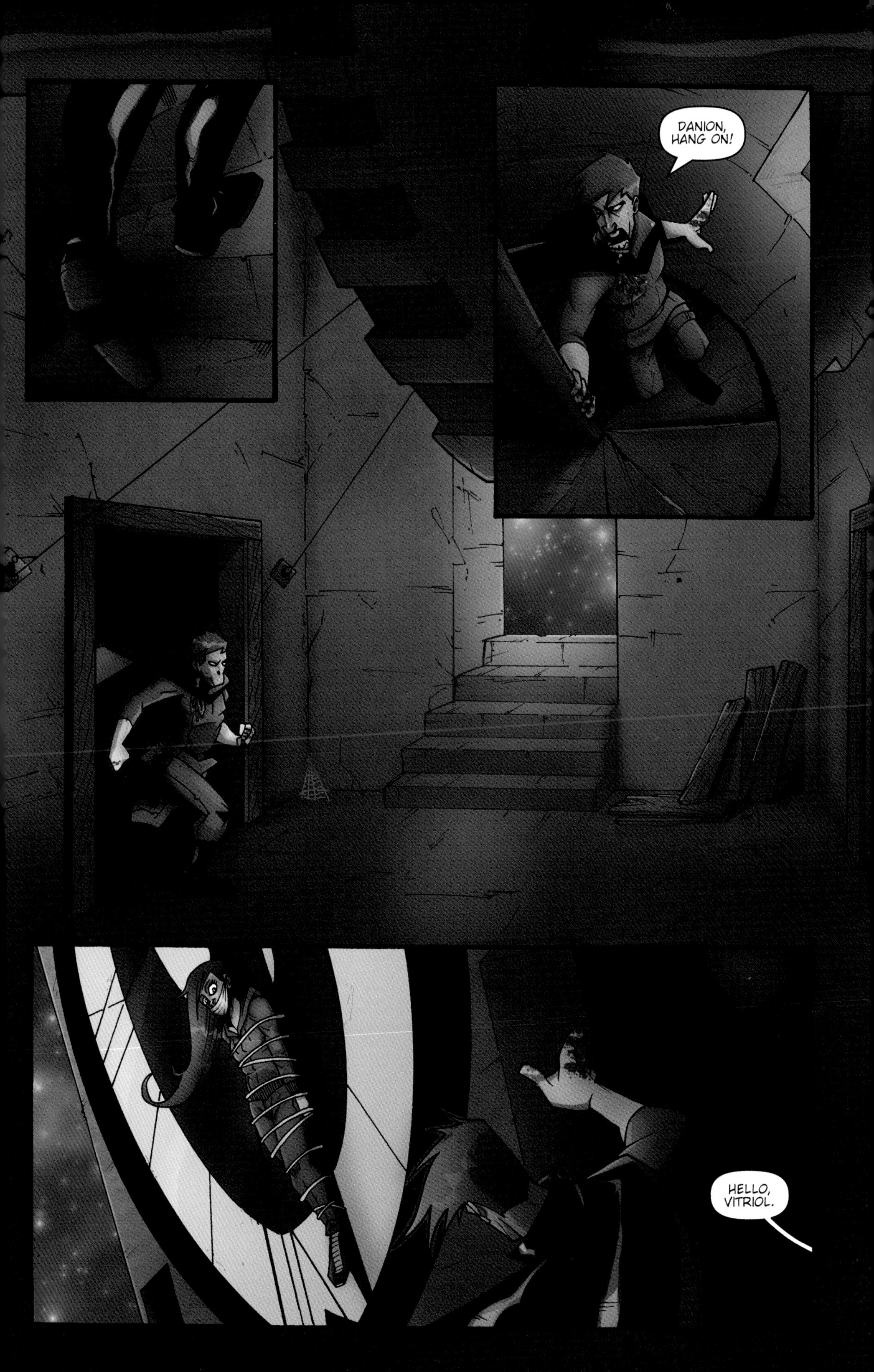
DANION, HANG ON!
HELLO, VITRIOL.

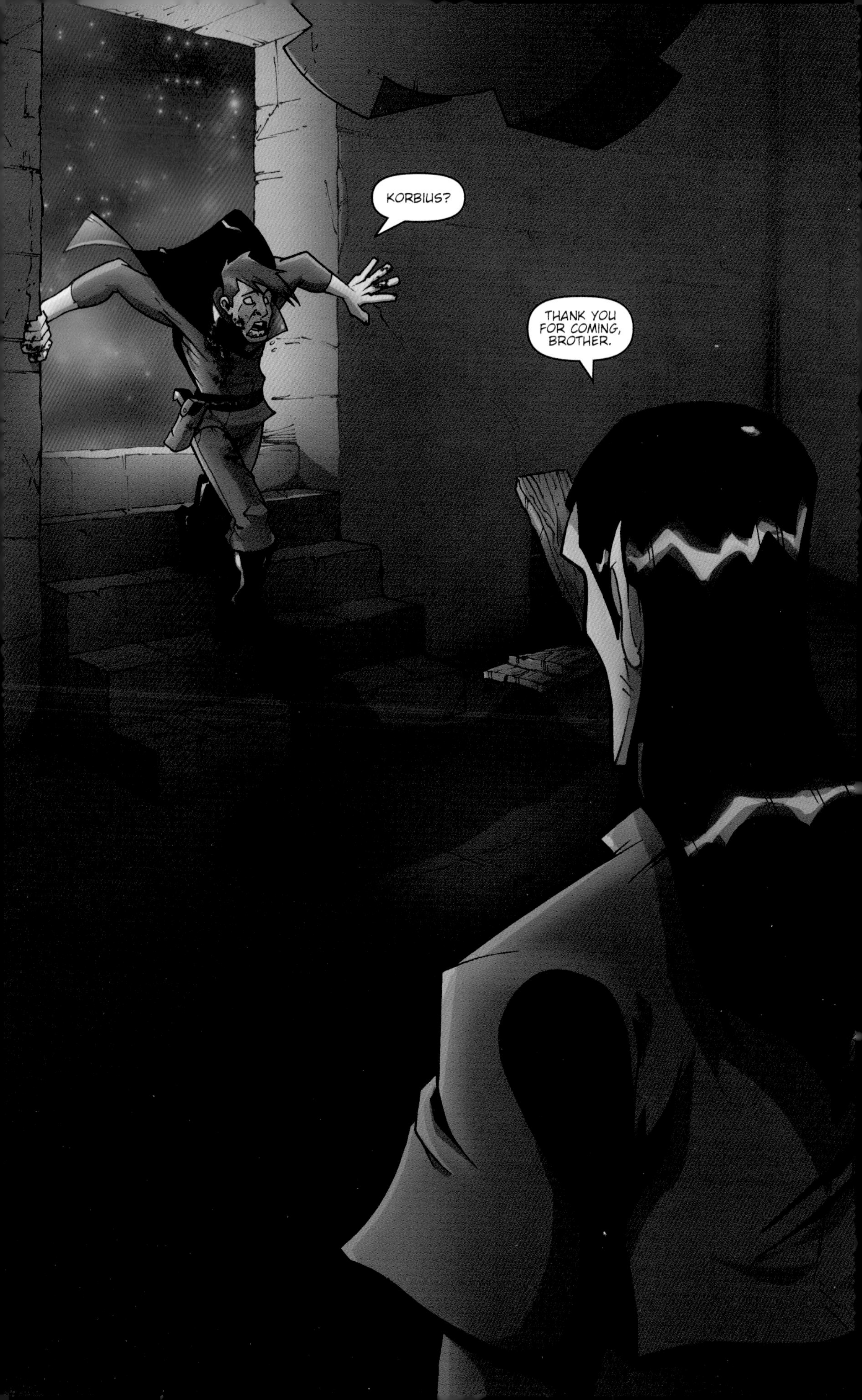
KORBIUS?
THANK YOU FOR COMING, BROTHER.

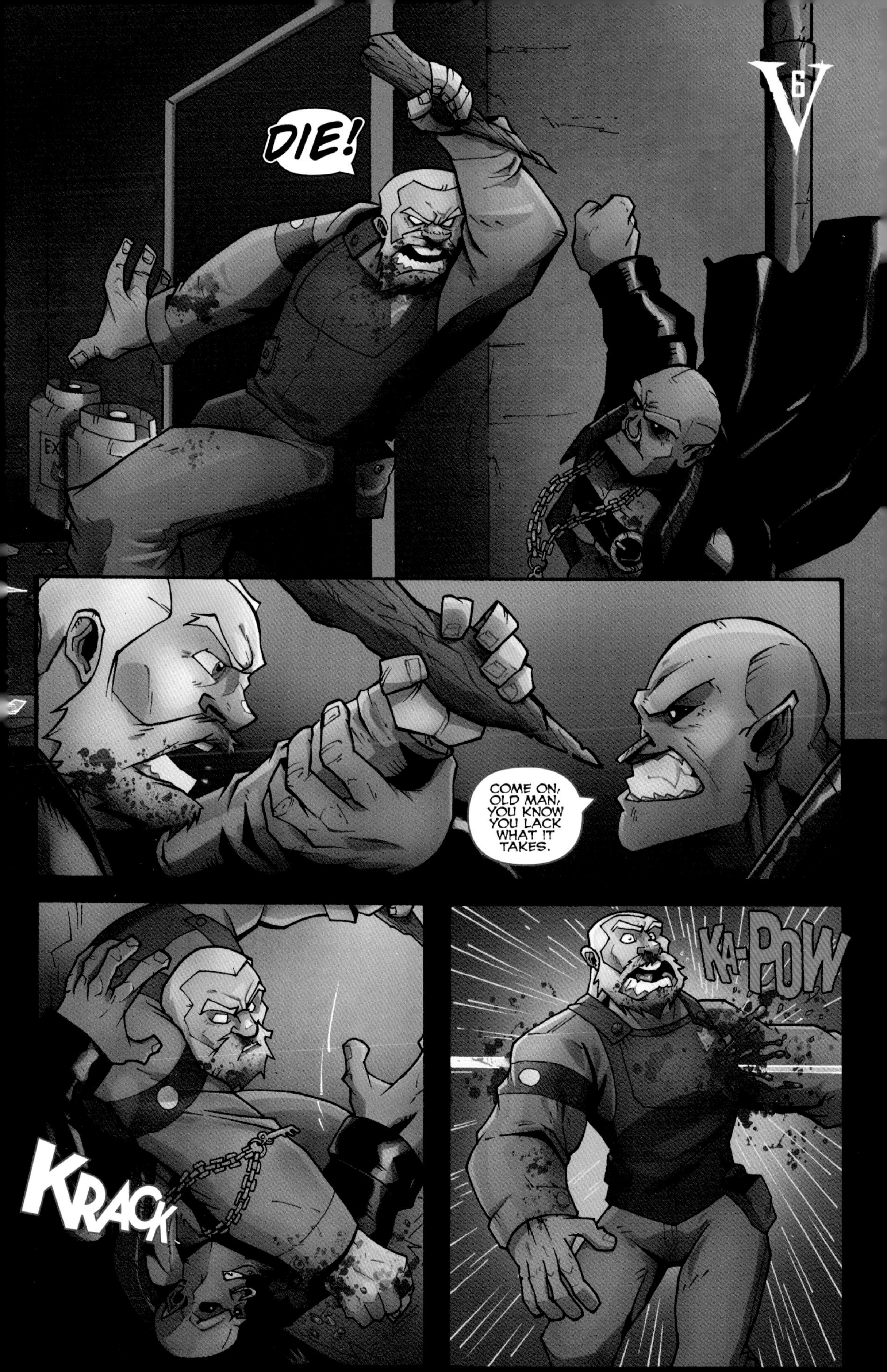
DIE!
COME ON, OLD MAN, YOU KNOW YOU LACK WHAT IT TAKES.
KRACK
KA-POW

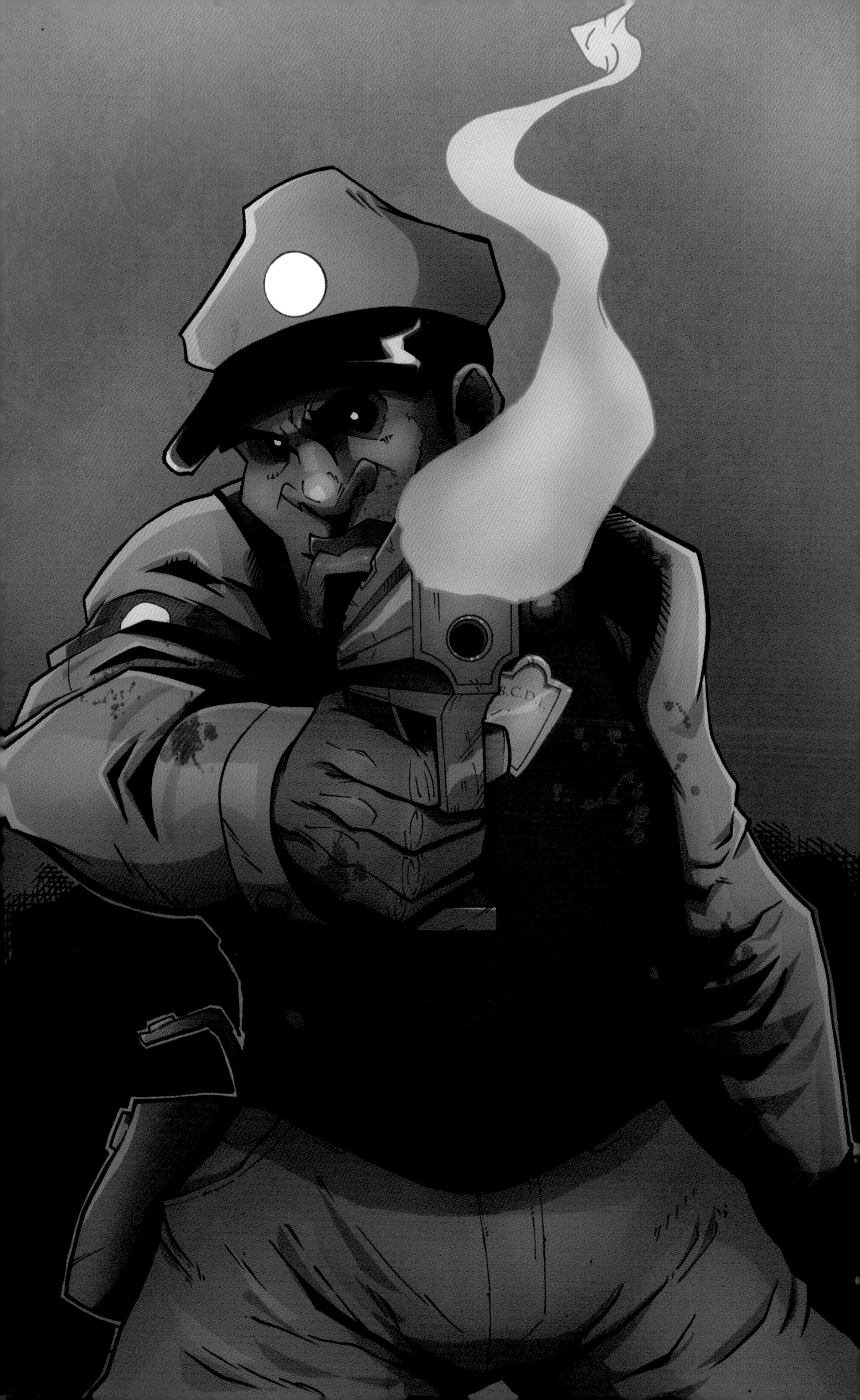

C.D.I.

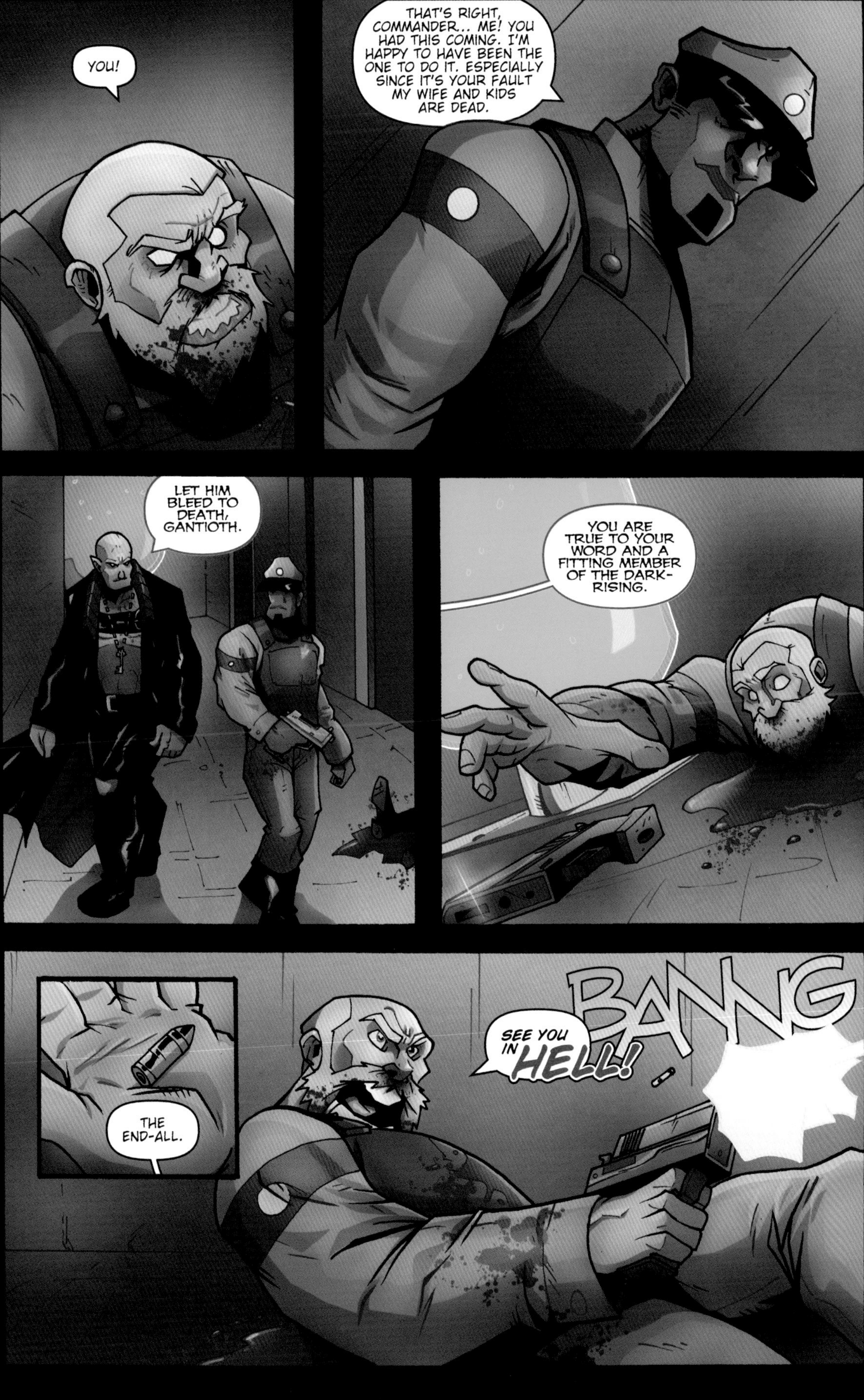
YOU!
THAT'S RIGHT, COMMANDER... ME! YOU HAD THIS COMING. I'M HAPPY TO HAVE BEEN THE ONE TO DO IT. ESPECIALLY SINCE IT'S YOUR FAULT MY WIFE AND KIDS ARE DEAD.
LET HIM BLEED TO DEATH, GANTIOTH.
YOU ARE TRUE TO YOUR WORD AND A FITTING MEMBER OF THE DARK-RISING.
THE END-ALL.
SEE YOU IN HELL!
BANNG

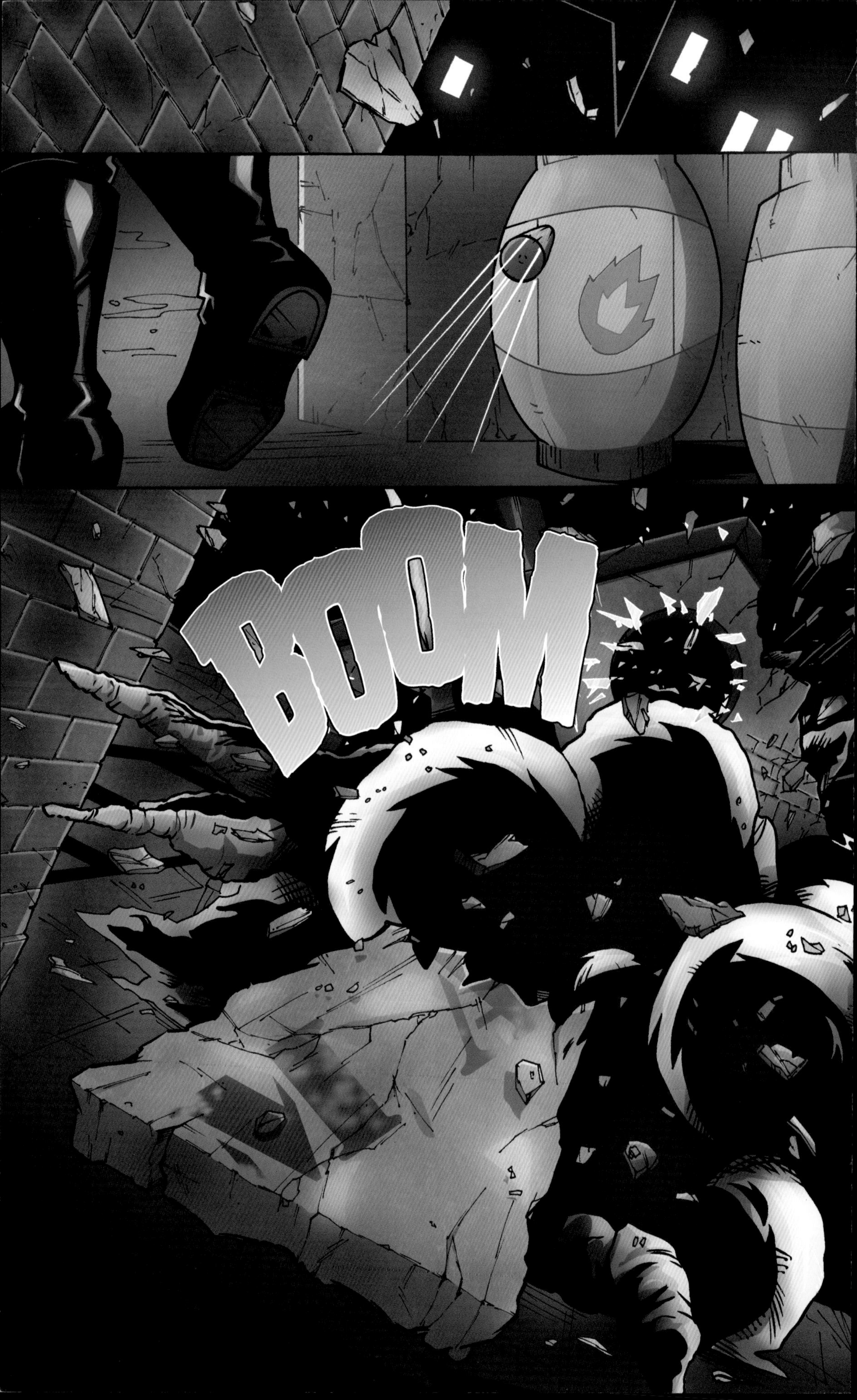
BOOM

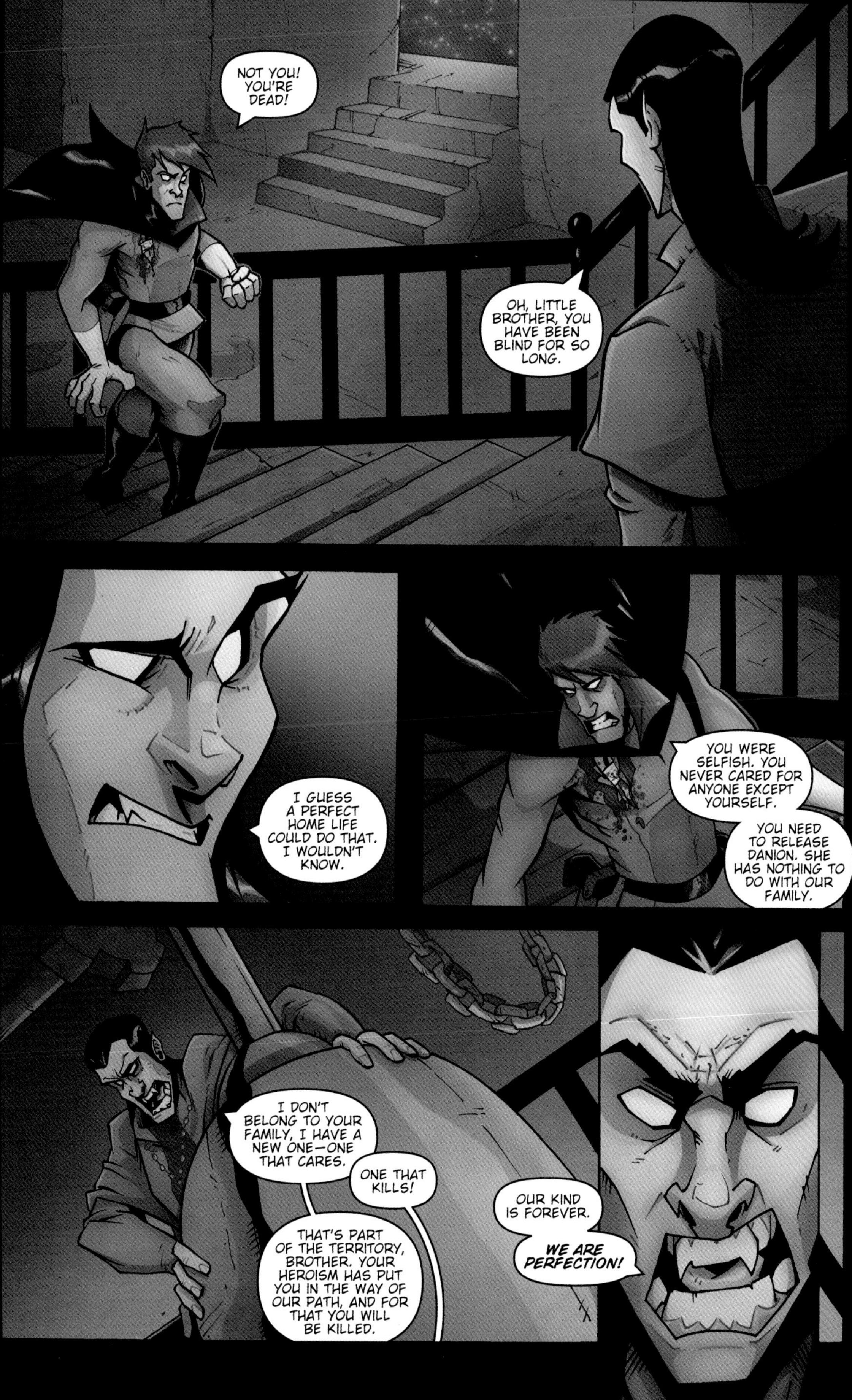
NOT YOU! YOU'RE DEAD!
OH, LITTLE BROTHER, YOU HAVE BEEN BLIND FOR SO LONG.
I GUESS A PERFECT HOME LIFE COULD DO THAT. I WOULDN'T KNOW.
YOU WERE SELFISH. YOU NEVER CARED FOR ANYONE EXCEPT YOURSELF.
YOU NEED TO RELEASE DANION. SHE HAS NOTHING TO DO WITH OUR FAMILY.
I DON'T BELONG TO YOUR FAMILY, I HAVE A NEW ONE—ONE THAT CARES.
ONE THAT KILLS!
THAT'S PART OF THE TERRITORY, BROTHER. YOUR HEROISM HAS PUT YOU IN THE WAY OF OUR PATH, AND FOR THAT YOU WILL BE KILLED.
OUR KIND IS FOREVER.
WE ARE PERFECTION!

MY OWN BROTHER.
THE CAUSE OF SO MUCH DEATH.
I THOUGHT HUMANITY'S HERO HAD MORE OF A FIGHT IN HIM.
THUDD
TELL MOM AND DAD I SAID HI.

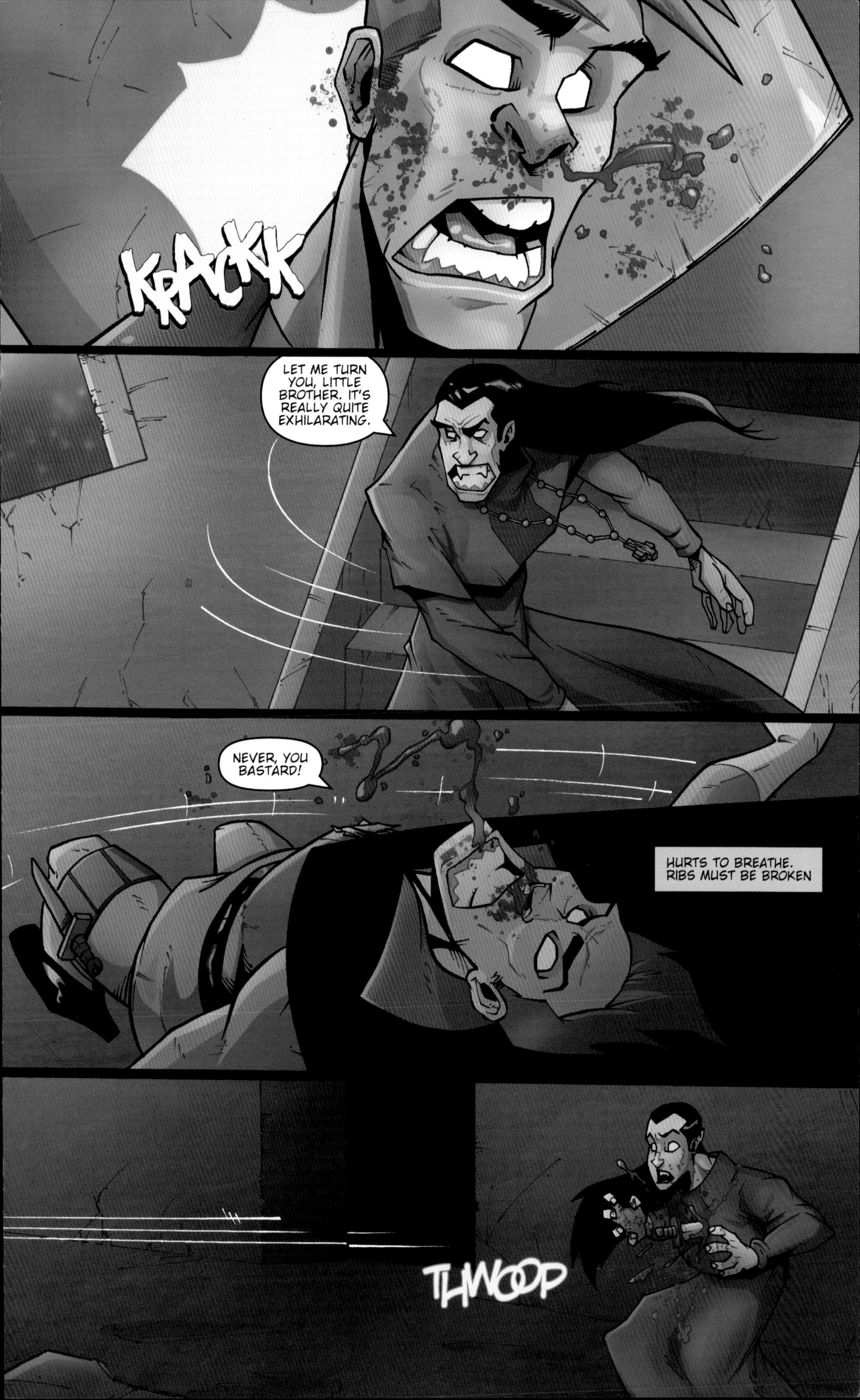
KRACKK
LET ME TURN YOU, LITTLE BROTHER. IT'S REALLY QUITE EXHILARATING.
NEVER, YOU BASTARD!
HURTS TO BREATHE. RIBS MUST BE BROKEN
THWOOP

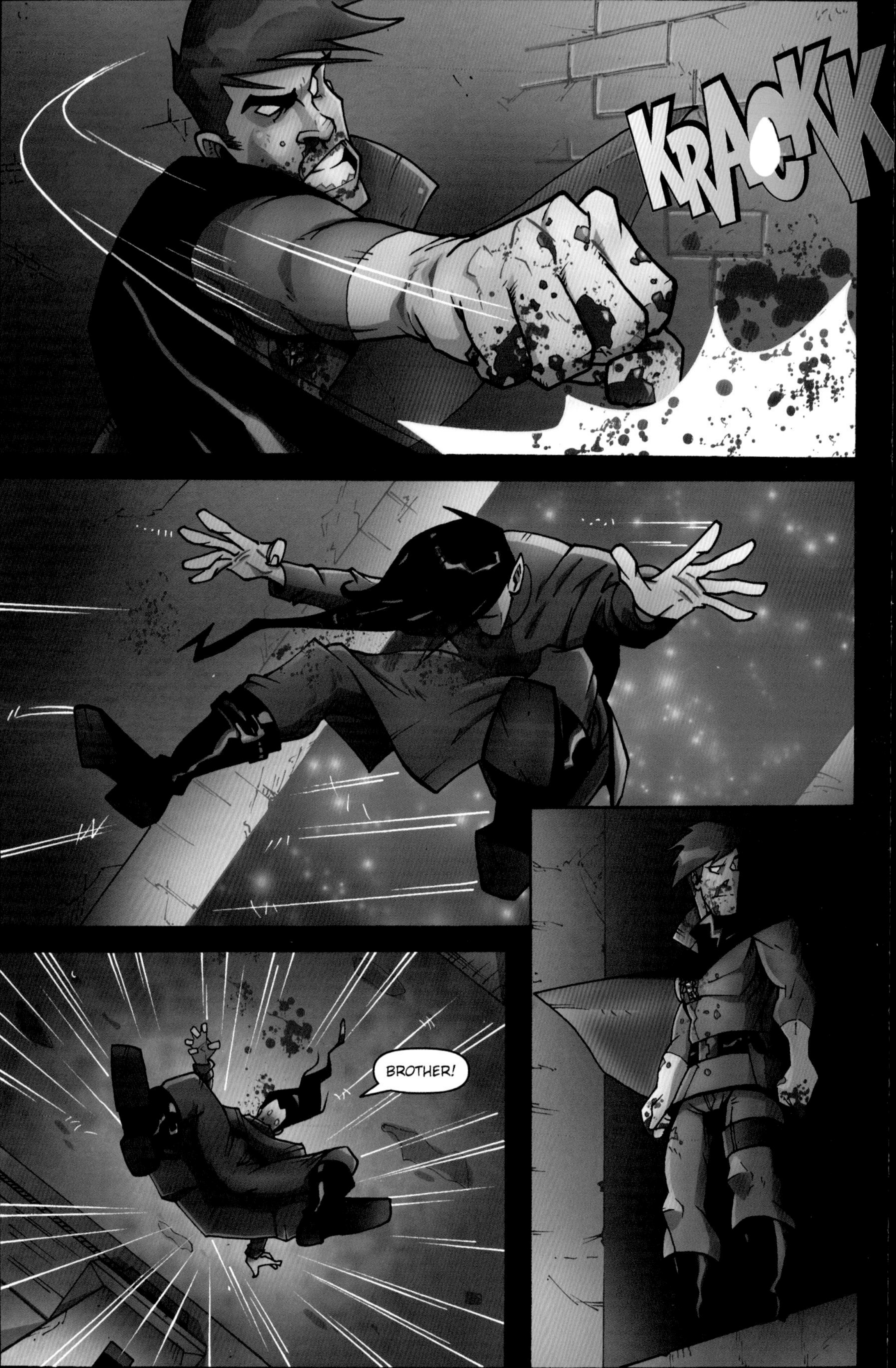
KRACKK
BROTHER!

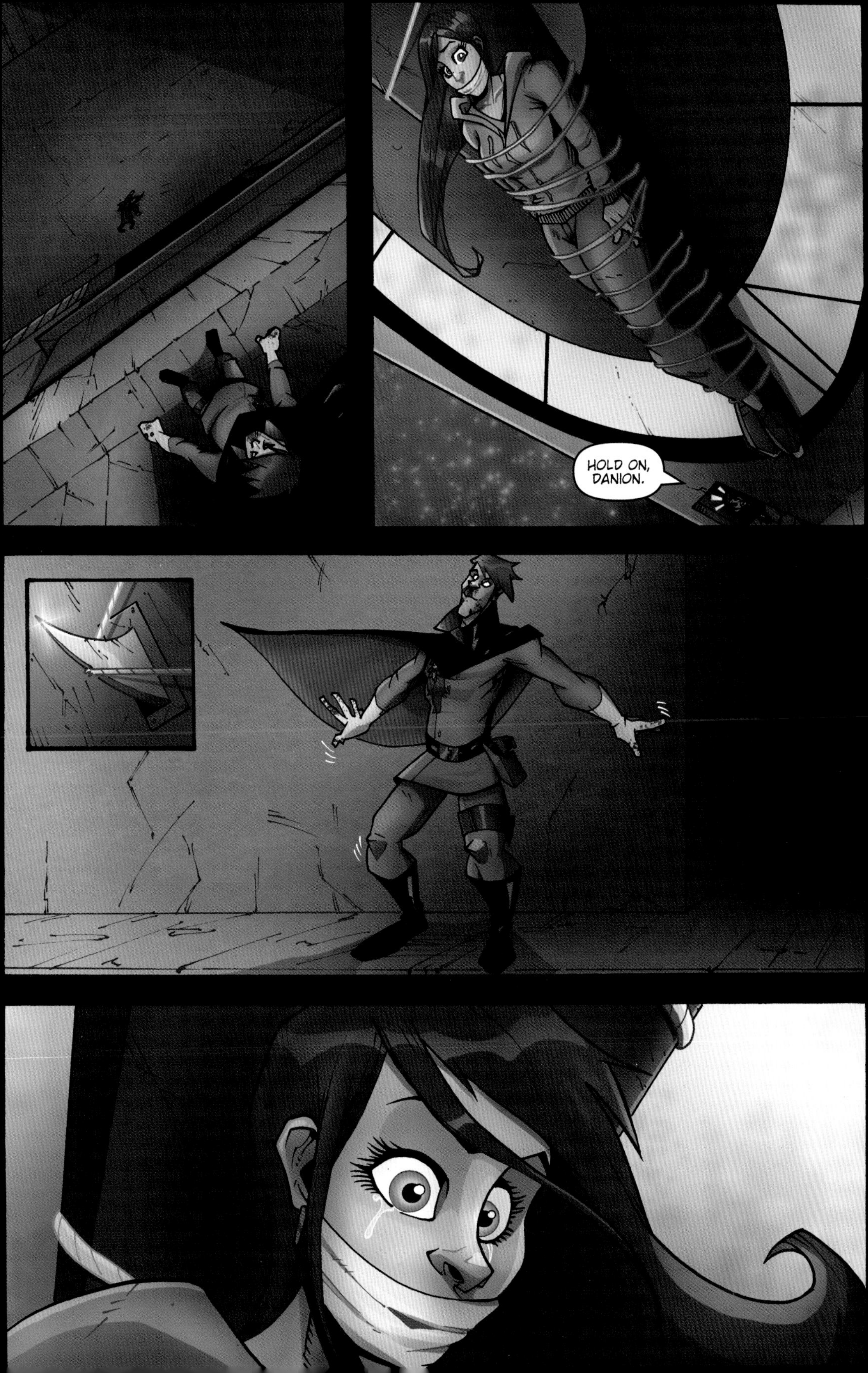
HOLD ON, DANION.

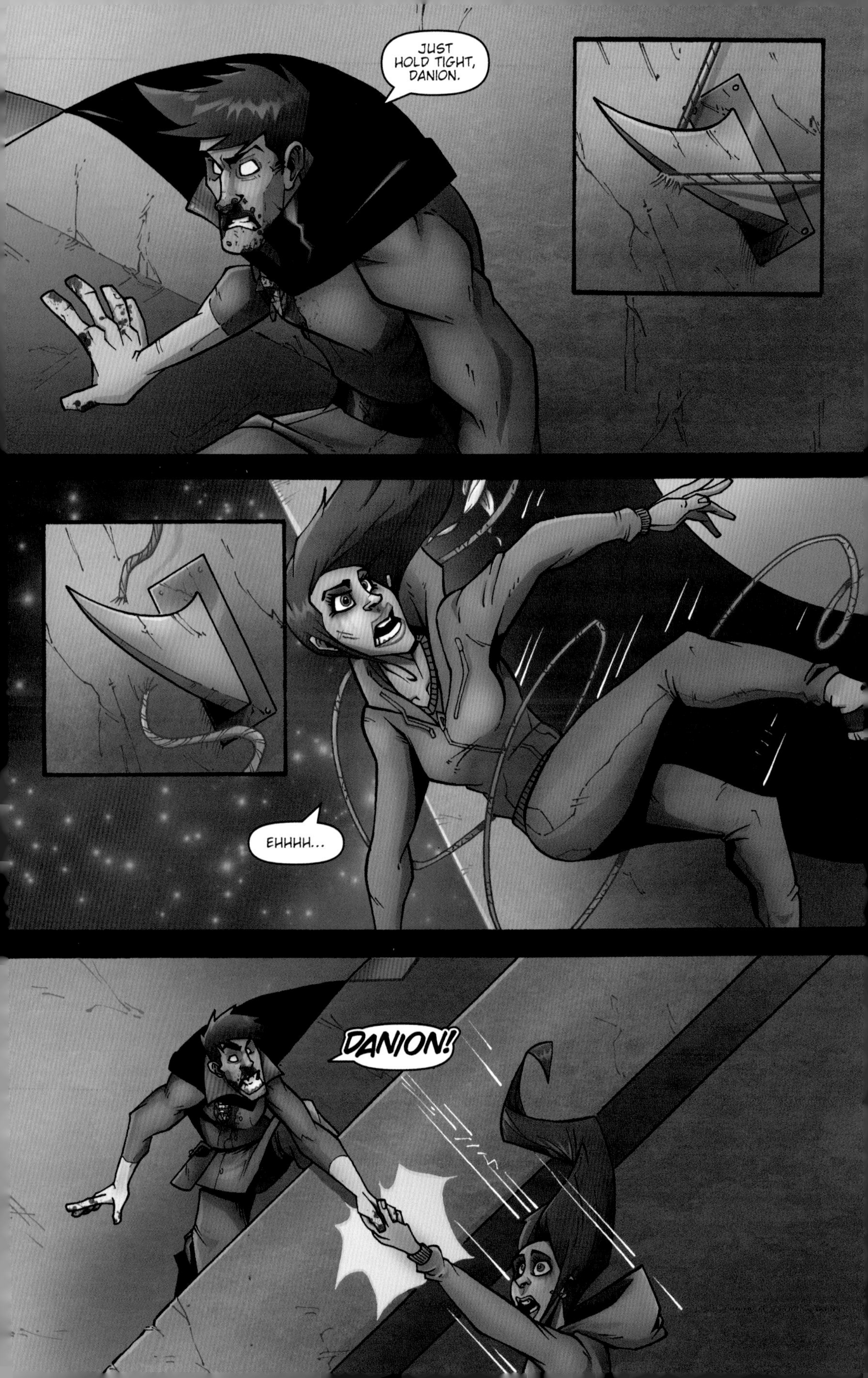
JUST HOLD TIGHT, DANION.
EHHHH...
DANION!

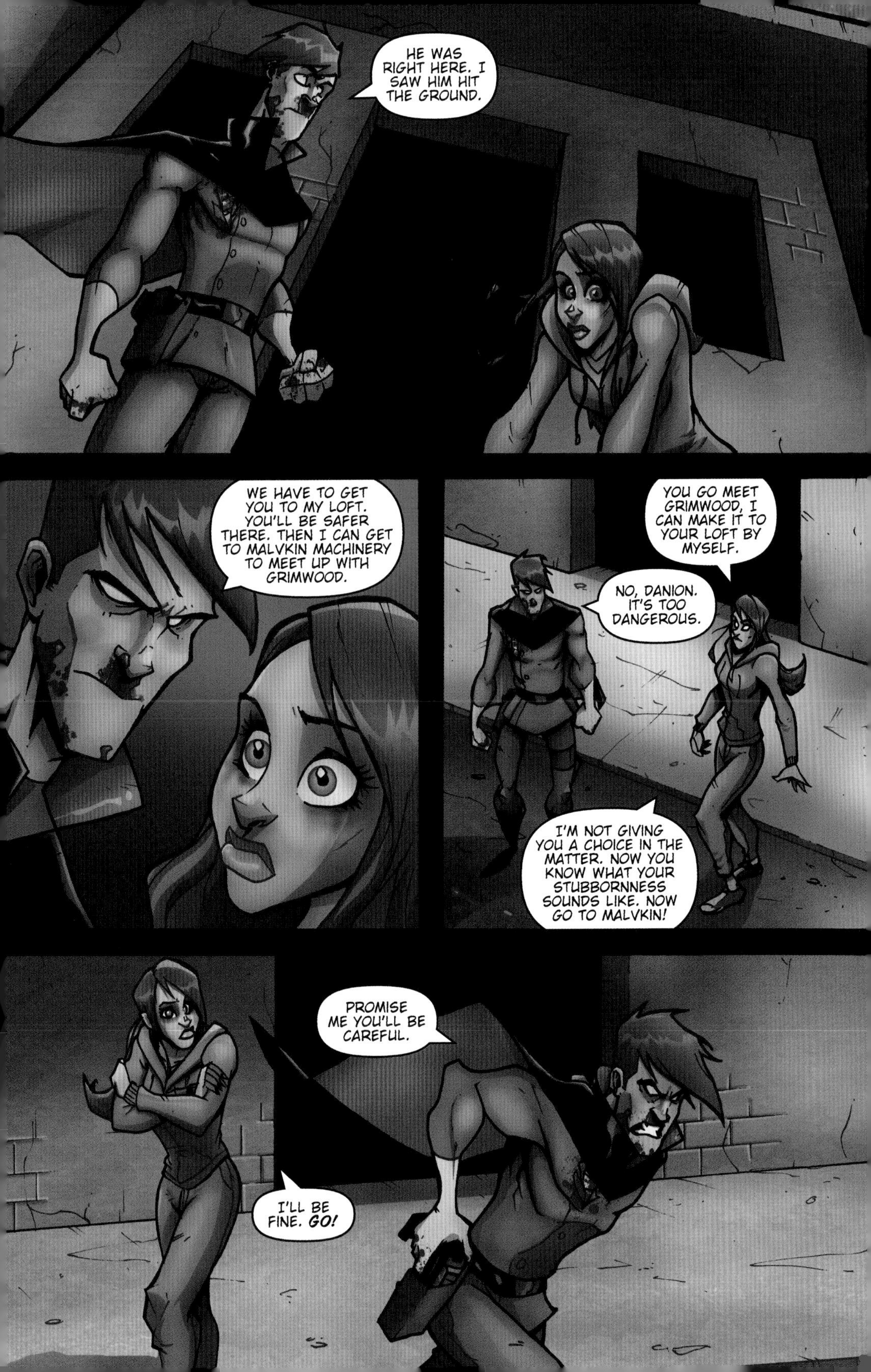
HE WAS RIGHT HERE. I SAW HIM HIT THE GROUND.
WE HAVE TO GET YOU TO MY LOFT. YOU'LL BE SAFER THERE. THEN I CAN GET TO MALVKIN MACHINERY TO MEET UP WITH GRIMWOOD.
YOU GO MEET GRIMWOOD, I CAN MAKE IT TO YOUR LOFT BY MYSELF.
NO, DANION. IT'S TOO DANGEROUS.
I'M NOT GIVING YOU A CHOICE IN THE MATTER. NOW YOU KNOW WHAT YOUR STUBBORNNESS SOUNDS LIKE. NOW GO TO MALVKIN!
PROMISE ME YOU'LL BE CAREFUL.
I'LL BE FINE. **GO!**

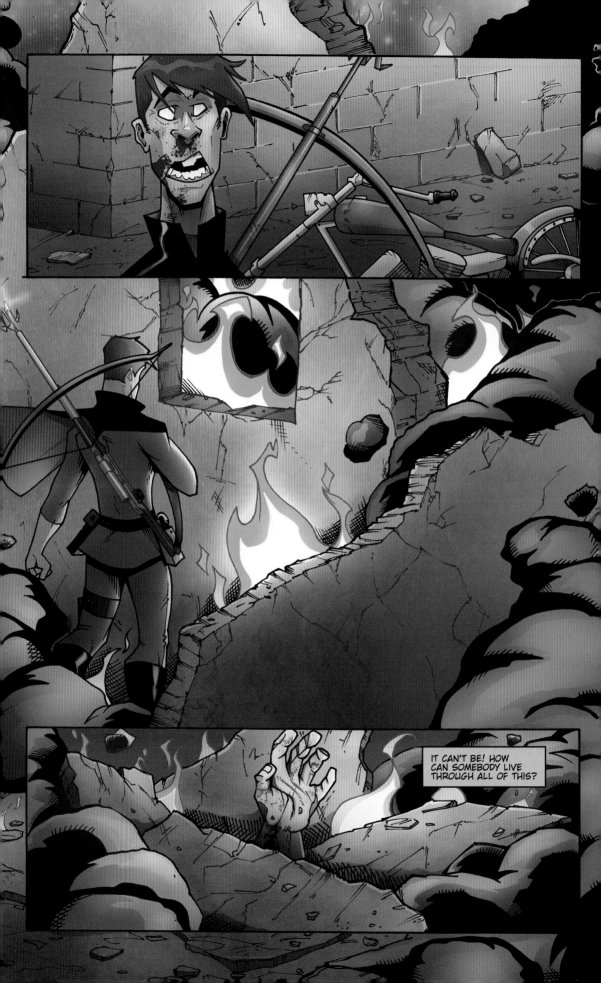

IT CAN'T BE! HOW CAN SOMEBODY LIVE THROUGH ALL OF THIS?

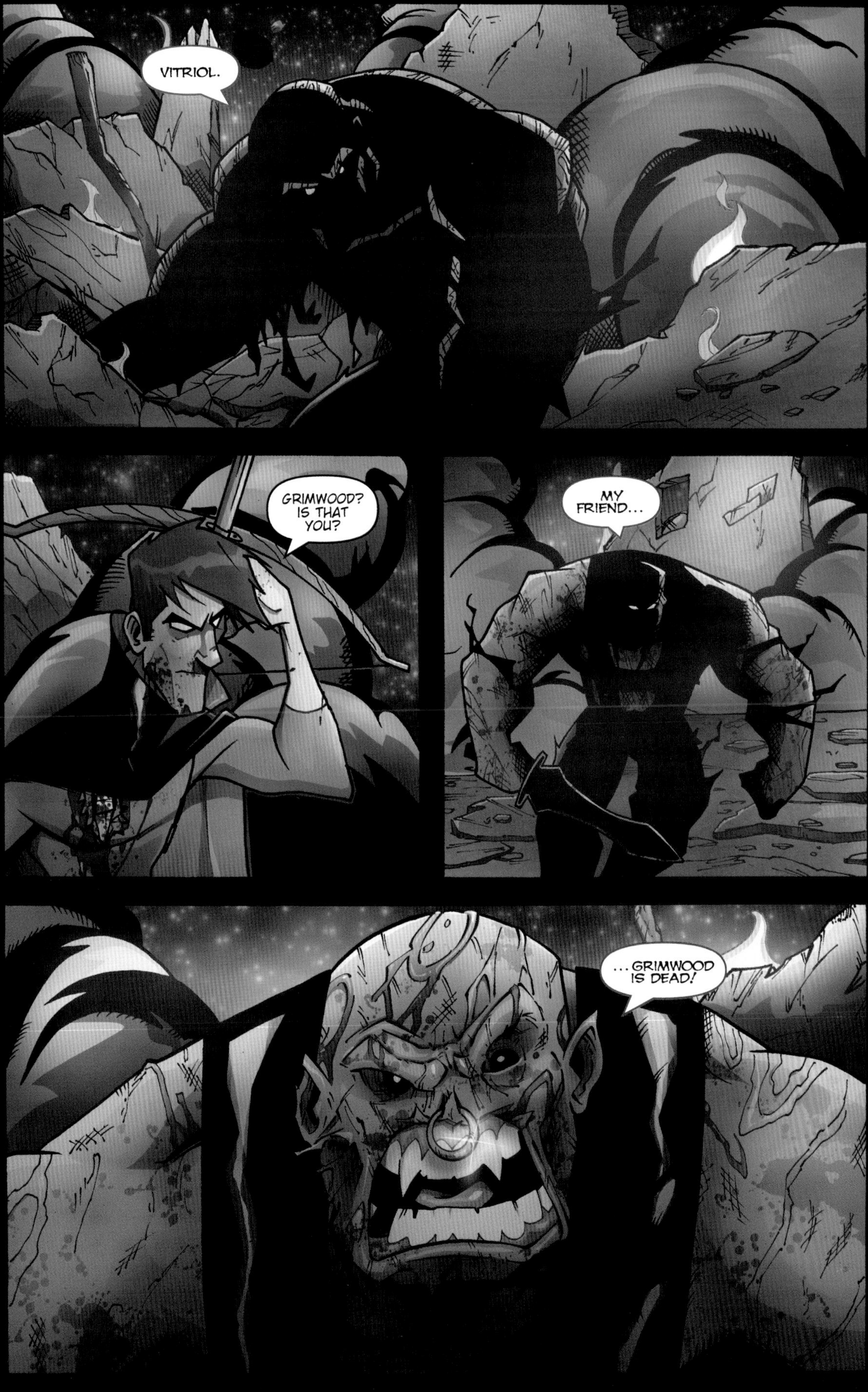
VITRIOL.
GRIMWOOD? IS THAT YOU?
MY FRIEND...
...GRIMWOOD IS DEAD!

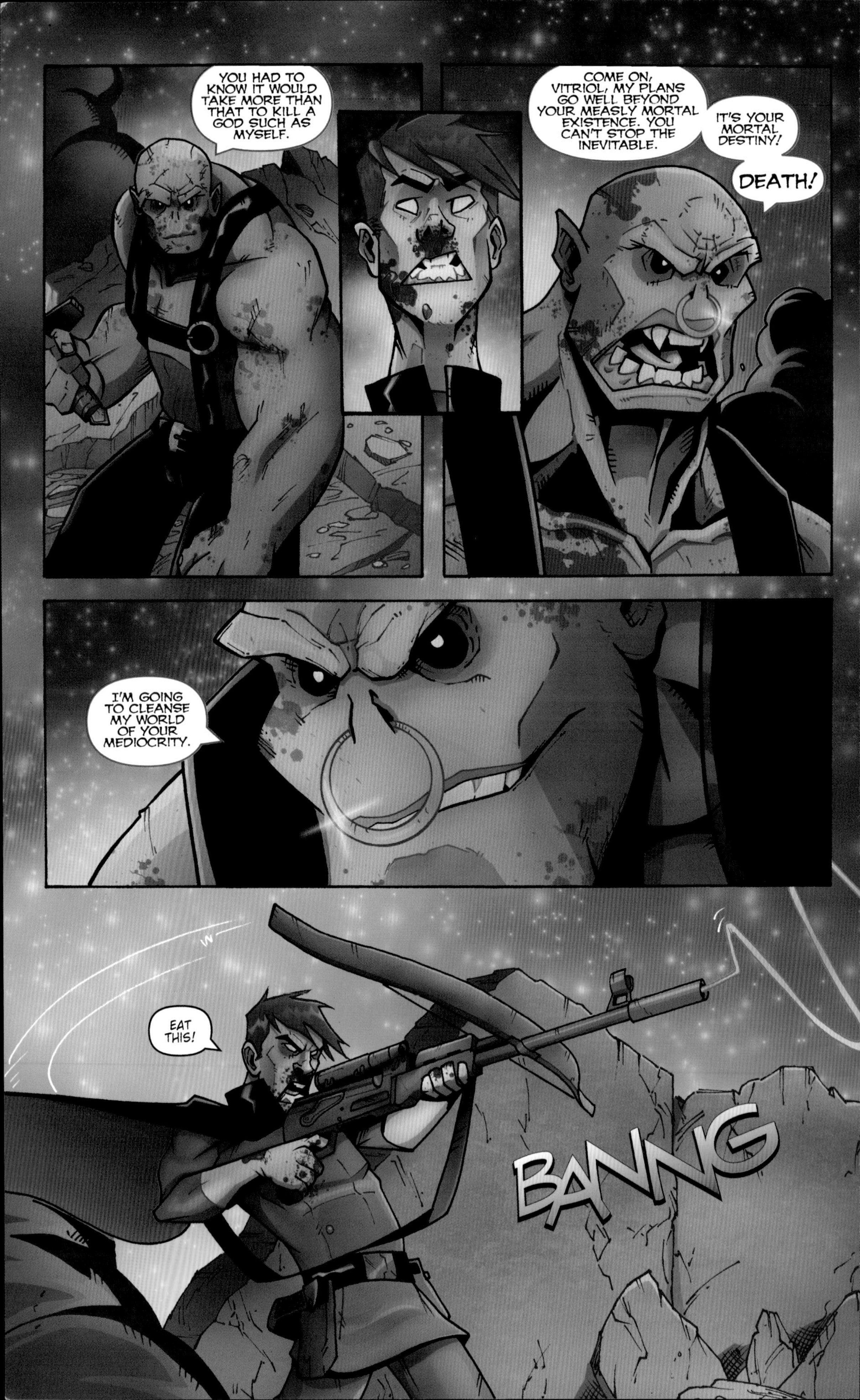
YOU HAD TO KNOW IT WOULD TAKE MORE THAN THAT TO KILL A GOD SUCH AS MYSELF.
COME ON, VITRIOL, MY PLANS GO WELL BEYOND YOUR MEASLY MORTAL EXISTENCE. YOU CAN'T STOP THE INEVITABLE.
IT'S YOUR MORTAL DESTINY!
DEATH!
I'M GOING TO CLEANSE MY WORLD OF YOUR MEDIOCRITY.
EAT THIS!
BANNG

THWAPP

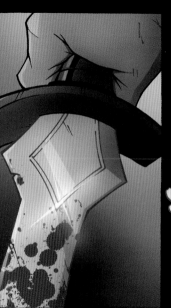

SHISSHH

YOUR LITTLE POP GUNS CAN'T HURT ME, VITRIOL. I AM A BREED BEYOND YOUR COMPREHENSION.

KRAGGK

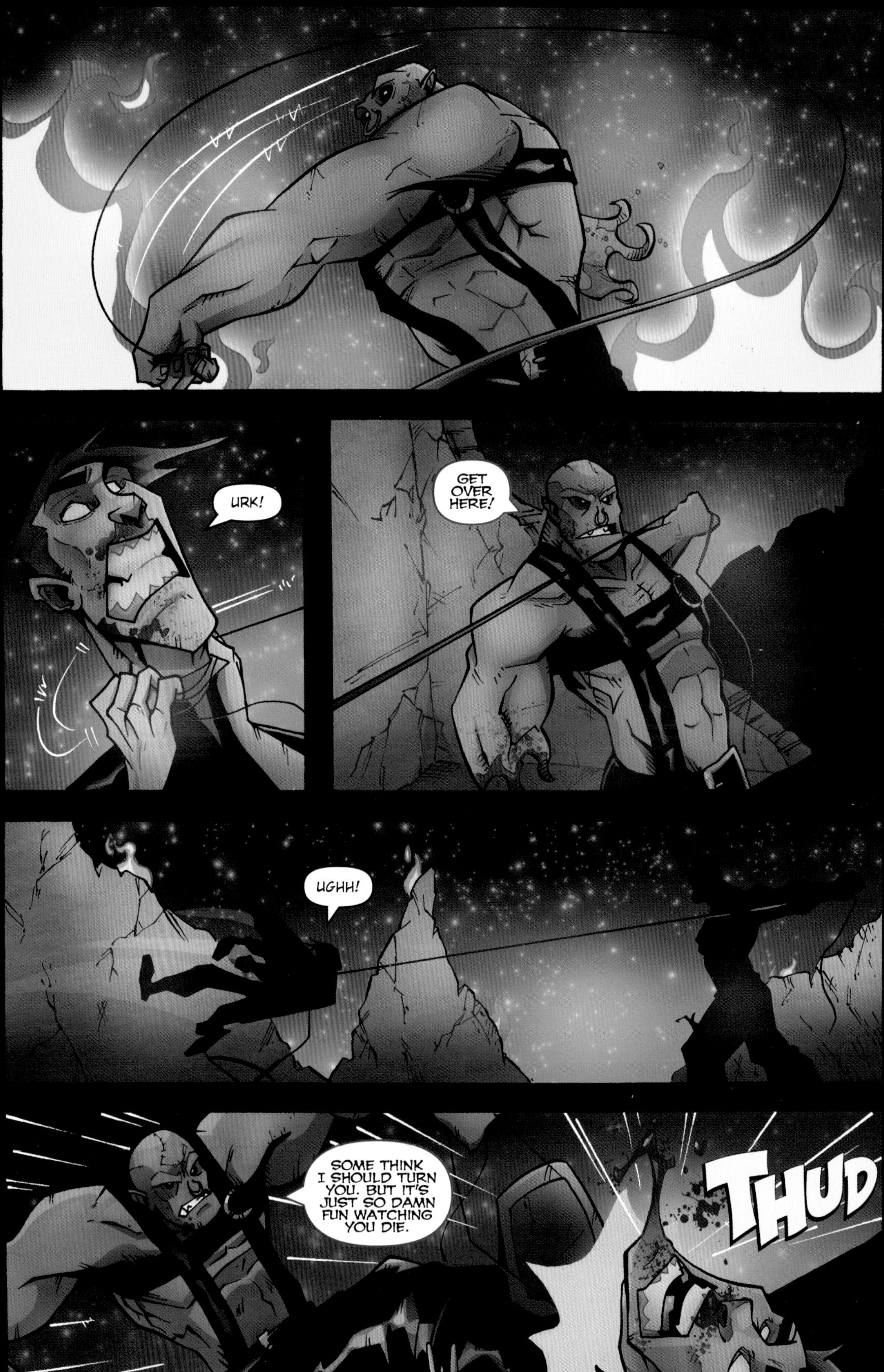
URK!
GET OVER HERE!
UGHH!
SOME THINK I SHOULD TURN YOU. BUT IT'S JUST SO DAMN FUN WATCHING YOU DIE.
THUD

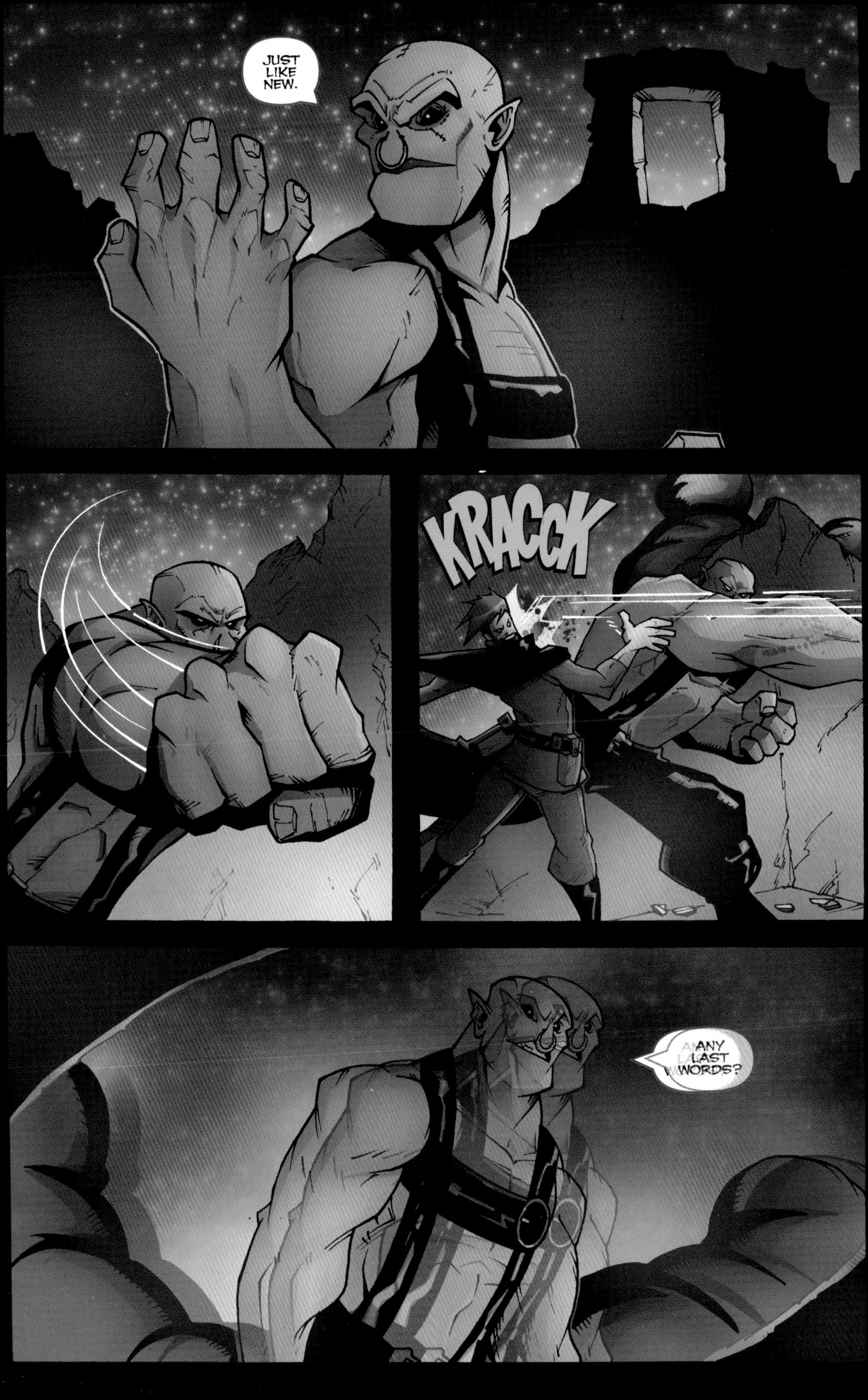

JUST LIKE NEW.
KRACCK
ANY LAST WORDS?

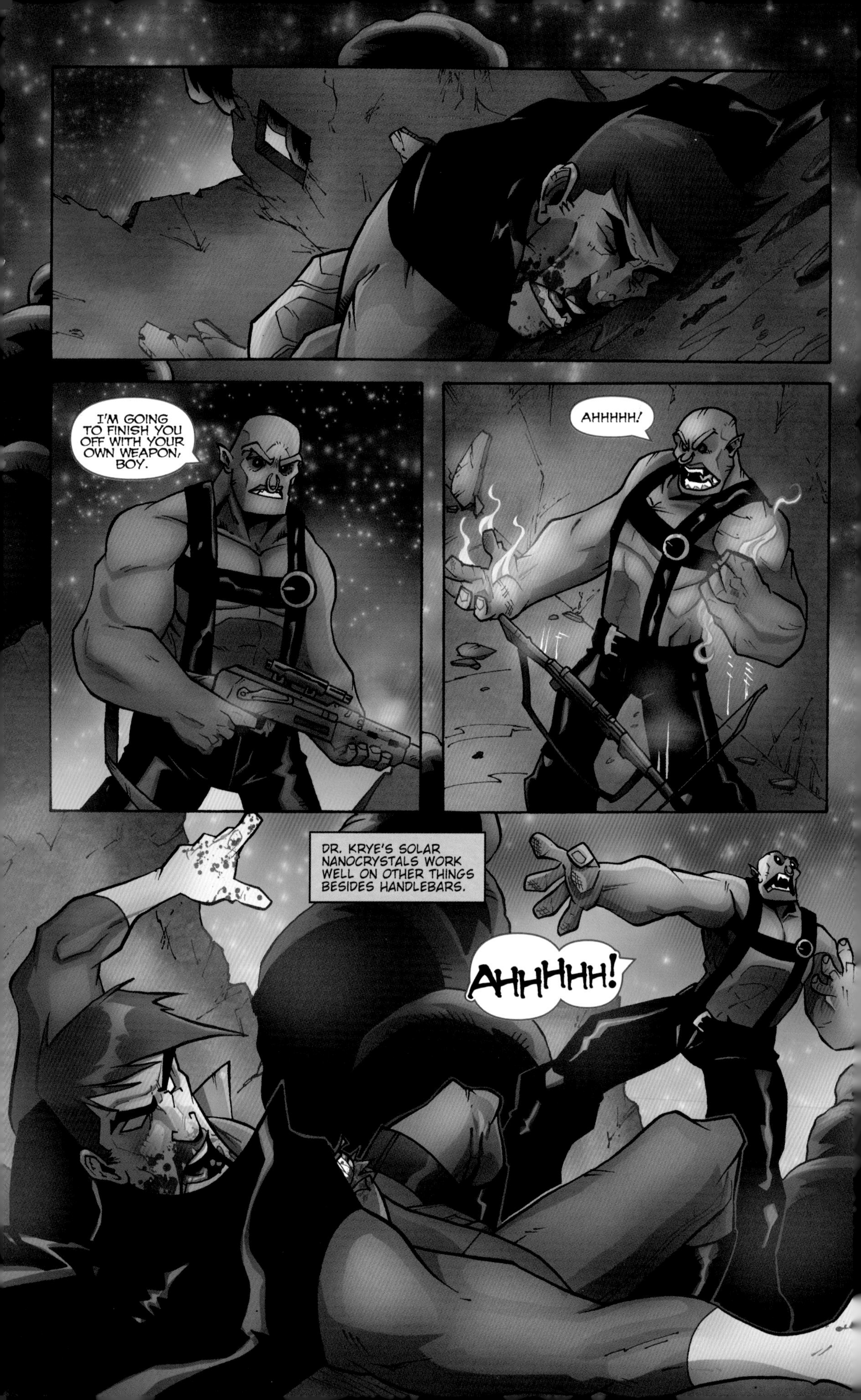
I'M GOING TO FINISH YOU OFF WITH YOUR OWN WEAPON, BOY.
AHHHHH!
DR. KRYE'S SOLAR NANOCRYSTALS WORK WELL ON OTHER THINGS BESIDES HANDLEBARS.
AHHHHH!

YOU'RE NOT GOING ANYWHERE.

HOW'S THIS FOR PERFECTION?

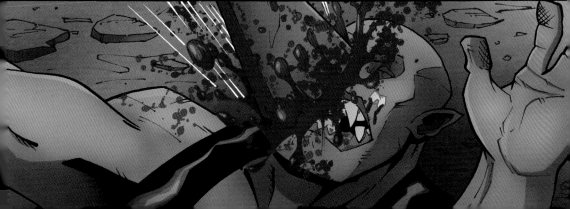

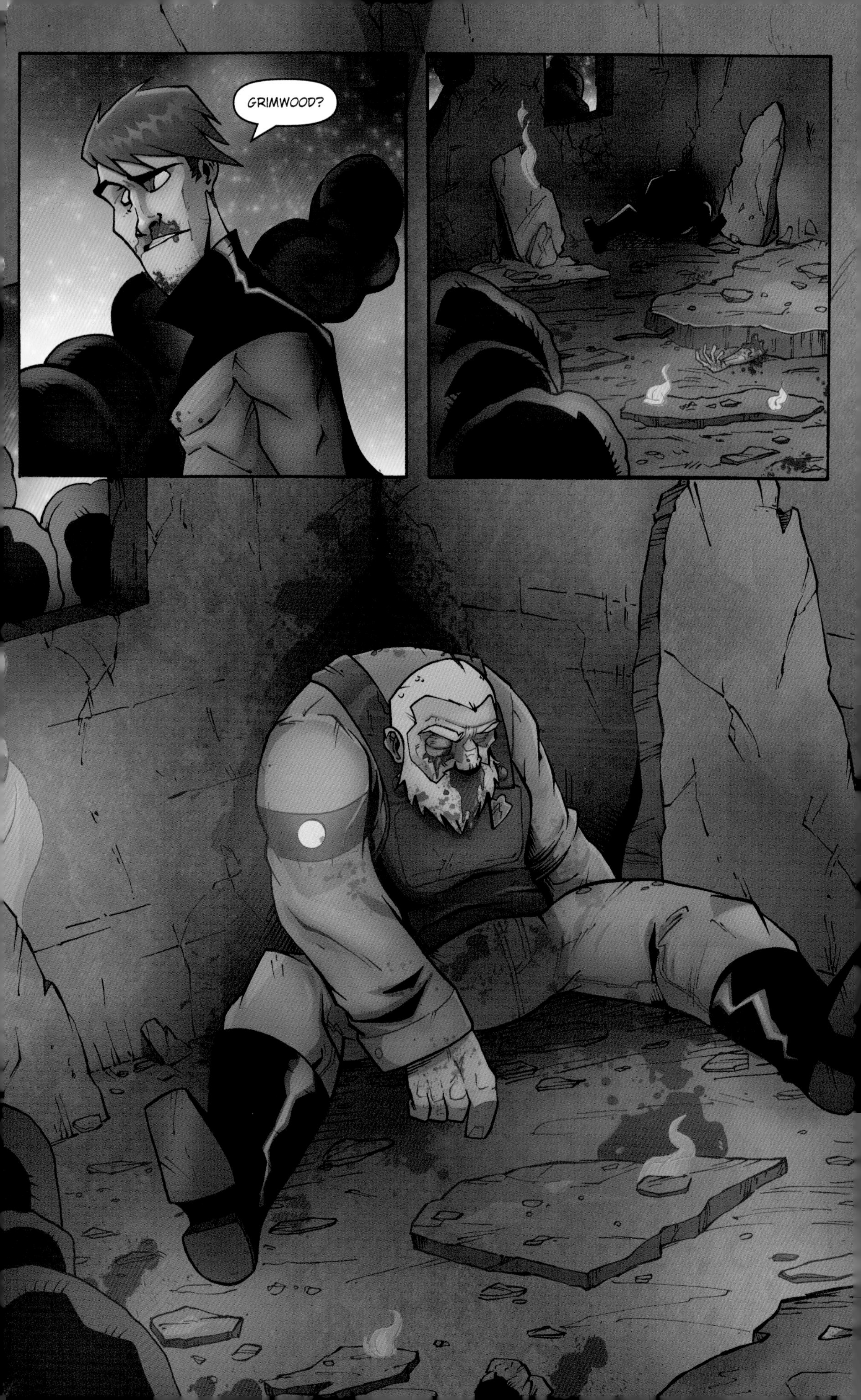
GRIMWOOD?

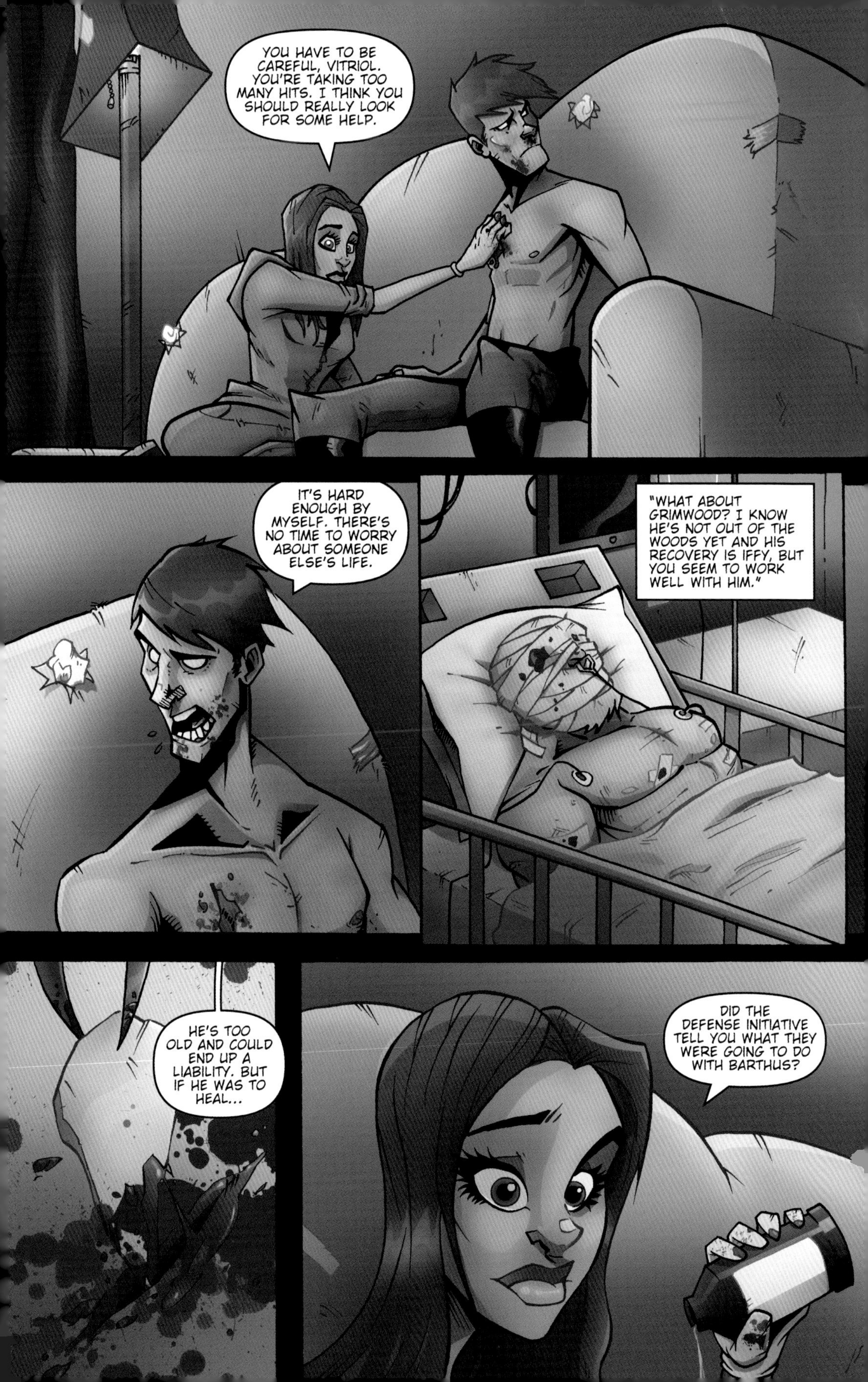
YOU HAVE TO BE CAREFUL, VITRIOL. YOU'RE TAKING TOO MANY HITS. I THINK YOU SHOULD REALLY LOOK FOR SOME HELP.
IT'S HARD ENOUGH BY MYSELF. THERE'S NO TIME TO WORRY ABOUT SOMEONE ELSE'S LIFE.
"WHAT ABOUT GRIMWOOD? I KNOW HE'S NOT OUT OF THE WOODS YET AND HIS RECOVERY IS IFFY, BUT YOU SEEM TO WORK WELL WITH HIM."
HE'S TOO OLD AND COULD END UP A LIABILITY. BUT IF HE WAS TO HEAL...
DID THE DEFENSE INITIATIVE TELL YOU WHAT THEY WERE GOING TO DO WITH BARTHUS?

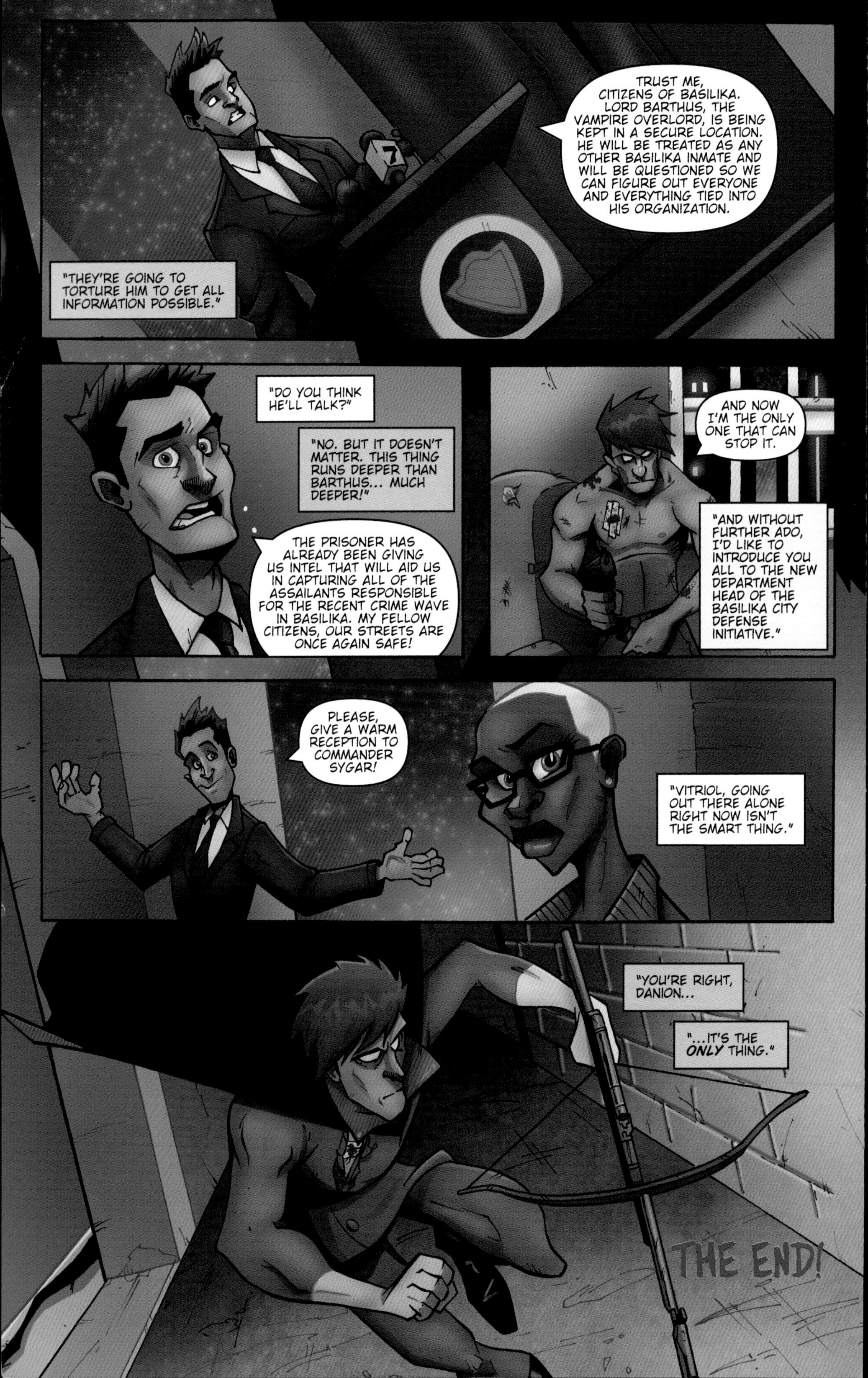
TRUST ME, CITIZENS OF BASILIKA. LORD BARTHUS, THE VAMPIRE OVERLORD, IS BEING KEPT IN A SECURE LOCATION. HE WILL BE TREATED AS ANY OTHER BASILIKA INMATE AND WILL BE QUESTIONED SO WE CAN FIGURE OUT EVERYONE AND EVERYTHING TIED INTO HIS ORGANIZATION.
"THEY'RE GOING TO TORTURE HIM TO GET ALL INFORMATION POSSIBLE."
"DO YOU THINK HE'LL TALK?"
"NO. BUT IT DOESN'T MATTER. THIS THING RUNS DEEPER THAN BARTHUS... MUCH DEEPER!"
THE PRISONER HAS ALREADY BEEN GIVING US INTEL THAT WILL AID US IN CAPTURING ALL OF THE ASSAILANTS RESPONSIBLE FOR THE RECENT CRIME WAVE IN BASILIKA. MY FELLOW CITIZENS, OUR STREETS ARE ONCE AGAIN SAFE!
AND NOW I'M THE ONLY ONE THAT CAN STOP IT.
"AND WITHOUT FURTHER ADO, I'D LIKE TO INTRODUCE YOU ALL TO THE NEW DEPARTMENT HEAD OF THE BASILIKA CITY DEFENSE INITIATIVE."
PLEASE, GIVE A WARM RECEPTION TO COMMANDER SYGAR!
"VITRIOL, GOING OUT THERE ALONE RIGHT NOW ISN'T THE SMART THING."
"YOU'RE RIGHT, DANION...
"...IT'S THE ONLY THING."
THE END!

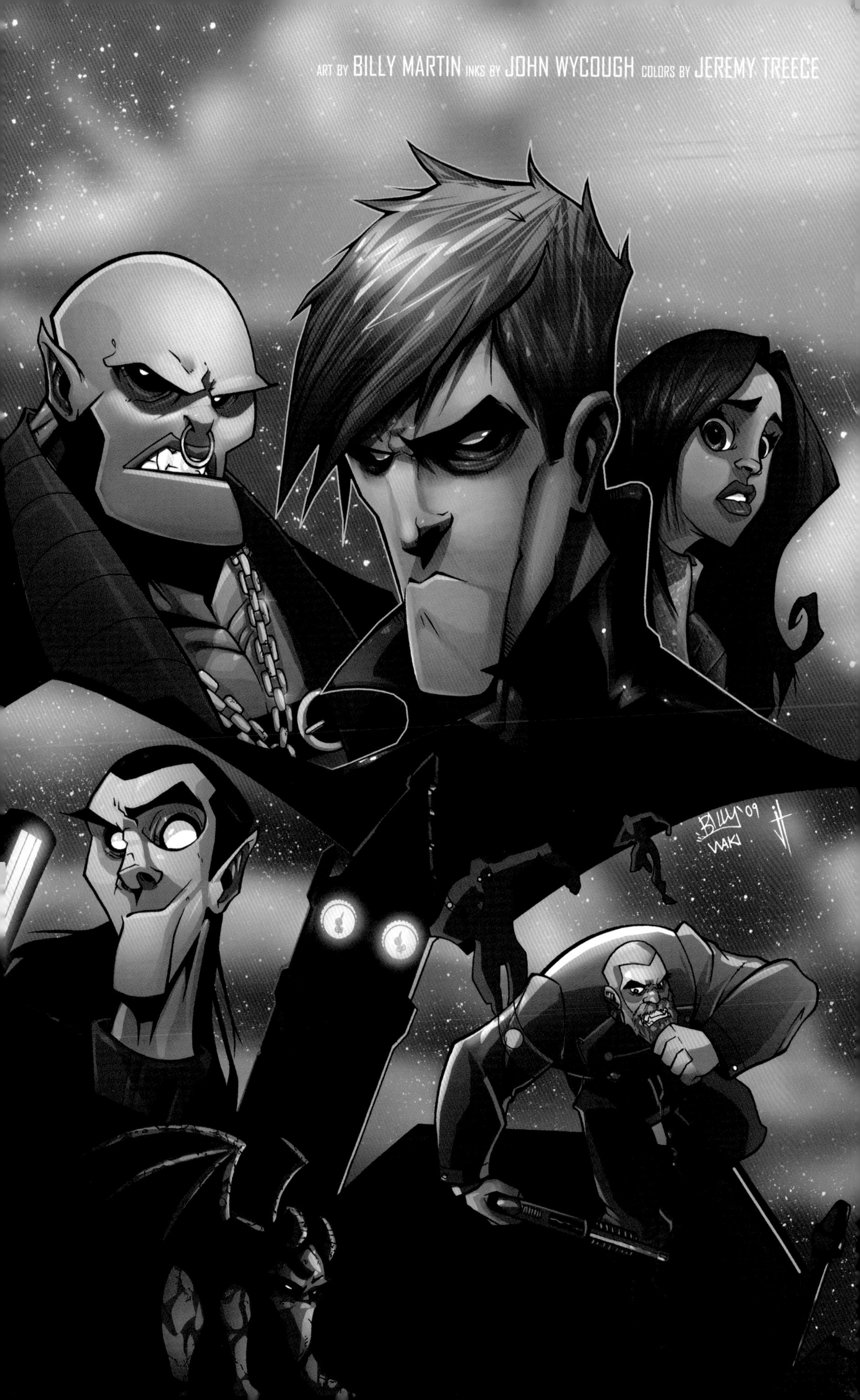
ART BY BILLY MARTIN INKS BY JOHN WYCOUGH COLORS BY JEREMY TREECE

ART BY BILLY MARTIN INKS BY JOHN WYCOUGH COLORS BY JEREMY TREECE

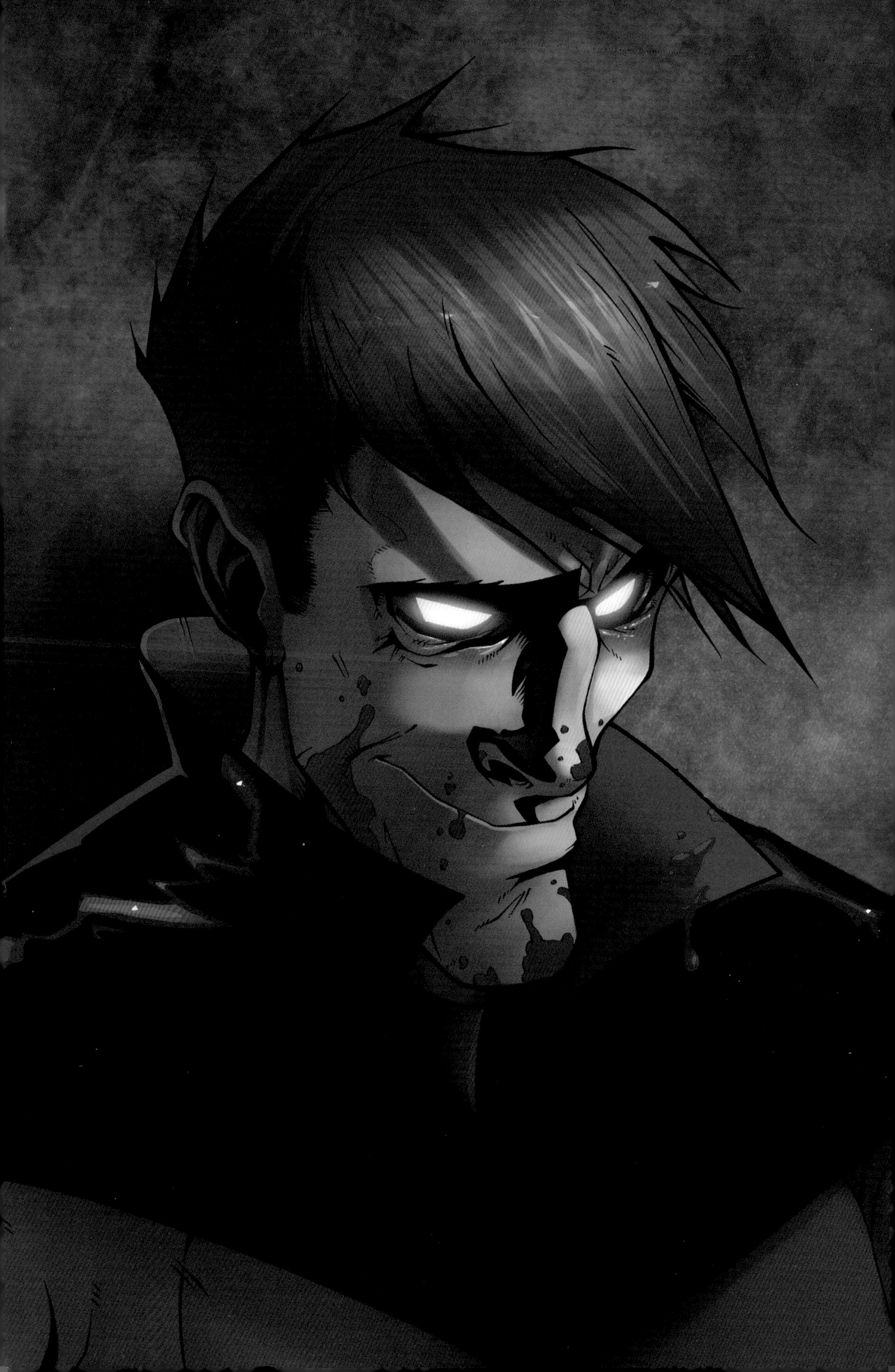

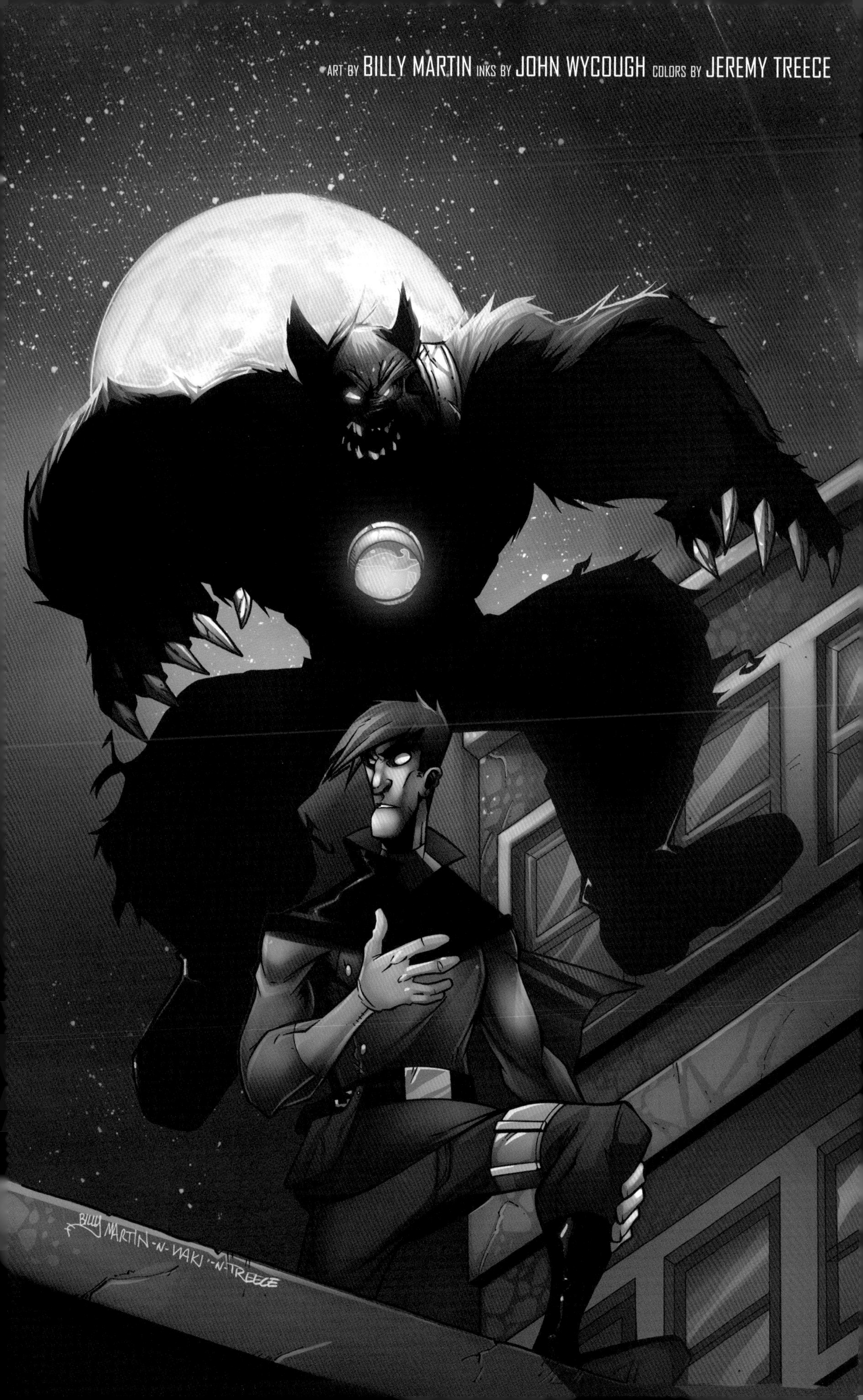
BILLY MARTIN -N- NAKI -N- TREECE
ART BY BILLY MARTIN INKS BY JOHN WYCOUGH COLORS BY JEREMY TREECE

ART BY BILLY MARTIN INKS BY JOHN WYCOUGH COLORS BY JEREMY TREECE
BILLY MARTIN
WAKI
TREECE

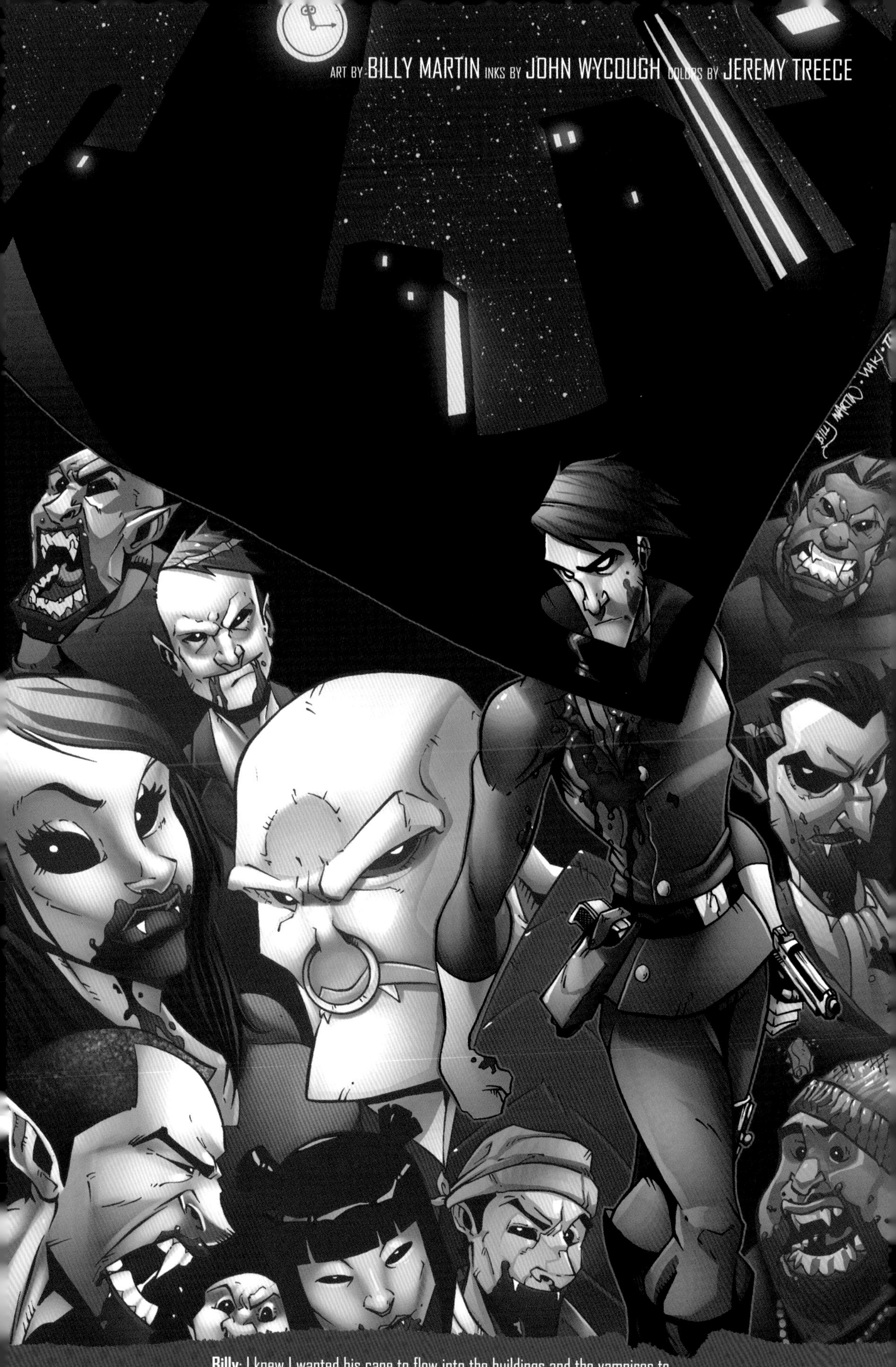
ART BY BILLY MARTIN INKS BY JOHN WYCOUGH COLORS BY JEREMY TREECE

Billy: I knew I wanted his cape to flow into the buildings and the vampires to be below the city in a metaphorical sense of them ruling the "underworld."

ART BY BILLY MARTIN INKS BY JOHN WYCOUGH

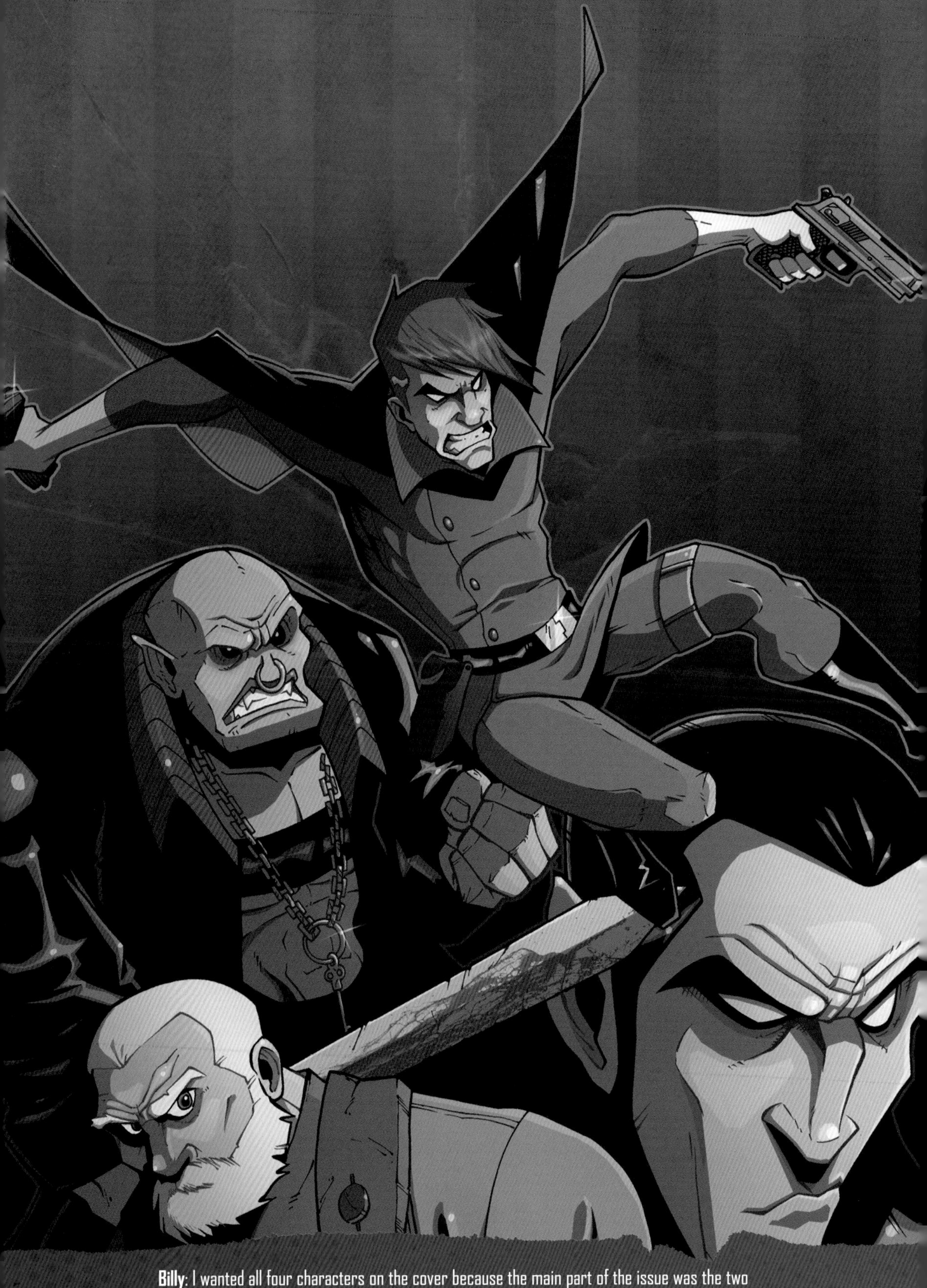

Billy: I wanted all four characters on the cover because the main part of the issue was the two separate battles taking place. I ended up swapping out Korbius for a big head shot to give the page better balance and more variety. This was actually the first thing I colored for *Vitriol*.

ART BY BILLY MARTIN COLORS BY SEAN "CHEEKS" GALLOWAY

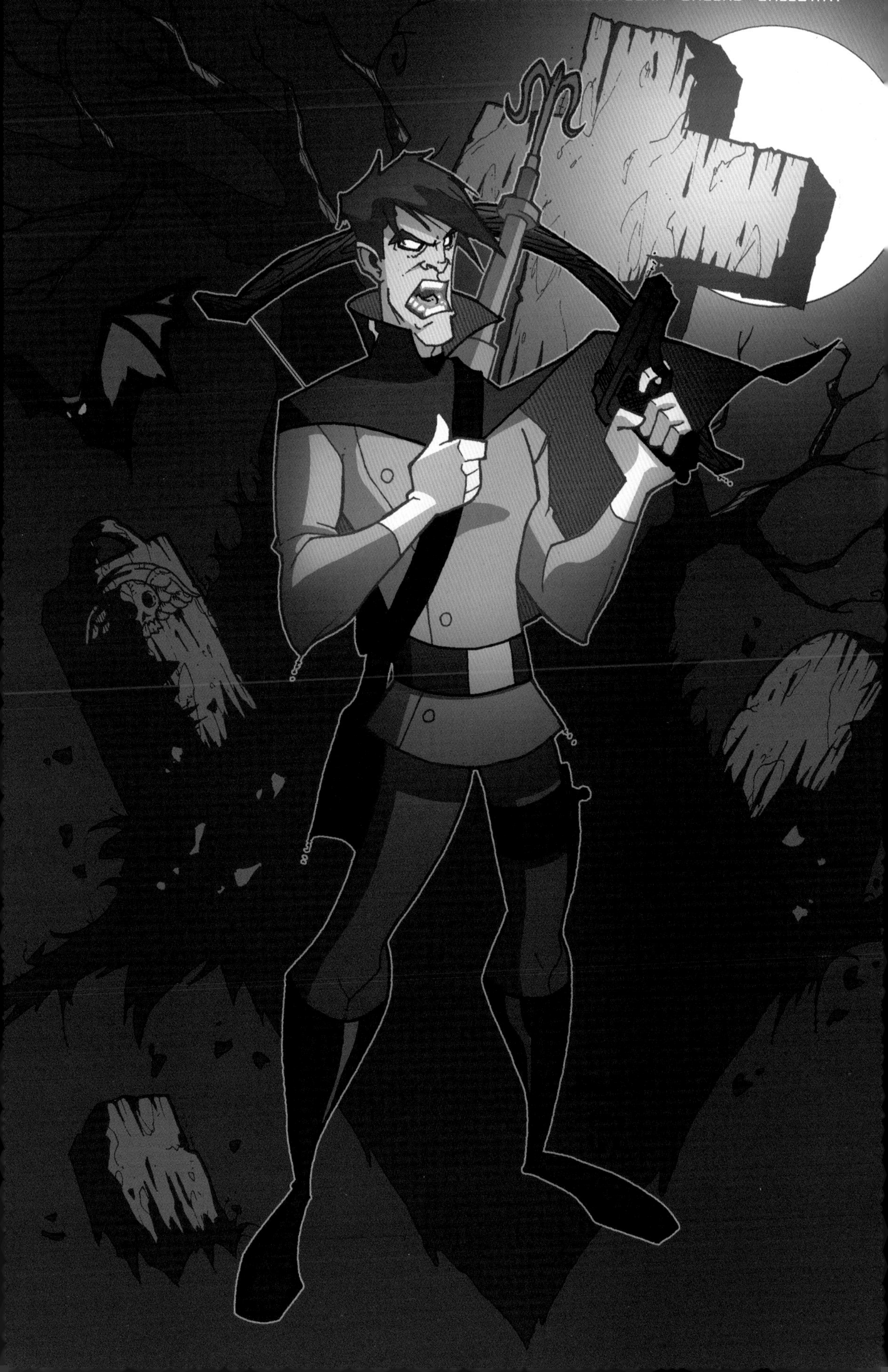

ART BY MIKE HENRY

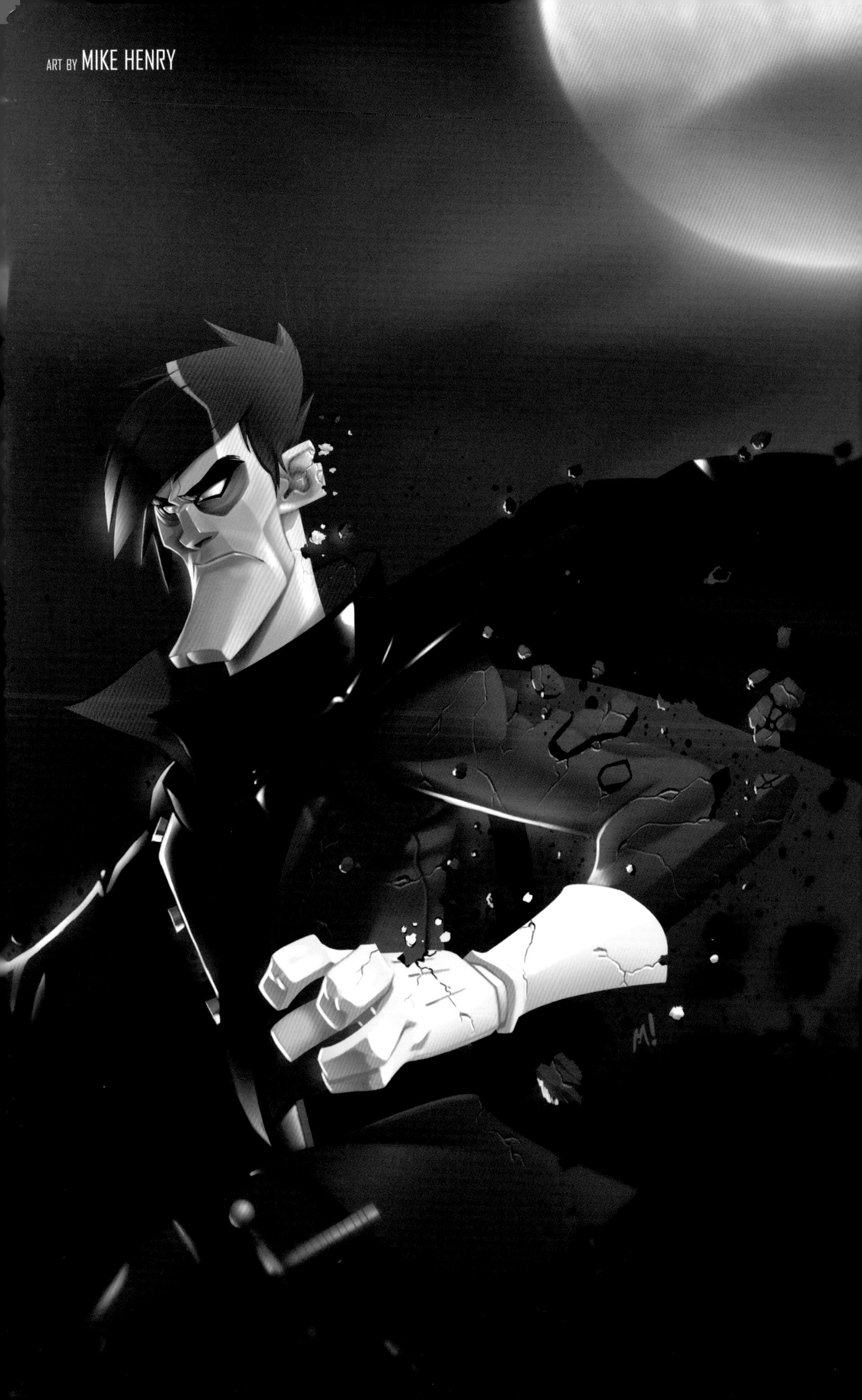

ART BY HUMBERTO RAMOS COLORS BY JEREMY TREECE

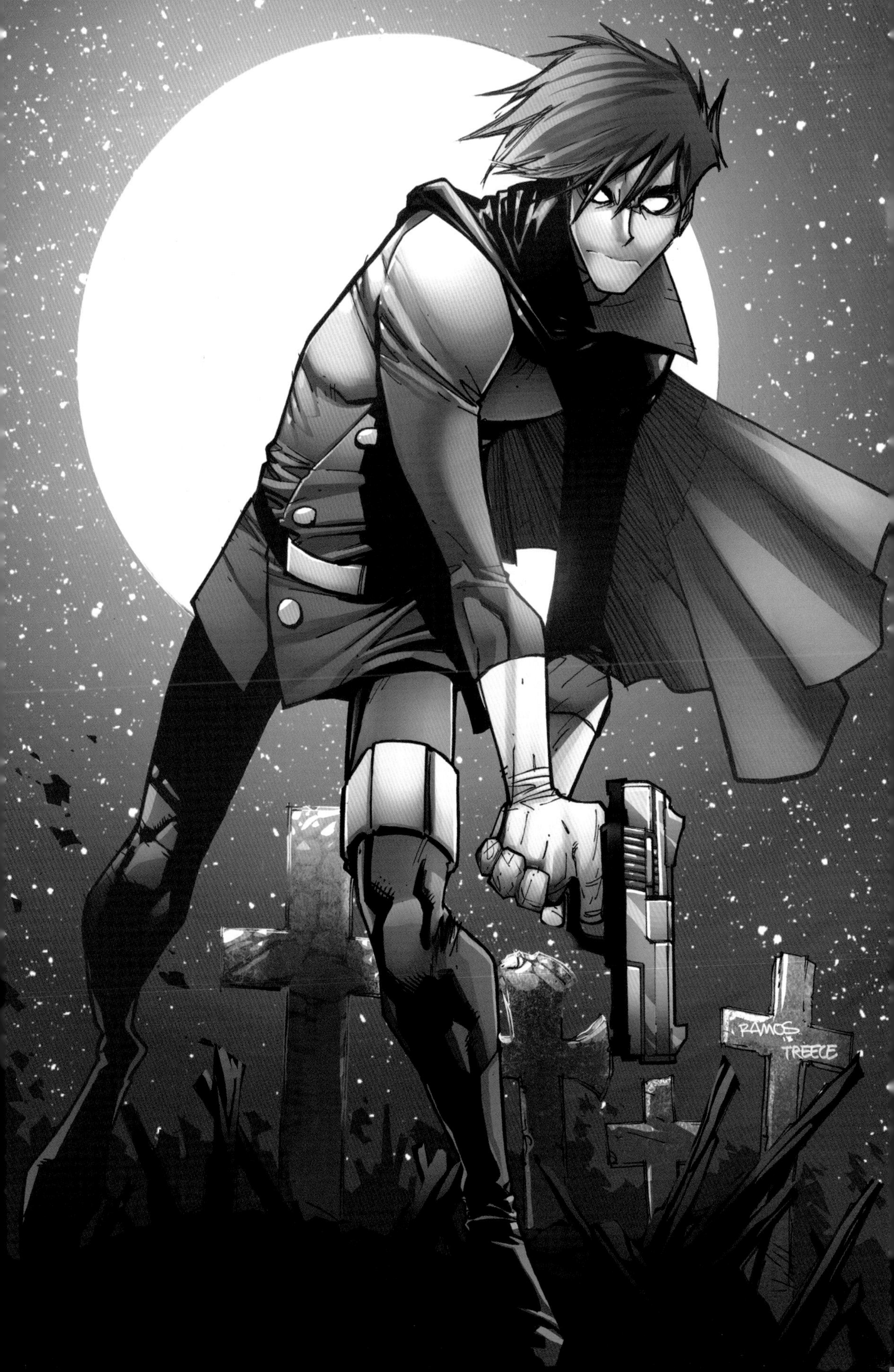

ART BY TABLE TAFFY'S SEAN "CHEEKS" GALLOWAY AND DEREK LAUFMAN

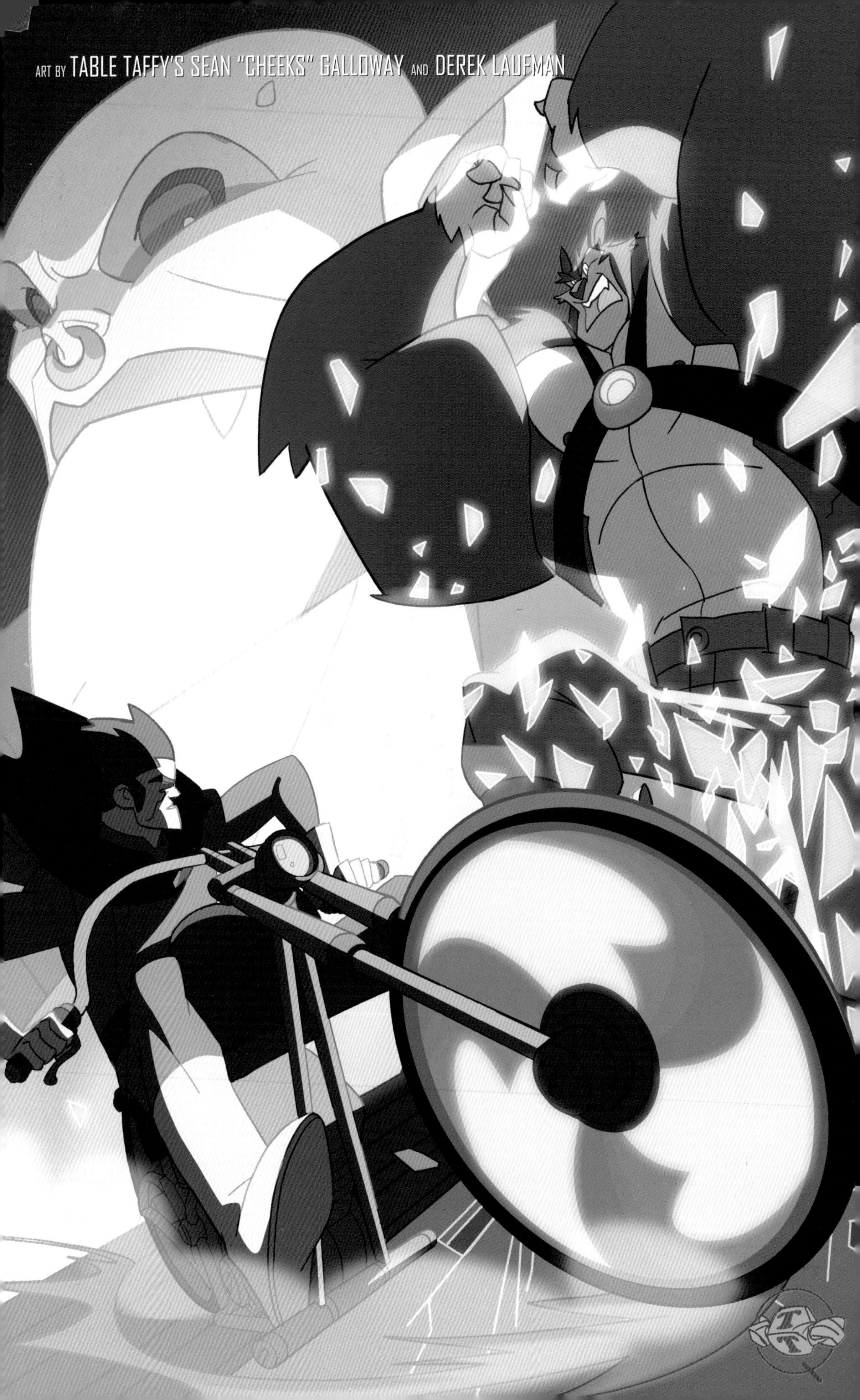

ART BY FRANCISCO HERRERA COLORS BY BILLY MARTIN

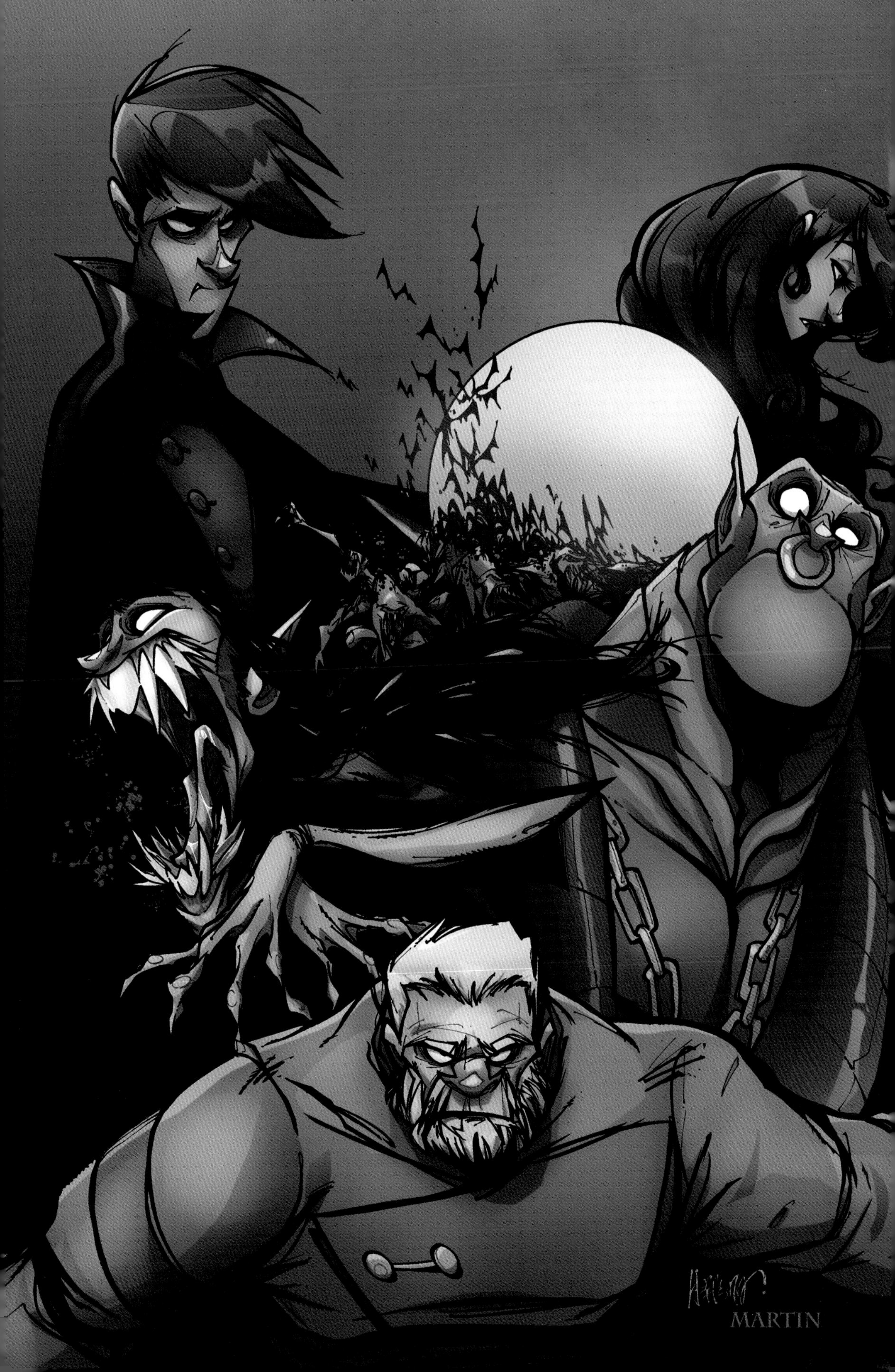
MARTIN

ART BY BILLY MARTIN

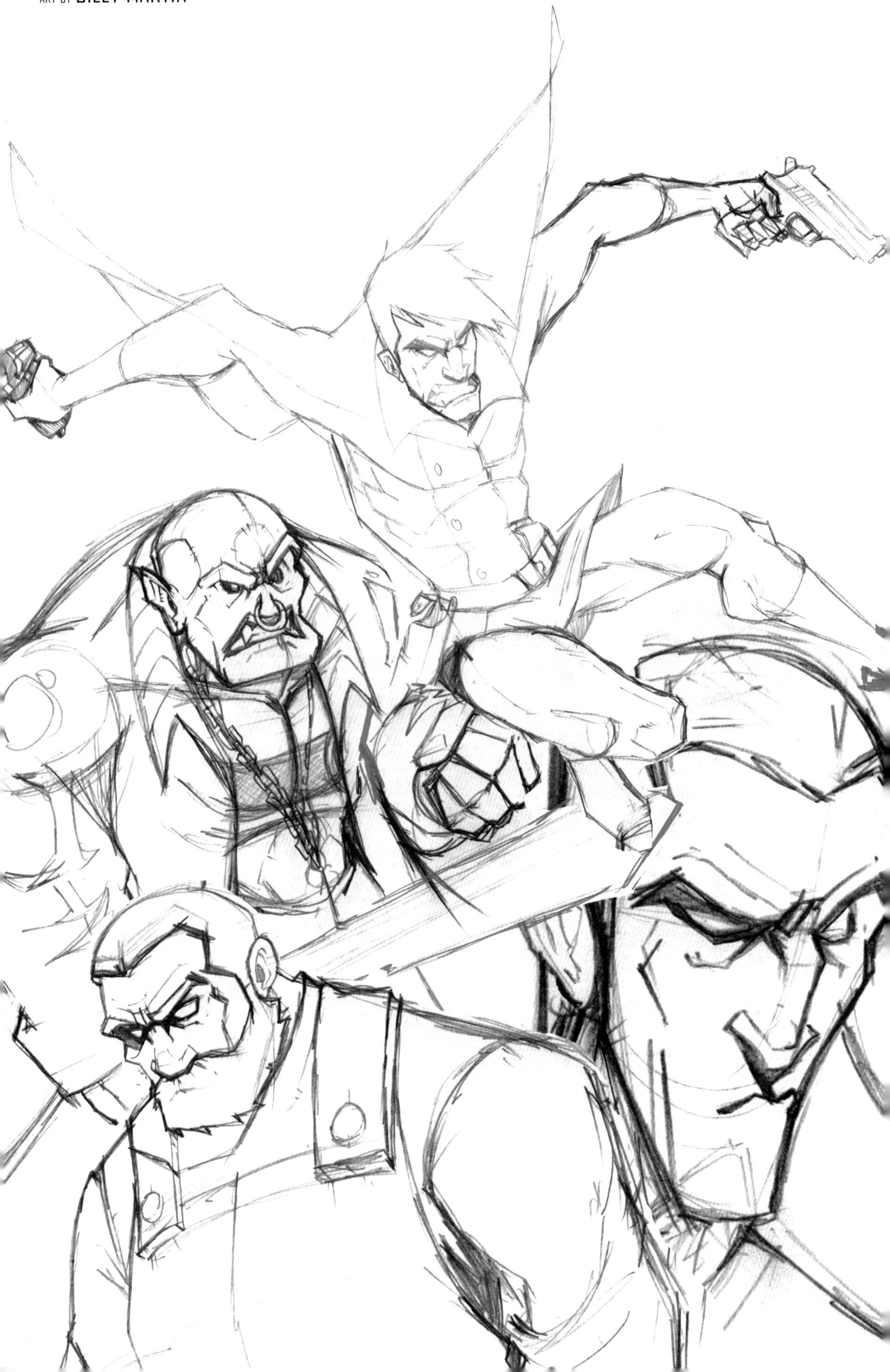

BlueLine Art
BOOK

ALL BLEED ART MUST EXTEND TO SOLID LINE

ISSUE _____ PG. # _____

STRATHMORE 300 (Regular) Item# BL1042

PRINTS AT 67%

KEEP ALL LETTERING INSIDE
OF BROKEN LINE

ART BY BILLY MARTIN

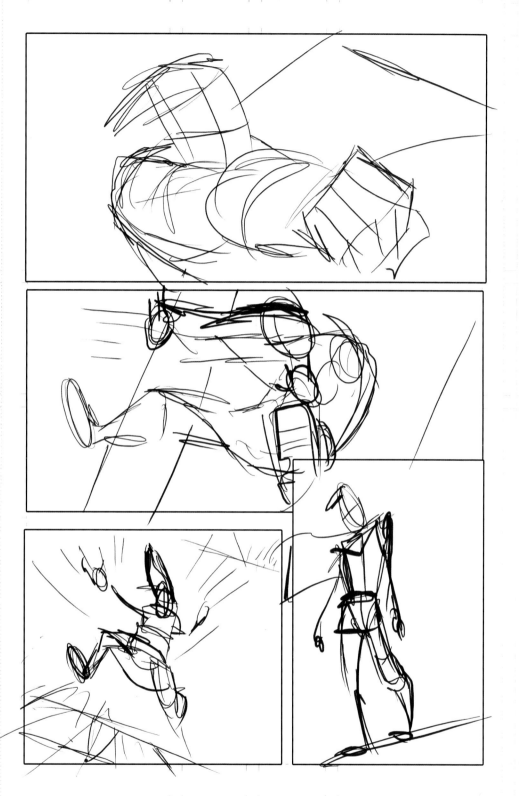

Brent: Denton was great for our book. He probably didn't know what half of the things we were doing were about. Haha. He was great at helping us organize this from start to finish and awesome at helping with these page layouts.
Billy: I keep the layouts very simple, I never really draw the backgrounds until later. I'm sure it was a pain for our editor (Denton) who couldn't tell what half of these were supposed to be.

ART BY **BILLY MARTIN**

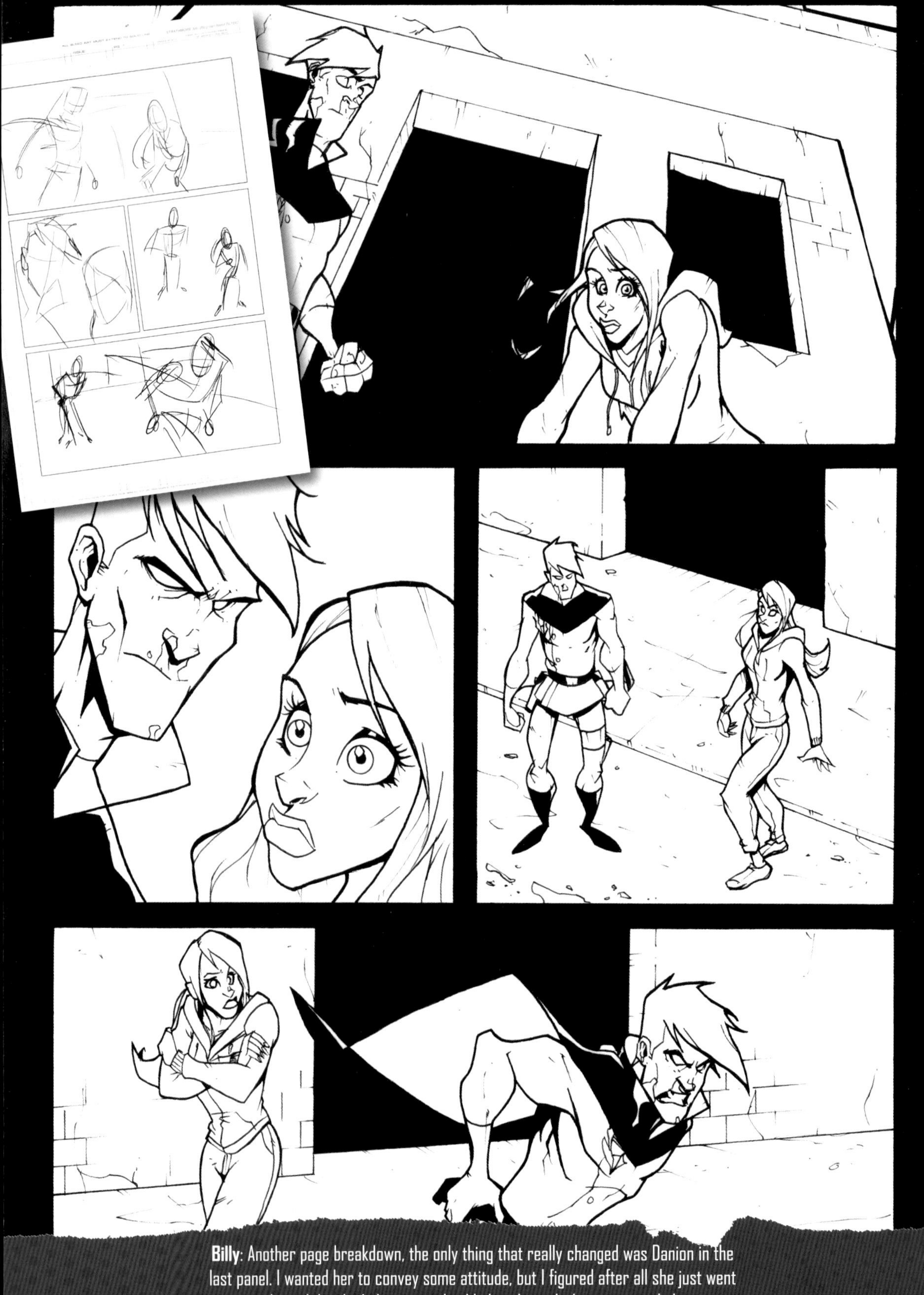

Billy: Another page breakdown, the only thing that really changed was Danion in the last panel. I wanted her to convey some attitude, but I figured after all she just went through her body language should show her a little more guarded.

Brent: Danion is a tough character to draw. She's kind of "the damsel in distress" but she also has a little attitude to her. Billy had his work cut out for himself when drawing her different moods.

ART BY BILLY MARTIN

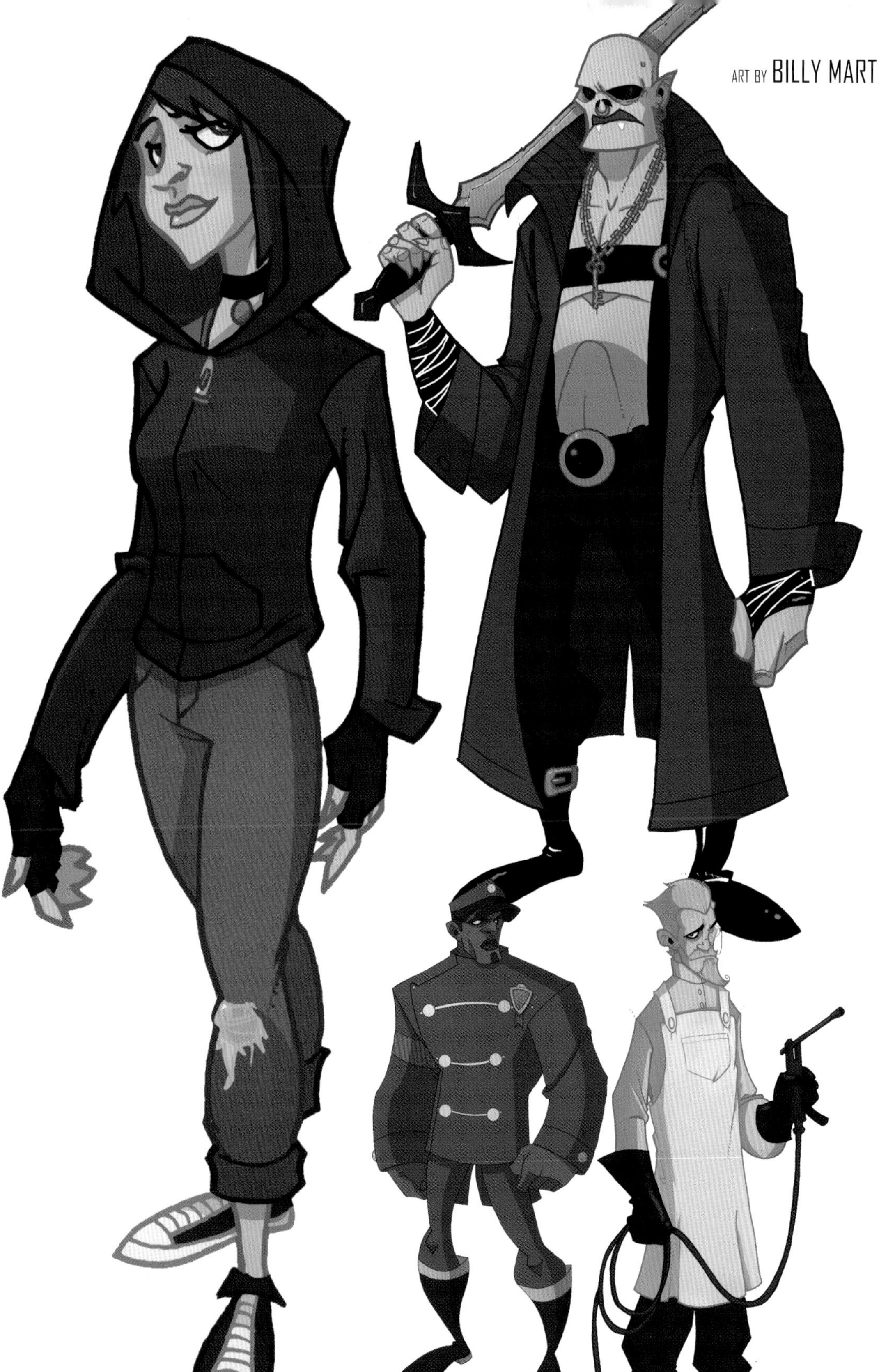

Brent: We wanted Vitriol's world to really show how it's been thrown through recessions and terrible economic troubles. It was important to show the characters dressed in futuristic clothing, however, it being old clothing altered into a futuristic feel. Gantioth's uniform really pushes this fact forward.

Billy: These are the original character designs I did back in 2008. Some of them changed a bit and some stayed pretty close. You can really see how much my drawing style has evolved between these and the actual Vitriol books.

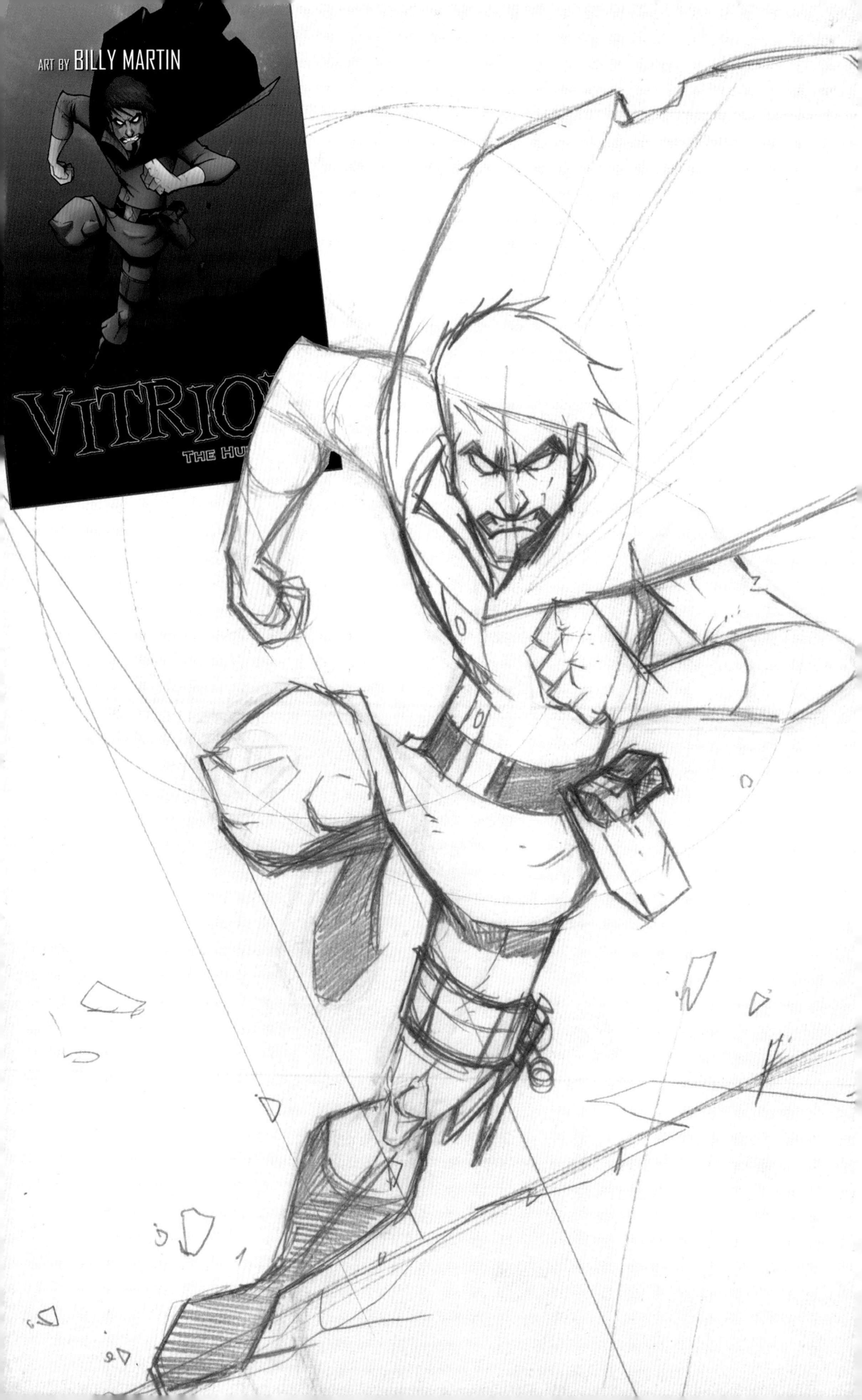
ART BY BILLY MARTIN

ART BY BILLY MARTIN

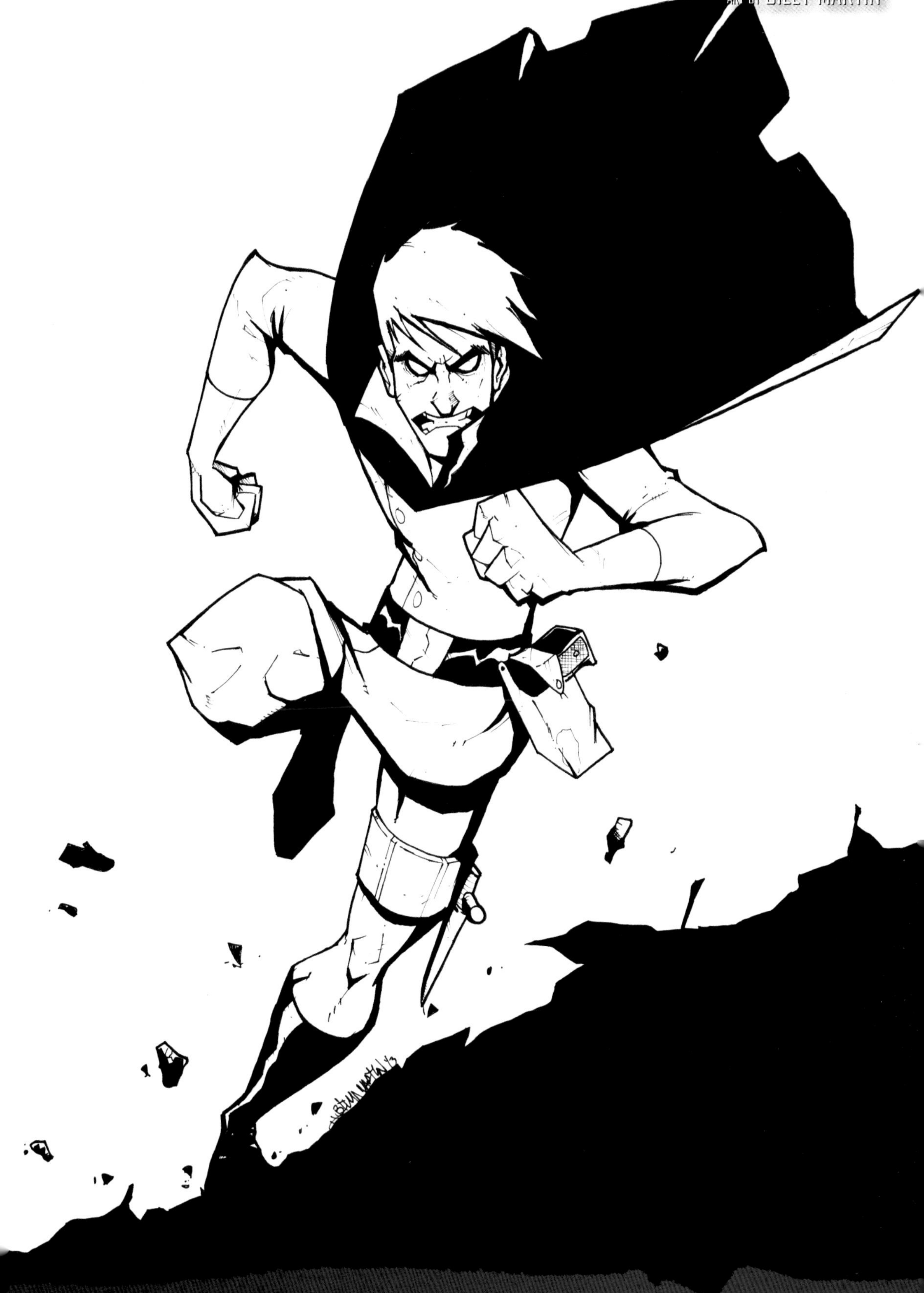

Billy: This is a promo image I did for stickers, prints, flyers and things like that. I considered using it for the trade cover, but I was itching to draw Vitriol and Co. one more time. You can see the initial pencil sketch as well as the cleaned up lines. I inked and colored this one myself.

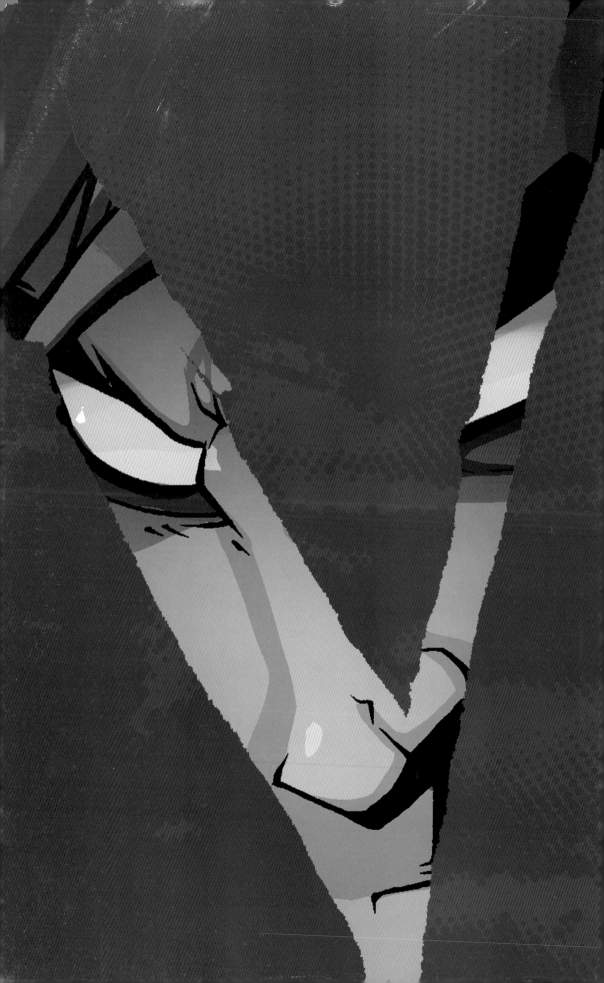